DIDN'T WE ALMOST HAVE IT ALL

DIDN'T WE ALMOST HAVE IT ALL

In Defense of
Whitney Houston

GERRICK KENNEDY

ABRAMS PRESS, NEW YORK

ABRAMS The Art of Books
195 Broadway, New York, NY 10007
abramsbooks.com

CONTENTS

FOREWORD
by Brandy

The first time I heard Whitney's voice, she was singing "Greatest Love of All." I felt feelings, emotions I'd never before felt in my body and in my spirit. I don't quite have the words to describe what her voice did to me. How it was able to move me. And how I was suddenly able to see all of her—her grace, her class, her beauty, her smile. She was an angel. She was the person I wanted to be exactly like. I knew I could never be *exactly* like Whitney Houston, but if I could just do a little bit of what she did with her voice, if I could make someone else feel the way she made me feel, then that's what I wanted to do. I was mesmerized by her. I spent my childhood practicing to all her records and imagining myself meeting her. Those were my dreams and prayers. I wanted to be a singer, and I wanted to meet Whitney Houston.

I was a young Black girl growing up in the South when Whitney took over the world. She was an effortless singer, and it inspired me to see someone with a voice as powerful as hers. She had every range you can imagine—her falsetto was as strong as her head voice, and she could do all these amazing things with her tone. Whitney made me feel like anything was possible, even though everything she was doing had been so impossible for Black girls to achieve. She was the result of so much, and she was the reason why I could be everything I wanted to be, why any of us who came after her could be anything we wanted to be. Whitney was the blueprint. That was the magic of her. I remember going to my mother and telling her: *"I want to be as big as Whitney Houston."* My mom encouraged me to dream big, but Black girls rarely saw the type of success Whitney achieved. Selling tens of millions of records, all the history she made, and all the accolades—we didn't see many artists, let alone Black artists, reach the levels Whitney did. I don't think I would've made it as far as I was able to make it as an artist if she were not the idol I looked up to most. Whitney was magical. She opened—literally—every door for every singer. Black, white, Hispanic—anyone who wanted to do this has Whitney in their Top Five.

When I was twelve years old, I sang my way down the audience of *The Tonight Show* in order to get backstage. BeBe and CeCe Winans were there to perform, and I wanted to meet them, not just because I loved them so much, but because I knew they knew Whitney and I wanted to meet Whitney. *"Is there a way you can just call her, so I can talk to her?"* I begged CeCe. She actually called Whitney, and I got to talk to her. I got to *hear* her voice. I couldn't believe it was her on the other end telling me to have a great summer and sweetly listening as I professed my love of her and my dream to be just like her.

And then I got a chance to go to one of her concerts. I was up in the nosebleeds, but I told everybody—all the ushers—that I was going to be a big star and I was going to pay all their bills if they let me move down. Just like at *The Tonight Show*, my charm got me backstage. But Whitney was already gone by then. I was crushed; plus, I missed the entire concert trying to get to her. As I stood in the rain outside the Forum in tears, my mother looked me in the eyes and told me: *"You're going to see Whitney at the top. That's where you're going to meet her."* Three years later, my first record came out and did pretty well. Whitney was hosting the 1995 Kids' Choice Awards, and I was performing on the show. We were going to be on the *same* stage. At rehearsals, I saw this woman coming toward me. I couldn't believe that it was really her. It was really Whitney Houston. I was so taken aback that I ran from her. It just didn't feel real. When she embraced me, she embraced me as if she knew me. And she did know me, because of my music, and that's exactly what my mother had told me would happen in the parking lot after missing Whitney's concert trying to meet her. *You will see her at the top.* Whitney gave me her jacket to wear, and I hung out with her for the whole day. It was a dream, one of the best days of my life.

To experience that moment of meeting my idol just as all my dreams were coming true was surreal. And then *Cinderella* happened. First of all, I didn't realize that I was making history with the role. For me it was, "Oh my God, I'm working *with* Whitney Houston." Just a few years earlier, I was at the Forum trying to meet Whitney, crying because I couldn't. And then I was in the studio with her? There was something about Whitney that made me feel like I could completely be myself. I was so happy to be in the same studio with her, to both hear her sing and sing with her. My voice was not even fully developed yet, and I got to ask her to do all these things that I wanted to hear her do vocally—all the things I dreamed of hearing her do with her voice. When I look back now it's like, *"Oh my God."* I was the first Black Cinderella, and it was because of Whitney that I got a chance to play such an iconic role. It was because of her that I became the first Black Disney princess. I couldn't really appreciate it in the moment because I was busy doing the work. But my life had quite literally become a Cinderella story. My dreams had come true—except I didn't care about finding a prince, because I had met my fairy godmother.

***

Whitney's support helped me realize my potential to grow as an artist. Whitney saw me, and she pushed me. *"You need to sing from your gut,"* she would tell me. *"You need to sing from your heart and choose songs for* you. *Don't try to be me. Be you, and that is what will carry you through."* I think about her in so many different ways, all the time. And I miss her so very much. Even when she lost her voice, when she lost it, Whitney still got up on that stage and sang from her heart, whether she could hit the notes or not. It speaks volumes that she still showed up and still tried to do what she had to do—no matter what. She was a different kind of lady. To go through everything she went through and still give so much to us is unbelievable. But that was her magic.

The day she passed, I woke up in the morning and didn't like the way I felt. It was my birthday, and I was supposed to perform with Monica at Clive Davis's pre-Grammys gala. I don't know if I was just afraid to perform or nervous about letting people down, but I woke up not feeling very good. My voice was weird, and there was something so off about the energy of the day. I went to my voice doctor, and when I got back to the Beverly Hilton there were paramedics outside. Nick Gordon saw me and shouted, *"Brandy! Brandy! Come in the elevator! Come in the elevator!"* Just seeing him, I immediately started praying. I knew him from seeing him with Whitney and her crew. I didn't know what the stretcher I saw was for, and I wasn't putting two and two together. As I was getting hair and makeup, I got the call that Whitney had passed away. I was in complete denial. I had just talked to her three days before. We had a long conversation. We talked about everything—from the beginning of our relationship to where we were at that moment. I couldn't understand that she was gone. It just wasn't registering for me. To this day, I still don't understand it. I feel like I could have been there for her more than I was. I could have loved her differently than the way she was being handled. There was a gap in our relationship, but that's just life—you go and do your own thing and grow. But I had a moment with her during those harder times. We talked about her coming and staying with me to get away. So for her to pass away, the way she did? I'll never be the same.

I really try to carry on in Whitney's tradition. She taught me not to allow fame to beat me and not to allow negativity to stop me. I never dealt with any of the negativity shown toward me or my brother after Whitney died. I didn't feed into it. Ray J and I, we're the same person when it comes to genuine love for Whitney. He had a genuine friendship with Whitney, and he had nothing but her best interests at heart. His respect for her was out of this world, and a part of him feels he couldn't protect her the way he wanted to. It's natural for people to want to place blame. I placed a lot of blame on a lot of people too, when it came to Whitney. We loved her so much and needed something or someone to attach blame to because it was so hard to accept that she was gone. We don't really have the right to speak on anything that she had to go through in her life. No one knows what she was running from. No one knows what she was trying to overcome. No one knows the costs that came with being Whitney Houston. That level of fame, that level of expectation, that level of pressure.

It's so important that we honor and respect Whitney's legacy. Her voice had the power to sit you still. The magic in her voice could help get you through whatever you were going through. Whitney's voice could bring you closer to God. There was so much love and joy in that voice. Listening to her voice has gotten people through heartbreak and anguish. Her music has been there for our darkest moments and our brightest days. There was such beauty and grace in her voice. Whitney could take you to so many places with *just* her voice. She has inspired generations of little girls all over the world to sing from their heart and guts. That was her magic, and that's her legacy. And we'll never see another Whitney Houston.

INTRODUCTION

I'm met with variations of the same three questions anytime someone asks me about writing a book on Whitney Houston: *Did you get Cissy to talk? What really happened with Robyn and Bobby? What's Clive got to say now?* Every time, without fail. But the question I'm asked the most? *Why do you want to write a book about Whitney Houston?* Typically, my elevator pitch about the motivation and intent behind this book is met with curiosity and enthusiasm. But I've lost count of how many times I've witnessed that same curiosity and enthusiasm drain from someone after I tell them I'm probably not writing the kinda book they think I am. I didn't write a traditional biography; nor did I write an exposé full of bombs about Whitney or her life. But I get it. We associate Whitney with the many scandals that befell her, and it's hard to see past that with a story that ends as tragically as hers does.

And I was no different. When Whitney died, I couldn't listen to her music anymore. It hurt too much. I had met her, and two days later she was dead. That was gutting enough on its own and hearing her was a painful reminder of that weekend, so I made the conscious decision not to play any of the Whitney albums I once loved and frequently listened to on repeat. I loved her so much, but her voice no longer reminded me of the euphoric feeling her music once gave me. In its place was regret for what could have been and deep sadness for what no longer was, and my love of her was now engulfed in guilt. There was guilt over how *we* treated her—all the crass jokes at her expense, the punch line she became, and how common it was for us to play into it. To indulge in tearing her down. My memories of Whitney evaporated into a fixation over thinking of all the ways her life and career should have gone. How things could have been different if we stopped speculating and taunting. If we were a little bit louder in our support for her to pin down her addictions than we were about her inability to come back swinging. For so long my guilt had eaten up the joy I found in Whitney's music. All I could see were the years that had stripped her of a dignity that has only been restored in the years after her death, once we learned of the burdens and shame she carried. So I understand why so many of us haven't moved on from the tragedies that swallowed Whitney whole. But I wanted to be able to rejoice in all that she was. I wanted to reconnect to the joy I found in her music. So I went back to the beginning, to our first time seeing Whitney on television, when she belted "Home" from *The Wiz*, and spent hours one night cycling through the decades of concert footage that has been preserved on YouTube. I watched the great ones that left goosebumps on my arms and the not-so-great ones that made me remember how much it broke our hearts to see her lose parts of herself. Then I moved on to her music videos, watching them all again and again. And then I went back to her movies and revisited the albums that once had permanent residence in my CD changer. Sitting in the past made me fall back in love with Whitney in the present, and it allowed me to see her fully, without her tragedies obscuring my view.

Didn't We Almost Have It All arrives just as we're marking a decade without Whitney. We now live in a time when the way she was treated by the press and the music industry wouldn't dare go unchecked. Millennials and Generation Z have transformed the way in which we see the world around us. Our understanding and language around all that makes us unique has broadened, which has diversified all facets of popular culture. There were so many barriers eviscerated by the power of Whitney's voice and the success she found. But chipping away at all those cultural barriers came with a cost, a mighty one, as we know. Whitney left this earth as a cautionary tale, but reading her solely through the lens of tragedy does her a major disservice, and it took projects like Kevin Macdonald's unflinching 2018 documentary *Whitney* and Robyn Crawford's 2019 memoir *A Song for You* to show us just how wrong we had gotten Whitney.

We missed so much the first time around. We were too busy judging and consuming her. And Whitney is overdue for a reexamination now that our dialogue around celebrity, addiction, sexuality, gender, mental illness, and Blackness in America has changed dramatically. We have undergone a degree of self-reflection on much of what tore her down. We now hold more compassion for celebrities battling addiction and mental illness, but it took the tragedies of losing Whitney and Michael Jackson and Amy Winehouse and Scott Weiland and Prince and Chris Cornell and Tom Petty and Lil Peep and Mac Miller to get us there. In a seven-year stretch, Michael, Whitney, and Prince died. The three biggest stars of the MTV generation—Black artists who challenged our ideas of race and sex, broke new ground for generations to come, and redefined pop music—dead. They all succumbed to addiction before we collectively shifted our thinking; before our views of the struggles to assert one's Blackness in America evolved; before our consideration of the spectrum on which sexuality and gender lines expanded; before our realization of the toxicity of celebrity culture and the role we play as consumers deepened; before our understanding of the lasting traumas of childhood abuse and the way we think about mental health faced a needed reckoning; and before our common vernacular included terms like "accountability" or "problematic."

These conversations have altered the way we've been able to reframe our icons in the years after their tragic deaths as we continue to confront the psychological toll of being a Black superstar in America. I've often fantasized about how their lives—our lives—would be different had they not fallen, if they had lived to see a time in which our thinking was generally more progressive. Would they still have lost themselves to drug abuse? Would the last years of their lives still be remembered more for their eccentricities than for their talents? The sad truth is we'll never know. Just as we will never really know who Whitney was. The woman behind the voice was an enigma, and that state of unknowability is remarkable on its own given how much the concepts of fame and celebrity as we've always known them operate on overexposure and oversharing. Even when Whitney was directly telling us who she was, she was telling us only what she *wanted* us to know, and all that we have discovered about her in death doesn't change the reality that she was the only one who could offer any real insight into her interior life and her motivations as an entertainer and she's not here to give that to us.

So why write a book about someone as unknowable as Whitney Houston? It's simple: There wasn't a book about her that was grounded in scholarship and reverence, and that absence felt profoundly unfair to her legacy. Plenty of books have gotten down in the weeds on the gossip and the scandals that formed our view of Whitney, but none of them have explored her importance or searched for any meaning in her triumphs and tragedies. Those closest to her—her mother, Cissy; her ex-husband, Bobby Brown; her mentor, Clive Davis; and her confidant, Robyn Crawford—have all written about their life in proximity to Whitney, and while each of those books has provided more clarity and insight into her life, those were stories born from the necessary burden of setting the record straight about her.

As I was researching this book, a central theme quickly presented itself. From watching Whitney's old interviews and tracking the ways she was covered in the media, this idea of shame began to crystalize. Not just the shame Whitney carried or hid behind, but the shame we projected onto her with our expectations and judgment. And that theme informed how I decided to write about her. If you're looking for a straightforward cradle-to-grave story, this isn't the book for you. This isn't a collection of anecdotes from her inner circle, and the answers to all the lingering questions of her fall aren't inside these pages. What you are about to read is a road map of memory, shame, loss, and love. This is a celebration of all that Whitney was and all that she was never able to be, as well as an interrogation of who we were when she first came to us and what we did with the Whitney we were given.

Didn't We Almost Have It All is an attempt to have a different conversation about Whitney. About her voice. About her power. About her triumphs and failures. About her tragedies. About her legacy. The entirety of Whitney's life and career is covered here, but there is no straight line through Whitney, nor is there a great deal of music to analyze, so our cultural study won't always be linear. We will travel between eras in Whitney's life and career and revisit them from different perspectives and themes.

The first chapter, "Didn't We Almost Have It All?," is a meditation on loss and memory, and how I found my way back to Whitney and the joy of her music.

In "Under His Eye, Blessed Be the Sound," I chart the almighty power of Cissy Houston by mapping her roots in the church and exploring the ground she and her siblings broke in gospel.

"Home" contextualizes Whitney's hometown of Newark, New Jersey, and the Great Migration that brought her grandfather north in search of the Black American dream that eventually gave way to her career. The chapter also looks at the decline of the Black American city and how Newark's transformation directly impacted a young Whitney.

The next chapter, "Stuff That You Want, Thing That You Need," charts the ways in which Whitney's ascent in the late eighties and nineties impacted the world. This chapter examines the power and brilliance of her voice, and it also revisits the racial politics of MTV and radio during the eighties and looks at how Whitney's mainstream success was critical in closing the gap of racially segregated pop music.

"My Lonely Heart Calls" covers the handwringing over her sexuality and the probing of her femininity, and "Miss America, the Beautiful" unpacks the burden of "The Star-Spangled Banner" and interrogates how her image, specifically her Blackness, was questioned.

"Bolder, Blacker, Badder" analyzes the ways in which our understanding of how Whitney articulated Blackness was transformed by *Waiting to Exhale* and the growing dominance of hip-hop soul and how both gave way to her greatest career triumph. The chapter also explores how our obsession with Whitney's presentation of Blackness and our view of her as a Black artist making pop music shifted at the turn of the millennium.

In "Tell the Truth and Shame the Devil," I cover the traumas that weighed heavily on Whitney and look at how tabloid culture exploited her shame and helped contribute to her fall from grace, and "The Undoing of Whitney Houston" explores the last years of her life, a time defined by her unending quest for redemption.

And the final chapter, "Won't They Always Love You?," is a reflection on Whitney's legacy and what she means to us now.

It's hard not to wonder where Whitney would be if she had made it to the proverbial light at the end of the tunnel. If she had conquered the demons that derailed her and was able to see how much the world around her would change. What type of artist would she be today? Would Whitney have gotten her voice in enough shape to fully regain her glory? Would she have continued to find film projects she was passionate about? What kind of third act would her career have taken? What kind of mother would she have become to Bobbi Kristina, who didn't make it much longer without Whitney around? What I believe to be true is Whitney Elizabeth Houston—a beautiful Black girl from Newark with an anointed voice—would thrive if she arrived now, just as she was. We would have been more appreciative of her artistry. We would have been kinder to her and Robyn. And we would have supported her when the devil on her back pulled her to darkness, instead of shaming her for her choices. The sad truth is we'll never know.

DIDN'T WE ALMOST HAVE IT ALL?

A Meditation on Loss and Memory

She was running through heaven. Her willowy, caramel-colored frame swaddled in a lush, white silk that vanished into the clouds behind her as she ran toward the camera. Statuesque and graceful, she was the vision of an angel. The magic of her voice—fiery, yet pure—was enough to catapult her to the skies, and we floated with her, carried by the airiness of the notes she sang. "Can't you see the hurt in me? I feel so all alone." And then came her greatest act of wizardry, that ability to take a single vowel and stretch it from a small whisper to a stratospheric boom: *"Iiiiiiiiii wannnna runnnn to youuuuu."* She was running through heaven, and her voice took me with her.

I fell in love with Whitney Houston inside a dingy movie theater on the outskirts of Cincinnati on a November day in 1992. It happened while watching her run across the clouds in a scene from *The Bodyguard* as she sang the operatic ballad

"Run to You." I was only five, but her voice sent me fluttering in my seat. Witnessing Whitney's first arrival wasn't a fortune I had—she was well into stardom by the time I heard her music or saw her awkwardly bopping around in the music video for "How Will I Know." I imagine the feeling would have been the same had I known a world before her and watched the early years of her ascent in real time. I was awestruck watching her onscreen. Her voice was enchanting—otherworldly, even. The sugary pop confections that made Whitney—and defined an era—form my earliest consciousness of music. I can still picture a much younger version of myself swiveling my hips to "How Will I Know" alone in my bedroom. Her music gave me the feeling I had whenever I heard Michael or Janet Jackson or Prince or TLC—the first artists I was enamored of. It was a feeling that took over my entire body, this feeling of ecstasy, as if I could launch myself into the heavens just off the power of it.

Infatuation swelled into an obsession with music and with dance. I would spend hours in my room mimicking the moves and routines I'd seen on MTV and BET. I learned the intricate steps from Janet's "The Pleasure Principle" and could perform the breakdown from her brother's hit "Remember the Time" on command, and TLC's *Ooooooohhh . . . On the TLC Tip* led to a (very short-lived) phase during which I wanted to wear only Cross Colours. But it was different with Whitney.

Whitney's voice had the power to make you feel invincible. Those intoxicating runs she so effortlessly belted, steeped in the church and anointed by a lineage that made singing her birthright. Though she was cut from gospel, it would be sticky dance records and towering ballads that propelled her to stardom. For a stretch of the eighties and nineties, Whitney *was* invincible. It took just four songs to make her the preeminent voice of a generation. Think about that. Four songs. Not four albums. *Songs.* "Saving All My Love for You." "How Will I Know." "Greatest Love of All." "I Wanna Dance with Somebody (Who Loves Me)." When counted together, it's not even twenty minutes of her vocal instrument on display. Just four songs and Whitney became the Queen of Pop—*the Voice.*

I was at an age when going to the movies felt like a major event. Sitting in a grand, dark theater and staring up at a screen a thousand times bigger than the one at home was a thrill. If pop music was an escape, film was the teleportation device that beamed me into faraway lands. In the last months of 1992, *The Bodyguard* was all that mattered—at least it felt that way to me, a kid who loved the cinema and pop music. Of the things I inherited from my stepmother, a fondness for schlocky romantic films is high on the list, and *The Bodyguard* wrapped a frothy romantic drama around Whitney's voice—*that voice.* I couldn't wait to see it. During one of my stays, I mustered all my charm to get my stepmother to commit to taking me to see *Home Alone 2* and *The Bodyguard.* The sight of Whitney running through the heavens to the tune of "Run to You" completely enthralled me. It was the beauty of her voice, a wonderous marvel unlike anything I'd heard. *"Iiiiiiiii wanna run to youuuuuuu."* So light. So pure. So angelic. I never wanted to come back down to earth.

By the time I discovered Whitney's music and fell in love with her onscreen as superstar singer-actress Rachel Marron in

The Bodyguard, she was already one of the world's biggest pop stars. My appreciation of Whitney informed the music I began gravitating toward. I was infatuated by anyone who could move me with the magnetism of their voice the way Whitney did. Powerful voices that knew no bounds, that could be stretched and manipulated, excited me the most. Loving Whitney carried me to Mariah Carey, and loving Whitney carried me to Mary J. Blige, and to Brandy and to Beyoncé. My obsession with Whitney began in elementary school. Like a lot of kids growing up at the intersection of the late eighties and early nineties, I first saw and heard Whitney on MTV. The visuals for "How Will I Know" and "I Wanna Dance with Somebody (Who Loves Me)" were my first favorites. They were bright, Technicolor fantasies that matched the sugary sweetness of the songs. I couldn't then identify what an extravagant, perfectly made pop song sounded like or recognize the influence those songs have on us. How they can occupy space in your brain—and your body—for a lifetime. How even just the hook or the first measure of a song can teleport you to a memory. It's a heady, almost delirious sensation, really. Whenever I hear the syncopated drum claps and pings at the start of "How Will I Know" or the rapturous "*WOOOOOOOO*" that Whitney releases on "I Wanna Dance with Somebody," a giddiness washes over me. It's intoxicating, even still. Watching the videos now, I can clearly see my younger self bouncing around and doing the same little two-step Whitney does and giving my body permission to move without fear of judgment or ridicule. In those moments, I felt so free. I felt invincible. And I was hooked on that feeling.

The first Whitney album I bought was *I'm Your Baby Tonight*. My stepmother would take me to used record stores and watch me forage for cassettes. I had successfully convinced my mother to buy me a Walkman for Christmas and spent all the money my grandparents gave me for pulling in As and Bs on my growing music collection. On the cover of *I'm Your Baby Tonight*, Whitney is sitting on a motorcycle in a casual, sporty look of tennis shoes, jeans, and a baggy sweater, her curly hair perfectly falling to her shoulder. I was oblivious to the weight of *I'm Your Baby Tonight*. The buzz that it was made to steer Whitney back toward the Black R&B listeners her bubbly pop had turned off hadn't made it to my young ears, nor did the whispers about Whitney's sexuality and her courtship with Bobby Brown that many saw *I'm Your Baby Tonight* as attempting to silence. I didn't know she was polarizing, or controversial, or that this album was meant to radically shift opinions. I just thought she looked so badass on the front of the cassette and I *had* to have it. Compact discs were a luxury then, something only those with far more disposable income than a kid who split his time between his hardworking single mother and a stepmother who filled in the gap for an absentee father had access to. I can't remember if it was intuition or incessantness on my part, but both my mother and stepmother supported an appetite for music that grew more voracious by the year. It helped that they also enjoyed the music I liked and took an interest in introducing me to artists I hadn't heard yet. I took so much pride in my little music collection. *Oooooohhh . . . On the TLC Tip*, *Too Legit to Quit*, *What's the 411?*, *Bad*, and *Totally Krossed Out* got frequent spins, and I wore out my cassettes of *I'm Your Baby Tonight* and *The Bodyguard* soundtrack on my Walkman to the point where I'd have to take a pencil and manually rewind the tapes. Eventually my mother surprised me with a CD player when she felt I was old enough to take care of one.

Music was my safe place, and I found solace in my headphones wherever I was. Whenever bullies ran me into my house, I'd lock myself in my bedroom and listen to music for hours. And when I was visiting my father, my headphones transported me away from his drunken slurs and the cries of a woman who didn't feel she had the power to escape his abuse. Trauma was holding me hostage, but I didn't have the language to articulate it then, and I wouldn't for years. And so the escapism I found through music, film, TV, and video games became my entire world. The voices pouring into my headphones were a vital lifeline, and not a day went by when I wasn't listening to music, searching for that feeling. I'm still that way. "Are you floating away?" my partner will ask when he sees me meandering about the house, earbuds poking out of my ears. The digital age of streaming has rendered the collection of jewel-cased discs I spent two decades treasuring irrelevant. I held on for as long as I could. The ritual of grabbing a disc and inserting it into a player instantly took me to a place and a time when my youthful insouciance was in full bloom. I didn't want to lose that to the practicality of streaming, but age and inconvenience made me relent. I carefully packed up the essentials of my collection, in the hopes that one day my child would want to discover Whitney, or any of my old favorites, the way I once had. For now, the ease of accessing her at the push of a button far outweighs the nostalgia of parsing the liner notes.

***

I met Whitney only once. It was a February afternoon in 2012, barely two days before she would leave this earth. Her final days were a haze of confusing public appearances that weren't entirely becoming of the regal presence so many of us—myself included—expected. Standing face-to-face with her in a room inside the Beverly Hilton, I connected with her smile—the same smile I'd seen splashed across countless magazine covers; the smile that lit up movies and made her music videos pop with girl-next-door flair. There was sadness in her eyes, the permanent residue of years of pain and heartache and public humiliation. But that smile, the same smile I remember seeing in *The Bodyguard* and on MTV, warmed my spirit. When I look back on the day our paths crossed and the brief conversation she and I shared, I try to remember only the feeling of *that* moment—being face-to-face with the woman who resided in my heart and is the bedrock for all I hold holy about an entire genre of music.

I think of her often. Whitney shifted the earth when she arrived with a barrage of wistful ballads and peppy dance jams so expertly sung it was clear she occupied a space that was entirely hers. There wasn't anything she couldn't do, nothing she couldn't sing. No note was too high. Whitney had an ability to imprint herself on everything her voice touched—so much so that it took me years to fully grasp the fact that "Greatest Love of All," "Saving All My Love for You," and "I Will Always Love You" didn't originate with her. She had that rare ability, reserved for only the finest vocalists, to make any song her own. Whitney didn't sound like anyone, but *so* many have tried to sound like her. And still do. I can hear her voice everywhere. I hear Whitney whenever Ariana Grande reaches the highest peak of her falsetto. I hear Whitney in the clarity of Adele and the stirring grit of Jennifer Hudson. And I hear her every time Beyoncé effortlessly soars across the melismatic scale Whitney perfected so well, stretching her voice from its raspy gospel bottom to a tender flutter while making sure to accentuate each note in between.

Whitney didn't leave us with much music to rediscover— just nine albums, including two film soundtracks and a holiday collection. At the beginning she was somewhat prolific, releasing an album every two or three years. But Whitney didn't churn out work the way some of her contemporaries did. She came up with Prince, Michael Jackson, and Madonna, artists whose radical sounds were shifting pop music in real time. But while their music was the blueprint for generations of acts, Whitney's influence was solely her voice and how she used it. Whitney's scarcity, we eventually learned, wasn't so much about being selective with material or her venturing into film as it was about trying to preserve a voice that was deteriorating under the pressures of constant touring and the vices that would strip her of her dignity in the latter half of her career and eventually claim her life.

I've always wondered whether Whitney remembered the first time her voice failed her. I imagine she'd give an exact answer, given that she was quite the perfectionist. I'm still astounded that she would cut records in just a single take. She did "How Will I Know" in one take? "The Star-Spangled Banner" in one take? Unreal. I've wondered what it must have felt like when she couldn't hit those notes the way she used to, the way we were so used to her doing. For so long, she had made it look natural. What it must have felt like when it wasn't as easy to get there onstage or in the studio. Her voice was a gift so rare we are still searching for it, even though we all know a voice like that comes around only once in a generation, if that.

And I wonder what her answer would be if I asked her about the first time she felt failed by *us*. And to be very clear, I mostly mean those of us who looked like Whitney and understood what it meant to be a Black girl moving through a world where she had to carve out space for herself wherever she went. But, yes, the collective "we" as well. What would the answer be? In the years since she's been gone, there has been a great deal of discourse around the ways in which we treated Whitney while she was alive. Because her music didn't fit squarely in the boxes expected of a Black girl making music in the eighties, she was seen as *not Black enough*. She was ridiculed. Brandished "Whitey." There were calls for boycotts. The endless speculation on her sexuality. The bets on her marriage—and on her life. Those moments have all been excavated and reassessed as we've unpacked all the tragedies that contributed to her undoing. We know better now but should have known better then. We reduced Whitney to a national punch line. The pain she must have felt when she couldn't even go to the supermarket without seeing her face on the cover of trashy tabloids—a sensational declaration of her demise written in large, bold letters. It's part of the gig, sure, but I wonder if it stung more when she saw Black folks gleefully making fun of her addictions and her career challenges. Not just comedians and radio hosts, but singers who looked just like her and walked through the doors she had opened. There was a time when the world seemed to always be laughing at Whitney Houston. We all had an opinion about what was going on with her and what she needed to do to turn things around—personally and professionally. We judged her marriage. We judged her flaws. Judging everything about Whitney filled the void when her voice couldn't deliver that feeling we all wanted so badly. And if the voice wasn't there, nothing else mattered. *She* no longer mattered.

But what would a world that never had Whitney be like? If she never gave us the magic of her voice and set a gold standard for pop singers? If she never broke down the barriers that allowed girls like her to become the heartbeat of America? How would music sound today if Whitney hadn't married glorious gospel melisma and sparkling pop arrangements with delirious aplomb and created the blueprint? Had she not shown the world that a Black girl could shatter glass ceilings with her voice and rule the charts—and our hearts—with love songs or a spine-tingling rendition of the national anthem? What if we never heard "I Wanna Dance with Somebody (Who Loves Me)" or her version of "I Will Always Love You"?

***

Ten months after Whitney's death, I was walking the streets of London, lost and alone. I had never been overseas before, and my gift to myself that year was the European vacation I had dreamed of ever since I was a kid in elementary school trying to pass the French courses my mother enrolled me in. The grief over losing one of my heroes was the extra push I needed to find the courage to plan an international trip with nothing more than a textbook knowledge of my destinations. I started in Paris before venturing to London to ring in the New Year. Days were spent in museums, and at night I barhopped and explored neighborhoods. One evening, I got completely turned around. It was cold and rainy, and the buzz from the pints of beer I had downed quickly turned confusion into panic. Unable to remember the route back to the tube station that would leave me closest to my hotel, I wandered along the Strand hoping to spot anything that would clue me in on the right direction. The night was getting chillier and I was feeling drunker, so I resigned myself to the idea that I'd have to blow my daily budget and spring for a cab. On one of my detours, I passed the Adelphi Theatre and saw a marquee for *The Bodyguard*, a musical production I had no knowledge of. What were the odds that my favorite Whitney Houston film—the one that made in love with her as a kid—had been adapted into a flashy musical? As I fumbled through my coat to retrieve my point-and-shoot camera, I contemplated buying tickets. Heather Headley, a phenomenal R&B singer my mother had put me on to, was starring in the role Whitney played in the film twenty years prior. I got close to the poster teasing the show. The leads had re-created the film's poster, where Whitney's Rachel Marron was draped in Kevin Costner's arms as his character carried our heroine out of a nightclub after a riot broke out at her show (Costner later revealed that a body double was actually used for the iconic shot). The musical would blend the tunes Whitney made famous in the movie along with the hits that propelled her to global superstardom. I was intrigued, but I just couldn't do it. It felt like such a deep betrayal of Whitney to sit through something like this so soon after her death. I wasn't even ready to hear Whitney again, and the idea of listening to these songs being sung by anyone else felt sacrilegious. I snapped a few blurry photos and kept on walking until I eventually found the station.

It wasn't until 2017, five years after my serendipitous London discovery, that I made it around to seeing the *Bodyguard* musical. By then my grief over Whitney had softened and I was again finding great joy in her music and her films. Two years prior, a somewhat panned biopic on Whitney directed by her *Waiting to Exhale* co-star Angela Bassett premiered on Lifetime. I enjoyed the film more than most, but that was largely due to Deborah Cox singing incredible takes of Whitney's songs in the film, which were then lip-synced by Yaya DaCosta, the actress playing Whitney onscreen. Seeing that Deborah Cox would play the role of Rachel in the musical compelled me to buy tickets.

I love *The Bodyguard* to the point where I never change the channel when I catch a rerun of it on television. Regardless of how far into the film the airing is, I'll stop what I'm doing and watch the rest in all its edited-for-TV splendor, ignoring the ridiculous cuts and overdubbing. It wouldn't take much to imprint the sappy romance of the film onto the stage, but I was unsure how the production would weave in Whitney's original music. How would her hits be incorporated in a way that made sense and not take away from what *The Bodyguard* was or turn the production into a haphazard jukebox musical? But Deborah was a knockout. She nailed the dizzying ecstasy of "I Wanna Dance with Somebody" and reveled in the tenderness of "Where Do Broken Hearts Go." It was a thrilling watch, and I found myself snapping and singing along the way I did when I was alone in my room. I braced for her rendition of "Run to You," which still remains my favorite Whitney Houston ballad. I closed my eyes and shut out everything except Deborah's voice. For a moment, as she perfectly mimicked the brilliance that made us connect with Whitney so intensely, it no longer felt like her. *"Iiiiiiiii wanna run to youuuuuuu but if I comeeeee to youuuuuuu, tell me, will you stay or will you run aaaaaway."* The magic in that moment, in her voice, was enough. Deborah was singing to the heavens, and to Whitney, and she had taken me with her.

I left the show thinking of you, Whitney. What you could have been if we had truly allowed you to bend and shift and evolve. We so badly wanted that voice. Those notes. *That feeling.* And you so badly wanted to give it to us, even when you knew you weren't quite capable of it. I haven't stopped thinking about what you could have been. Where you could have gone. What was left to accomplish. Who you would work with. Who you would be. We'll never know what could have been. But didn't we almost have it all?

UNDER HIS EYE, BLESSED BE THE SOUND

Faith, Gospel, and the Almighty Power of Cissy Houston

It's quite fitting that one of the last songs Whitney recorded in her lifetime was "His Eye Is on the Sparrow." She had sung the hymn plenty, going back to when she was a young girl in Newark finding the depths of her voice under the stringent direction of her mother, Cissy, who was around the same age as her daughter when she discovered her own vocal gift. Whitney wanted to sing, this much she knew. And so Cissy decided that if her daughter was to sing, then she would become a student—a top-notch one at that. She would learn how to sing, really *sing*, from her abdomen; from her chest; from her head. "Heart. Mind. Guts," Cissy would remind her daughter. "His Eye Is on the Sparrow" was embedded in Whitney's soul, the way songs of faith and worship tend to be for those of us who spent Sunday mornings praising in church, had grandmothers or aunties who played hymns throughout the house whenever they wanted to be moved by the spirit, or felt the call to sing for the Lord, where mastering standards like this one comes as an unspoken requirement.

The foremost thing to understand about "His Eye Is on the Sparrow" is that it's a song that requires you to really *sing* from the heart and the mind and the pit of your guts. That's the only way the song makes its point. Put simply, it's the kind of song that requires you to *SANG!* Now what, or who, did you picture when you saw *SANG!*—italicized and capitalized for added emphasis? Did your mind place you in a pew at Sunday service or a homegoing celebration where everyone in the congregation is enraptured by a vocalist wailing with all their might—their faces moist with beads of sweat and their arms reached toward the heavens like an athlete claiming victory at the finish line? Or did you go to a specific performance, one of the many cover versions that might have taken space in your record collection? Perhaps you thought of the great Sister Rosetta Tharpe and how she shredded her guitar and turned the hymn into a rollicking foot stomper. Or of Mahalia Jackson, who interpreted the song so gloriously—and in so many different ways—that she made it her own more than anyone outside of Ethel Waters. Maybe you thought of the soulful intensity Marvin Gaye brought to it when he covered it in the late sixties or, if you're a Millennial, your mind possibly drifted to the scene in *Sister Act II* where Tanya Blount and a pre–The Fugees Lauryn Hill belted a stirring version. Regardless of where you sit generationally, the image your brain most effortlessly accessed is one rooted in Blackness, considering that "His Eye Is on the Sparrow" is so deeply enmeshed in the Black gospel experience that even if you didn't grow up in or around the church, your entry point to the record was most likely vis-à-vis a Black vocalist.

It's ironic, then, that a song so closely associated not only with the Black church but with the great resilience of Black people in America was composed by two white people—one from Iowa, the other Canadian. The story goes that the song's lyricist, Civilla Durfee Martin, was moved to write the hymn in 1905 after befriending a couple who brought comfort to everyone around them, despite facing debilitating health challenges. When Civilla's husband asked the couple how they remained so steadfast in their commitment to filling their lives and the lives of others with hopefulness, the wife responded, "His eye is on the sparrow, and I know He watches me." Inspired by that display of unwavering faith, Civilla quickly wrote out lyrics and mailed them to her collaborating partner and composer, Charles Hutchinson Gabriel. Basking in the gloriousness of hope is the crux of "His Eye Is on the Sparrow," the song's power determined by how the words are interpreted—starting with the questions asked at the top of the first verse. *"Why should I feel discouraged? Why should the shadows come? Why should my heart feel lonely?"* Taken on their own, these questions are somber. But the answer comes quickly: *"When Jesus is my portion and my constant friend, you know His eye is on the sparrow."* Why be afraid when I know I'm covered and watched over? That's the point driven home in the song's second verse: *"I sing because I'm happy, I sing because I'm free / His eye is on the little sparrow, and I know He watches over me."*

Ethel Waters might have made "His Eye Is on the Sparrow" famous with her performance in 1952's *The Member of the*

Wedding, but it was Mahalia Jackson who truly found excep-
tional meaning in its lyrics. Her cover during her landmark
appearance at the Newport Jazz Festival in 1957 is an exquisite
listen. She's not overly exerting the power of her voice, which
could easily swell into a colossal roar whenever she wanted it to.
Instead, she's tenderly stretching out the words, almost doing
a little dance with each line as her voice glides like a bird in the
wind. It allows the sunniness of the more optimistic lyrics to
stick. Mahalia makes these words feel like a nourishing meal
after a hard day or a warm hug from your grandmother, far different from other recordings, where she's letting the questions
linger mournfully, her voice lowering to its gritty bottom. She
could make the words smolder, her voice literally cradling whatever pain or sorrow flowed through her—but she could also make
the hymn soar and feel entirely sweet and heavenly.

Mahalia Jackson was intentional in how she approached
her songs. How she interpreted them. Like nearly every great
singer who's given us their all, the intensity of her voice was
shaped from a life of overcoming astonishing odds. Born into
poverty and orphaned at five, Mahalia migrated from New
Orleans to Chicago as a young teenager and held down menial
jobs like cotton picking, scrubbing floors, and other domestic
work. She had found her voice in the children's choir of her
Baptist church and became a fervent student of the craft. She
primarily pulled inspiration from gospel, blues, and jazz—genres
of music born from the souls of Black folks searching for solace.
Mahalia would merge the supercharged blues she learned from
queens like Bessie Smith and Gertrude "Ma" Rainey with the
sanctified spirit of gospel to shape her opulent contralto, a voice

the Reverend Martin Luther King Jr. said came along once in a millennium. Mahalia preferred to sing only righteous songs of worship—God's music—because it made her feel free. It gave her hope, unlike the blues, which lingered in her bones long after she'd expelled them through voice. Her performance at the 1957 Newport Jazz Festival was critical, for myriad reasons. Considered one of her finest showings, it was the first time gospel had been performed in front of an audience that large and that white. In fact, it was Mahalia's appearances at Newport and Carnegie Hall that helped introduce gospel to wider audiences.

That historic showcase of gospel at the Newport Jazz Festival in 1957—and Carnegie Hall a few years before that—also included Whitney's mother, Cissy, who was twenty-three and pregnant with her first child while making a name for herself in gospel alongside her family group, the Drinkard Singers.

***

To fully appreciate the anointing that graced Whitney's voice, it's essential to understand the almighty power of Cissy Houston.

Born Emily Drinkard in Newark in 1933 to Nitcholas and Delia Mae Drinkard, Cissy—as she preferred to be called—was the youngest of the Drinkard clan. She fell in love with the church at a revival her parents took their kids to when Cissy was five. It was the middle of the Great Depression, and the Drinkards found solace in their faith the way Black folks tend to do in times of uncertainty. They lived crammed together on the top floor of a three-story tenement in Newark. Church was the center of life for the Drinkards. Delia was a steward at their church, St.

Luke's African Methodist Episcopal, and Nitch—a strict man who could sometimes have a nasty temper—was a trustee. They were both moved by the songs of worship that boomed out of storefront churches and at revivals, the first place a young Cissy witnessed Black bodies singing poetic hymns and getting lost in the power and conviction of giving glory to the goodness of God. Cissy was enraptured. Her entire family was. Church was the only reason Delia ever left the house. Her mother was quiet and soft-spoken, but she wasn't shy about praising the Lord—she even sang a rendition of "His Eye Is on the Sparrow" during one service. "She had a beautiful voice that just rang out so clear—it was like bells when you heard it," Cissy's cousin Honey remembered. Delia died far too young—a cerebral hemorrhage took her when Cissy was eight—and everyone turned toward their faith and songs of worship to cope.

For much of her childhood, Cissy sang with her siblings. The Drinkard Singers, as they were called, was a dream of Nitch's after discovering the blessed voices his children possessed. He relished hearing the sweet harmonies his children could carry perfectly, and he wanted to share their voices with the congregation. Cissy, tiny enough she needed to be propped up on a crate, was the alto, and her sister Anne was lead. Brother Larry was the bass; her other brother, Nicky, the high tenor; and her sisters, Rebbie and Lee, coached. They practiced constantly, much to the chagrin of Cissy, who was barely six when the family group began. Cissy loved singing with her siblings, but she also yearned to be a regular kid and play with the other kids in the neighborhood. But the thought of her daddy and how happy it made him to hear their voices singing together was always enough to silence her protests. Cissy enjoyed the Billie Holiday, Dinah Washington, and Jimmy Witherspoon records her sister Anne would crank up on the family's old Victrola, but it was the songs of worship that she held closer to her heart and what she was committed to using her voice for. As Cissy would say, "Singing anything else—the devil's music—was unheard of."

The Drinkard Singers' profile rose, and they began traveling on the gospel circuit. Around the time Cissy graduated from high school, the Drinkards ramped up their bookings. They performed alongside the Dixie Hummingbirds and the Davis Sisters, groups that helped pioneer the "hard gospel" style of shouting and harmonic innovation that came to define gospel's golden age. Their widening exposure caught the attention of Joe Bostic, a journalist turned disc jockey who made a name for himself with his *Gospel Train* program. Joe was positive he could make the Drinkard Singers gospel stars. He had taken his knowledge of the burgeoning gospel scene and his access to record labels, promoters, and advertisers and parlayed that into managing and promoting gospel acts. Mahalia Jackson was a client, and Joe was interested in helping secure the Drinkard Singers a record deal, along with touring and management contracts. Lee despised the idea, as she wasn't ready to commodify the family's sanctified sound. Joe was able to encourage the group to join the lineup of the Negro Gospel and Religious Music Festival he was producing for Carnegie Hall. It was the second year of the gathering, which had been the first to bring gospel acts to the prestigious Manhattan venue. Mahalia Jackson was again headlining, and the program also included Sister Rosetta Tharpe, the Gaye Sisters, and Clara

Ward. The chance to spread the good word was precisely what Nitch dreamed of for his gifted children, but shortly after the Drinkard Singers sang among the greats, they were devastated by the loss of their father to stomach cancer.

In the summer of 1957, Joe Bostic got the Drinkard Singers a slot at the Newport Jazz Festival on the same bill with Mahalia Jackson and Clara Ward. It was a watershed moment, as this was the first time gospel was being presented to an audience of that magnitude. Cissy was pregnant with her first child, Gary, from a short marriage to Freddie Garland—a fine man she just didn't love as madly as she wanted to. The Drinkard Singers' appearance at the Newport Jazz Festival changed everything. Joe Bostic kept his promise and brokered the group an album deal with RCA Victor, making them the first gospel group signed to the label, and in 1958, the Drinkard Singers released *Make a Joyful Noise*, a live recording from Webster Hall that turned Elvis Presley on to the group. Elvis wanted the Drinkards to record and tour with him. But Lee wasn't for it, and so the offer was rejected. Much too secular of a move, she believed. The Drinkard Singers would make their live TV debut shortly after passing up Elvis's offer, performing on a gospel show that was broadcast from Newark's Symphony Hall. Watching one of those broadcasts was John Houston. A self-professed gospel groupie, John asked a musician friend of his to introduce him to Cissy. John grew up in the First Ward section of Newark, among middle-class Blacks, Italians, and Jews. The son of an electrical engineer and a schoolteacher, John was brought up Catholic and went to prep school before serving in the military during World War II. He was tall and handsome, and Cissy was smitten with his movie-star looks. Her siblings didn't care too much for the age difference between the two—thirteen years, to be exact—but Cissy was especially charmed by John's devotion to gospel music. The couple wed and supported themselves between Cissy's gig at the RCA assembly plant and John's hustle as a cabdriver. After Cissy had her second child, a son they named Michael, the Houstons sent the kids to relatives and family friends so they could continue working. John traveled with the Drinkard Singers and wanted to help them expand the network of venues that booked the group—an idea Lee didn't support. Lee's daughters, Dionne and Dee Dee, however, weren't opposed to the idea of allowing John to take the reins. The young women had formed a group with a few of the girls from the Young People's Choir at New Hope Baptist that Cissy directed whenever she wasn't on the road with the Drinkard Singers. The group called themselves the Gospelaires, and John drove them to churches and gospel concerts.

The Gospelaires, like the Drinkard Singers, quickly found their footing. By chance, John met a trumpet player backstage at an Apollo Theater gig the Drinkard Singers booked. The musician was looking to put together a recording session and needed background singers. Where Cissy and the Drinkard Singers would scoff at secular work, her younger nieces Dionne and Dee Dee didn't balk. The Gospelaires quickly became in demand for studio sessions in New York. John happily accompanied the ladies to the city by bus. John was a charmer, and he got close with the engineers, producers, and musicians, which only led to more session work for the Gospelaires. Seeing the money to be made in the secular world, John tried to convince Cissy that her sweet, soaring voice could go far. But Cissy wasn't interested in using her gift for anything other than God's music—even if her family needed the money. The way Cissy saw it, she didn't want to be a "backslider" the way she'd seen Dinah Washington and Sam Cooke and the Staple Singers branded when they ventured outside the gospel world. Cissy held firmly to her conviction, until her husband found himself in a jam. John had booked a session for the Gospelaires singing background for Ronnie Hawkins and the Hawks, but Dionne had committed to a session with the Shirelles. Dionne was the top voice, the key component to giving the background vocals their gravity. John didn't want to look like he couldn't deliver, so he pleaded with his wife to fill in for her niece. Not wanting her husband to lose potential work, Cissy agreed. She left the kids with her neighbor and best friend, Ellen White—a genteel woman her kids affectionally called Aunt Bae—and went to the studio with John. She knocked the session out of the park and came back the next three nights to finish recording.

With more coaxing from John, Cissy continued to lend her voice to more sessions. She eventually joined Dionne and Dee Dee for sessions, and the trio started doing session work for Jerry Leiber and Mike Stoller, a young songwriting duo who made a name for themselves by writing for Big Mama Thornton, the Drifters, Ruth Brown, the Coasters, and Elvis Presley. Producers loved the ladies because they sang effortlessly and had an impeccable connection with their voices. Cissy created a sound for the backing group by adding a fourth voice to the mix. The fourth vocalist mimicked the harmony Cissy was singing, creating a fuller and richer sound. While working out the vocals they planned on cutting for the Drifters' "Mexican Divorce" at Leiber and Stoller's office, the record's composer, Burt Bacharach, dropped in. He was struck by Dionne's crystalline voice and began calling her in to demo the records he was making with lyricist Hal David. Cissy and her girls got enough work with Leiber and Stoller that she could quit her gig at the RCA plant, a savvy economic move considering Cissy made in two days at the studio what it would take her a week to earn at the plant.

Dionne was the next in the family to catch her break after graduating from being Burt's demo singer to recording her own music. Her soaring pop ballad "Don't Make Me Over" reached the Top 10 on the R&B charts in December 1962. Cissy and Dee Dee were on the background vocals, and the hit was the beginning of a celebrated partnership between Bacharach-David and Dionne, who would become one of the top female vocalists of the rock era. At the same time Dionne's career was taking off with "Don't Make Me Over," Cissy learned she was pregnant. She decided this would be her last child. She was *tired* of having babies. After two boys, Cissy prayed she was pregnant with a girl. A baby growing in her belly didn't stop Cissy from wrapping secular recordings with her glorious voice. That's Cissy's voice on Solomon Burke's "Can't Nobody Love You" and on the Drifters' "On Broadway," and Cissy is the reason why the melody of Garnet Mimms's "Cry Baby" floats as divinely as it does. In those days, Cissy was largely recording for Jerry Wexler's Atlantic Records, which at the time was pushing forward the gospel-drenched rhythm and blues that would become known as soul music.

When Jerry Wexler signed a twenty-four-year-old Aretha Franklin, he knew the former child gospel prodigy would flourish with the backing of Cissy and her girls. Cissy was quite familiar with Aretha. Those from the church knew her—and *that* voice—very well. She had heard Aretha's father, the formidable Reverend C. L. Franklin, on the radio for as long as she could remember and knew his church, as well as the Franklin home, served as a way station of sorts for touring gospel singers. James Cleveland, Sam Cooke, Mahalia Jackson, and Clara Ward would stop at the Franklin home and fill it with the joyful noise of praise and worship. Clara Ward and Mahalia Jackson mentored a young Aretha. She was next up, and everybody knew it. Her genius was unmatched, even as a child. Between the sessions for Aretha and Gene Pitney and Wilson Pickett and her niece Dionne, Cissy struggled with a difficult pregnancy. She was overdue, and false labor pains and the fierce summer heat didn't make things any easier. Finally, on August 9, 1963, her baby arrived. It was indeed a girl. John and Cissy named her Whitney Elizabeth Houston.

Little Whitney was a few months shy of four years old when her mother helped Aretha shift pop music with her 1967 Atlantic debut, *I Never Loved a Man the Way I Love You*, a force of an album brimming with bold, Black anthems that laid the foundation for Aretha to become "The Queen of Soul." With Dionne and Dee Dee recording on their own, Cissy had assembled a new group of Black female vocalists from her church choir. Cissy and her girls traveled to Muscle Shoals in Alabama with Aretha to record alongside an assortment of genius artists that included Eric Clapton and Bobby Womack. The combination of southern blues musicians, deep-rooted gospel wailing, and piano pounding from Aretha and the angelic, octave-stretching background vocals from Cissy and her girls created something magical. A deluge of classics spilled out of their sessions: "I Never Loved a Man (The Way I Love You)," "Respect," "Do Right Woman, Do Right Man," "Ain't No Way," "Chain of Fools," "(You Make Me Feel Like) A Natural Woman," "(Sweet Sweet Baby) Since You've Been Gone"—records that helped Aretha transcend into an iconic American voice, one that we spent decades turning to in times of great joy—like the inauguration of Barack Obama as the country's first Black president—and of deep sorrow, like when Aretha belted "Take My Hand, Precious Lord" at Martin Luther King Jr.'s homegoing. When she died from pancreatic cancer on August 16, 2018, at age seventy-six, Barack and Michelle Obama credited Aretha's music as instrumental in defining the American experience, releasing a statement that read in part, "In her voice, we could feel our history, all of it and in every shade—our power and our pain, our darkness and our light, our quest for redemption and our hard-won respect."

Working with Aretha solidified Cissy's voice as a marvel of its own, and Atlantic signed her and the girls to the label, branding them the Sweet Inspirations. Though Whitney was a child, she was old enough to be infatuated with the sound that came out of the Sweet Inspirations and Aretha, whom she knew as

Auntie Ree. Cissy was ecstatic to have a little girl to dote on. She put her in frilly dresses and neatly braided her hair, and Cissy proudly brought her daughter along to recording sessions in the city whenever she could. A young Whitney bore witness to her mother and Aretha Franklin stretching their voices over each other, absorbing their tone and range and watching the depths of emotion they found in their instruments. It's astounding to sit with the image. Two magnificently blessed voices—one of which was among the finest the world has ever seen—singing freely in front of a little girl who would one day become the voice of her generation.

In the spring of 1967, the Sweet Inspirations recorded by themselves for the first time. They cut a take of the Staple Singers' bluesy civil rights anthem "Why (Am I Treated So Bad)," which drew its inspiration from the group of nine Black kids who integrated Little Rock Central High School in 1957, and a soulful cover of "Let It Be Me," a French record made popular when the Everly Brothers and Betty Everett and Jerry Butler interpreted it for pop and R&B audiences. The Sweet Inspirations' records were enmeshed in the soul sound the ladies had successfully crafted alongside Aretha, but the group didn't take off with their first album, at least not in the way the ladies had seen their peers take off. The Sweet Inspirations did score a Top 20 pop hit with "Sweet Inspiration," a record Barbra Streisand would later cover. They followed up their 1967 debut with several more records, including a collection of gospel tunes written by Cissy and the group, *What the World Needs Now Is Love* and 1969's *Sweets for My Sweet*. None of the albums pushed the Sweet Inspirations to the level of fame expected of the group of singers who had backed the great Aretha Franklin. Cissy knew how fickle the record industry could be. She had seen it firsthand for years, and she was growing more and more racked by the guilt of leaving her three kids in order to tour and record. Cissy wanted to spend more time with her family and less time on the road. After backing Elvis Presley at his comeback shows in Las Vegas and recording another album with the Sweet Inspirations, Cissy departed the group.

Cissy missed her kids and her family, but she also longed to be back in church, directing the choir. Being on the road took her away from singing with her brothers and sisters and the choir at New Hope. She wrote in her 1998 memoir *How Sweet the Sound* that she felt she had lost touch with what kept her grounded. So Cissy got right back to her old routine, which couldn't have happened at a better time for her daughter, who had already discovered the gift of her voice. Whitney would slip into the basement of the family house and sing along to the records her mother and Aretha made, belting at the top of her voice the way she'd seen her mother do. She loved the feeling that washed over her when her voice exploded out of her chest. Naturally Cissy put her daughter in the Youth Choir at New Hope. Little Whitney—or Nippy, as John had lovingly nicknamed her—thrived in the choir and worked her way up to helping her mother direct. Whitney saw the choir as her second family. The blessed voices in her family were all members of the church, of course—and there was Cissy, who could be tough as nails. Mother and daughter would butt heads over rehearsals, and their arguments were known to carry from choir practice all the way home. Whitney might not have always appreciated her mother's tough approach, but she knew that Mother knew best, and so Cissy shaped her like a coach training an Olympic athlete. She taught Whitney how to guide her voice like an instrument—from singing four-part harmonies and a cappella effortlessly, to breath control and changing tempos with ease. Cissy conditioned Whitney to sing with the full force of her body, using her feet as drums and her hands as the tambourine. "By taking me to church," Whitney later recalled, "my mother gave me two wonderful gifts: my foundation in gospel music and a godly heritage."

The image of a young Cissy Houston sharing the bill with Mahalia Jackson is a riveting one. Think about all that Cissy must have absorbed through osmosis before Whitney even formed in her belly, like singing with her relatives and bearing witness to Mahalia and Sister Rosetta Tharpe at the height of their powers. Think about Cissy taking her little girl to recording sessions with Aretha Franklin and how she surrounded her with some of the finest gospel voices to come out of Newark. And think about how the Black church, for so long, has been the primary incubator of the prodigious voices we cherish. Whenever she was asked about her daughter's vocal talent, Cissy would typically say her daughter sang the *"right"* way—the way she had instructed her, which was really just the way she had learned from church. The same way Dionne and Dee Dee had learned. The same way Aretha had learned. The same way Mahalia had learned.

It's no surprise, then, that the earliest evidence we have of Whitney showcasing the lessons she learned from her mother comes from her days at New Hope. There's grainy footage out there of Whitney standing in front of the congregation, leading the choir through "Just a Little Talk with Jesus" when she was thirteen or so. Dressed in a chalk white robe, her hair slicked back into a neat, tiny bun, Whitney sings with all her might into a microphone nearly bigger than her face. *"Now let us, have a little talk with Jesus / let us, tell Him all about our troubles,"* they all sang as Cissy conducted. Whitney's voice was muscular and pristine, carrying over the congregation with a force unbefitting her youth. "Heart. Mind. Guts." The sensation that washed over her when she sang for the Lord was magnified by the approval of a congregation brought to its feet by her voice. I imagine it's the same feeling Mahalia had at the Newport Jazz Festival all those years earlier, and the same feeling Cissy's father had when he watched his little girl singing in perfect harmony with her siblings. As Whitney sang, full-bodied, for the love of the Lord, it was clear she had the anointing of a blessed voice that, given the lineage she was born of, seemed as if it were touched by God.

***

I first went to Newark for the sole purpose of visiting New Hope Baptist Church. On a windy autumn afternoon, I pulled up to 106 Sussex Avenue and marveled at the red brick building. New Hope has that immediate, familiar warmth, the way so many neighborhood churches I visited in my childhood felt. The gravity of its history was only ever on the periphery of my mind. This was one of the oldest Black churches in New Jersey, the place where Cissy first developed her voice as a young woman, then shaped the voice of her only daughter, but I didn't feel any connection to the place until I livestreamed Whitney's homegoing with teary eyes and a broken heart. Not too far from this building is the home where Cissy and John lived when Whitney was born and the house in East Orange they upgraded to, but it was inside this hallowed house where Whitney's journey began and ended, and I wanted to see it for myself. I needed to see where Whitney discovered the voice she spent much of her life giving to the world.

Standing in the church's dimly lit basement, I waited in a back corner while a Narcotics Anonymous meeting wrapped up. I pictured a young, wiry Nippy bounding into the room for choir rehearsal. I imagined the nooks and corners where she might have ducked off to play and the hours she must have spent here learning music and fussing with Cissy over arrangements and absorbing all the anointed voices that shared their gift in this house. I had arranged a private tour of the church, which mostly consisted of a security guard unlocking doors and leaving me alone with my thoughts—with the exception of pointing out tiny details I might have missed on my own, like the small red brick with Whitney's name etched into it that sat near those of her siblings and other relatives who contributed to the church. I made my way to the pulpit and sat in one of the rising pews meant for the choir. The room felt grandiose, imposing even, with its vaulted oak ceiling and arching windows. A trio of white crosses hanging high above bathed the room with a soft golden glow that made the red cushioned pews and matching carpet radiate a calming warmth.

An oak communion table rested at the foot of the pulpit. The words *"This Do in Remembrance of Me"* were inscribed across the front of it. The table was adorned with white candlesticks and a large, gold-lined King James Bible that was propped up on a decorative base. Standing at the communion table, I got lost in the memory of Whitney's voice. At Whitney's homegoing, her golden casket rested where this table sat. The room was silent, save for the scratching of my pen racing across the tattered notebook I brought along. In that moment, I felt so close to her. Closer than I did when I listened to her records or watched her music videos or her films. I felt her spirit, flowing through the place and finding its way into me. I traced the center aisle of the church, where she walked so many times—and where she made her final exit in her casket as "I Will Always Love You" played over the speakers, my cheeks warm from the steady stream of tears that fell.

Before leaving, I circled back to that Bible propped atop the communion table. It was open to Psalm 120. *In my distress I cried unto the Lord, and he heard me.* I ran my fingers across the page, soaking in the full weight of the legacies created in this sacred house for a few more moments before seeing myself out.

***

Whitney recording a gospel standard like "His Eye Is on the Sparrow" at the end of her life—and not for *The Preacher's Wife* soundtrack—makes perfect sense when considering where she was in life during both projects. *The Preacher's Wife* was a jubilant affair. It came after *Waiting to Exhale,* a film that let Whitney channel some of her marital strife with Bobby Brown into a dramatic role and a set of lush R&B records produced by Babyface for the soundtrack. But *The Preacher's Wife* is a feel-good family film with Christmas and inspirational gospel music as the backdrop. And the album reflects the ethos of the film, with music that is uplifting and rooted in the jubilance of praise and worship. Whitney focused on traditional songs of faith and upbeat records that made for a gospel record that would be accessible to her wide fan base, which is how we get an exhilarating flip on an Annie Lennox B-side and a somber gospel standard like "Somebody Bigger Than You and I" reworked into a funky stomper (it's worth pulling up Mahalia Jackson's version from 1960 and playing it next to Whitney's version to see how far she stretched it). She was working hard to move us and fill us with the spirit of the church. *The Preacher's Wife* may be Whitney's only gospel album, but the music had always been at the center of her artistry. Because she didn't use gospel as a stepping-stone into secular music the way her mother's generation had, Whitney's connection to the genre and the way she performed it throughout her career didn't face the same kind of scrutiny or pressures her contemporaries who came up through gospel and crossed into the mainstream with music influenced by R&B and hip-hop did. And so the gospel standards Whitney held close to her heart like "I Love the Lord" and "The Lord Is My Shepherd" were paired with sweeping pop ballads and soulful, R&B-forward records she made with pop hitmakers like Babyface, Diane Warren, and David Foster. At the time, Whitney's life wasn't at all devoid of the pain or the troubles that would eventually undo her, but she was still able to shrink those parts of herself to a public that craved the heavenly highs of her voice and were largely unaware of the challenges she faced. "His Eye Is on the Sparrow" is a song about the comfort of being wrapped in the arms of the Lord. It's a song about exorcising whatever trials and tribulations test us. Whitney was always so steadfast in her belief that her faith would keep her covered, comfort her when the world got weary, and protect her when temptations of her demons grew loud. But when she made *The Preacher's Wife* in 1996, she still wasn't ready for us to hear any of her pain—but how could she have been? Her voice was one of love and escapism. Not of sorrow. She had channeled the love for her mother and the Lord when she sang "His Eye Is on the Sparrow" at the Rhythm & Blues Foundation Pioneer Awards the year prior. There was such unrestrained joy in her voice as she wailed, *"I sing because I'm happy."* Some of her struggles were public by then, but her voice was still untouched by the vices that later took some of the sheen off her gift. The raspy, mature voice in the last years of her career was imprinted with the torments of the darkness that consumed her offstage. On what ended up being her final tour in 2010, Whitney paired "His Eye Is on the Sparrow" with "I Love the Lord," another one of her favorite gospel standards to sing that she recorded for *The Preacher's Wife* soundtrack. Her voice didn't pour out as effortlessly, though, and often cracked and split under the pressures of singing live. Whitney's challenges to rise to the full power of her peak overshadowed the tour, but there's a flash of brilliance in that gospel medley. It's where she typically gave it her all—*heart, mind, guts*—despite how tiring it was for her.

When Whitney recorded "His Eye Is on the Sparrow" for 2012's *Sparkle*, life was far more complicated for her than her days as a young girl singing at New Hope. The voice she shaped in church had taken her across the globe and made her the preeminent vocalist of a generation. But the world no longer saw her that way. They no longer saw the extraordinary talent that could move us to tears or euphoric joy with stunning effortlessness. They saw a woman who had weathered years of storms, someone whose demons had gotten the best of her—the best of *that* voice. It was unlikely that Whitney would ever recapture the glory of her past. We always hoped she would, even as our support was drowned out by a sea of headlines that made it apparent how far away she was from her best days. But that's the thing about faith: Whatever challenges await us, we can brave them if we just believe. Whitney believed this, and she wanted us to believe it too.

Growing up in the hood, I never understood how anyone held on to their faith. I believed in God and the power of spirituality—even if the concept of religion was far more complicated for me to grasp as a child. But what I struggled with the most was faith. For a kid who heard the symphonies of gunfire, police cruisers, and wailing sobs from grieving mothers on a frequent basis, faith seemed much harder to fathom. Something about being surrounded by all that death and violence, the gangs, the drugs, and the poverty made the idea of trusting God's grace seem ridiculous. How could I have faith when everything around me was so grim? When everyone around me was struggling to get by? I had friends and classmates who went to church two or three times a week, while my family only ever saw the inside of a church at holidays, weddings, and funerals. It wasn't a relationship I had because it wasn't a relationship my mother had, nor was it one her mother had. I never envied any of my friends who felt a closeness to religion. All I ever saw was what they *weren't* allowed to do and who they *weren't* allowed to be. The holidays they couldn't celebrate. The rules they had to abide by.

Their rolled eyes when I'd talk about the rap music my brother was putting me on to or the soulful secular music that filled my body and mind with euphoria or the discomfort they felt when I stopped caring who knew that I liked boys. It always felt like such hypocrisy to me when I'd see elders sinnin' freely—getting high, drinking, bed-hopping, gambling, cursing like sailors—and then shouting in tongues during the rare times I found myself in church. I would always spend the entirety of the service with my head staring down at the floor or up at the ceiling, or flirting with the boy in choir I snuck around with when nobody was home. I was always so deeply uncomfortable by the display of public worship. The shouting. The Holy Ghost. Speaking in tongues. It was all so frightening and confusing. And then there were the sermons, so full of fierce judgment and shame disguised as the good word. But there's church, there's religion, and then there's God and a relationship with God. A belief in religion can be found and sustained without the church. People can find God anywhere, and many of us find it in gospel music.

Though I had no connection to church, I loved hearing choirs sing. Their voices working together to create harmonies sent shivers down my spine. The music was all I could connect with. Didn't matter the church. If there was music, I could be moved. It informed my love for the gospel music I was exposed to by way of the records that crossed over to mainstream R&B radio in the early nineties. I was drawn to Karen Clark Sheard and Yolanda Adams and Kim Burrell for the same reasons I was pulled toward Whitney. It was the way they used their voices—the glorious highs and the dizzying runs and the deep growls from the pits of the guts that they delivered so effortlessly. As I was struggling to make sense with my complicated feelings around religion, gospel music was moving closer to mainstream in a major way. Kirk Franklin exploded with his sleek R&B-infused gospel, and Whitney had the best-selling gospel album in the country with *The Preacher's Wife*. Gospel was my entry to God, and I loved the music so much that I joined a choir in elementary school, despite having no real knowledge or interest in any religion. The youth choir was packed with kids like me—outcasts who didn't fit in anywhere else at school. It wasn't like a traditional choir. We were the Gospel Posse. We wore track pants, T-shirts, and sneakers instead of robes, and our repertoire was a blend of contemporary gospel tunes and inspirational R&B. We'd load up in yellow buses and shuttle to nursing homes and sing Kirk Franklin and covers of "Joyful, Joyful" and "The Greatest Love of All." I'd whoop and holler about a revolution that was coming to take away our troubles with full aplomb to the delight of elderly audiences that loved pinching my chubby cheeks after our encore. Then I'd return to school, where I was teased and taunted, before going home to hide from the torment of the hood with my collection of records and books, magical worlds where I never had to stare down danger. That gospel choir was a refuge for a chunky Black kid who loved reading and dancing to Kriss Kross and TLC and Janet Jackson and singing along (or at the very least trying) to Whitney and Mariah and Brandy. And when I traced my footsteps on the same pews that held the choir at New Hope during my visit to Whitney's church home, I imagined the refuge she found in hearing her voice float and blend in with the harmonies of the choir. I thought about how fervent her belief in God was, and how much her connection to her faith was rooted in the gospel and the ministry she found in the music.

One thing about comebacks that we always tend to forget is that they really only work if there's faith. Doesn't matter how great the project is, if there's no faith in the person putting in the work or if the person putting in the work doesn't have any faith in the work itself—or in those who will receive said work—then there's no real shot at making a comeback. *Sparkle* was supposed to be that comeback for Whitney after fifteen years of being absent from films. The rags-to-riches yarn set against the backdrop of the music industry originally came out in 1976, when Whitney was thirteen, an age when she had already decided, rather firmly, that she wanted nothing more than to share her voice with the world. There's a cautionary tale at the center of *Sparkle*, which follows three sisters from Harlem who form an R&B group that crumbles under the weight of their individual issues. It's a dark saga that's better known for the gorgeous soul records Curtis Mayfield wrote and produced for Aretha Franklin to sing for the film's soundtrack. When *Sparkle* was released, Whitney trotted down to the theater every Saturday for months to watch it. Twenty years later, when she was a monolithic talent, her production company acquired the rights to the film. Mounting a remake was a passion project for Whitney that, sadly, couldn't escape tragedy—first the death of its original lead, the shape-shifting R&B songstress Aaliyah, who perished in a plane crash in 2001, at the apex of her career, and later the death of the woman who yearned for so long to bring it back to the screen and so desperately wanted a comeback.

In 2011, Whitney's dream of remaking *Sparkle* was starting to come to fruition. *American Idol*'s Jordan Sparks signed on to play the titular role, with Carmen Ejogo and Tika Sumpter as her sisters. Whitney took the role of their mother, her character rewritten from a housekeeper to a failed R&B singer who coped with alcohol before turning her life over to the Lord. The Curtis Mayfield tunes that made the original soundtrack a soul classic were reworked by new producers, and R. Kelly was hired to craft several original songs (this was before his crimes against women were actually taken seriously in the industry and he was jailed over numerous allegations of sexual assault). Whitney recorded two new records for her remake: a sparkling upbeat duet with Sparks titled "Celebrate" and her take on "His Eye Is on the Sparrow."

By the time Whitney stepped into a studio with the production duo the Underdogs to record the hymn, her voice was no longer the muscular instrument it once was. She'd put her voice through so much that it had lost much of the fiery, octave-spanning range that once drew comparisons to Mahalia Jackson and to Aretha Franklin and was so greatly inspired by her mother's divine lilt. Whitney's version of "His Eye Is on the Sparrow" echoes the mournful approach Mahalia took with the hymn during her defining appearance at the Newport Jazz Festival in 1957. It begins with just a little piano and organ. Whitney had lost some of the top range of her voice, which always seemed to receive far more attention than any of the material she was releasing. But it's actually the rasp in her voice that makes her rendering of "His Eye Is on the Sparrow" so moving. The days of perfect, rafter-rattling singing were over, but loving Whitney meant never counting her out. Before *Sparkle*, she had stripped herself of the goodwill she earned from her 2009 comeback album *I Look to You* with a world tour she knew she wasn't in any real shape to go on. Fans were furious that Whitney couldn't nail the powerhouse notes that were her signature, and the tour is mostly remembered for the disastrous footage that was circulated online and the headlines about angry ticket buyers jeering or walking out of shows. Those last years of Whitney's career felt like a spin cycle as drug addiction undid her. There was excitement over the music (she was, after all, Whitney Houston), then judgment on her failure to hit a high note or land another number one hit. The disappointment in her inability to replicate her former glories then led to a deluge of embarrassing headlines that always speculated on her drug use and rehashed the details of her dysfunctional personal life, which had become center stage.

Whitney needed another win, which is part of what drove her to get herself together to film *Sparkle* in the fall of 2011. She wanted to restore her voice—and her reputation—and inspire her daughter, who had slipped into peril after watching her parents in turmoil for so long. Whitney wanted the world to celebrate her for what she had given, and not spend as much time focused on her fall. And yet, she'd be dead three months after filming and recording what was to be her next comeback. The grief of Whitney's death was fresh when her recording of "His Eye Is on the Sparrow" was released in June 2012. I didn't listen to the record much when it first came out. It was too hard, and the scene in the film in which she performs it felt like a painful goodbye, so the sunny and upbeat "Celebrate"—with its retro flourishes and vibrant hook—became the last Whitney song I actively played for quite some time. But I put her version of "His Eye Is on the Sparrow" on repeat while revisiting the soundtrack in the early days of researching this book. It was the first time I truly sat with Whitney's interpretation. I listened to the voice working its hardest to soar the way it once had. Whitney believed she could find salvation through her faith, and she held on to it—intensely—in times of trouble. She sings like a woman praying her way out of the shadows, with nothing more than her faith to keep her covered. By the time she makes it to the song's declaration—"I sing because my soul is happy, I sing because I'm free"—it sounds as if she had found the light. But that was Whitney. She always sang the way Cissy taught her. *Heart. Mind. Guts.*

HOME

Newark and the Black American Dreams That Birthed Whitney Houston

Two generations before Whitney came into the world, her grandfather on her mother Cissy's side, Nitcholas Drinkard, left behind all he knew in a small farm town east of the Chattahoochee River in Georgia and headed north to Newark, New Jersey. There was no plan, or much money, but Nitch had his faith—the bedrock of the Black American dream. A third-generation farmer, Nitch raised cotton and grew sugarcane, peanuts, corn, and sweet potatoes on land that belonged to his family—a rare achievement for Black families in the Jim Crow era. Still, the terrors of life that befell Black people in the American South pushed up against Nitch. It was before the age of civil rights. Segregation and discrimination were the law of the land. Nitch witnessed the terror unfurl around him. Blacks were strung up in trees. Their property was pillaged. Homes set ablaze. Violence could arrive at any moment. Nitch wondered if he and his family were next, a crippling trauma that still lingers for Black people in America nearly a century later. The racists may have never come knocking, but the Great Depression did, unraveling whatever dreams Black Americans dared to conjure for themselves. In the end it was a misstep of his parents—forgetting to pay taxes on the family land—that crushed Nitch's earliest ambitions. County officials repossessed the family property, and Nitch, overcome with grief and shame, packed up his parents, his wife, and their three children and abandoned Early County, Georgia, for Newark.

Like most cities from the West Coast to the East Coast beckoning millions of Black families during the Great Migration, Newark was at the intersection of promise and hope. When Nitch and his family descended upon Newark, it was a densely populated city that held the state's largest population—10 percent of which was Black at the time. The Drinkard family settled in a ghetto once inhabited by German and Jewish immigrants. A ramshackle three-story tenement in Newark's infamous Third Ward became home for Nitch and his wife, Delia Mae. Their brood would grow to eight, with the birth of their youngest daughter, Emily, in 1933 on the same September day that Nitch's mother passed away. Delia would become pregnant two more times, with twins each time, and lose the babies at birth. Nitch was a strict man, with steely gray eyes and a temper that commanded respect and fear. But he too was a man of devout faith. His father and his grandmother preached at Ebenezer African Methodist Episcopal back in Early County. He learned the spirituals that were passed down from a generation that survived the horrors of the Middle Passage and poured the pain and rage coursing through their bodies into song—tunes that would evolve into the blues and eventually gospel. They sang with their whole being, clapping their hands with fervor and intensely patting their feet, creating their own syncopation with their limbs and voices and whatever they could use as drums. The music of the church is what drew Nitch in. The sternness he held over his kids was how he had been brought up. He didn't want his kids to find temptation in the speakeasies and brothels dotting the city's red-light district. Nitch clung mightily to his faith. It was the Great Depression, and life up north was tough with a house full of kids and a collapsed economy. He found the family a church home, settling on St. Luke's African Methodist Episcopal near their tenement. The Drinkard clan devoted themselves to St. Luke's. Before the family would file into service at St. Luke's, the Drinkard children would go to Sunday school at the Church of God in Christ. It was a deal Nitch made with the missionary who helped the family after a fire destroyed their tenement. The spirituals Nitch learned as a young boy in the South were a cornerstone of the weekend revivals at the Church of God in Christ. Nitch had been enamored of the world-famous Fisk Jubilee Singers and the male quartets that traveled across the South singing old Negro spirituals with near-perfect voices. He was delighted that his progeny gravitated toward the music too, and after discovering that his kids could replicate the glorious harmonies they heard in church, a new dream was born. Nitch believed his children were called to spread the word of God through song, and he wanted them to answer the call. The Drinkard Singers, as they were christened, would go on to travel the circuits integral to popularizing gospel music at the dawn of the twentieth century, perform with Mahalia Jackson, and make history as the first to record a gospel album for a major label. But it was young Emily Drinkard, affectionately known as Cissy, who would push her father's dreams the furthest by going on to use her voice to shape the golden era of soul—and by giving birth to the voice that would eventually modernize pop music.

Cissy had Whitney—her first daughter and the youngest of her three kids after sons Michael and Gary—in August 1963, right at the tail end of the Boomer generation. The world Whitney entered into was ripe with change. America had rebounded from the Eisenhower recession, there was Martin Luther King Jr.'s landmark "I Have a Dream" speech and its bright optimism, the technological advances of the space race, and the tragic assassination of John F. Kennedy. And then came Beatlemania, shooting excitement and delight across the globe and ushering in a new era of rock and roll that shaped youth counterculture and defined popular music for decades to come.

The Black American dream was as much about surviving as it was about upward mobility. After Jim Crow racism and the pull of better labor opportunities in the North had lured six million Blacks out of the South during the Great Migration, the burst of populations in cities across the Midwest and in the West and Northeast gave way to the birth of Black epicenters. This was especially true for Newark, which had become one of the country's first majority-Black cities by the late 1960s. But Newark's promise was blighted by the recession. The city's industrial center was imploding. Manufacturing jobs shrank dramatically as manufacturers left the city and breweries shuttered their doors. The jobs that were left at the port area and in business districts were earmarked almost exclusively for whites, many of whom had already fled the city for the suburbs, leaving the waves of Black folks pouring into Newark from the segregated South to take up residence in overcrowded housing projects. Between the rise in unemployment and Blacks being denied political power despite being the majority, Newark was rife with conflict and repression. A nearly all-white police force violently brutalized the Black community it vowed to protect and serve. Landlords gouged tenants, and retail merchants cheated their Black patrons. Schools were substandard, and a rash of urban renewal projects only further cut up neighborhoods and pushed people out. The promise and hope that had lured Cissy's parents to Newark from the South had eroded by the time she was raising her kids. In its place was frustration and anger that was ready to combust at any given moment in a city controlled by white politicians ignoring the needs of a majority Black constituency. Newark needed only a fuse, and it came during the long, hot summer of 1967, when over 150 uprisings erupted in cities across the country following years of racial tensions. Cincinnati. Milwaukee. Birmingham. Chicago. Plainfield. Saginaw. Rochester. Cambridge. Detroit. Newark. All cities that saw uprisings from their Black citizens that summer. In Newark, it was a rumor that a Black cabdriver had been beaten to death at a police precinct after being arrested by two white officers. The cabdriver wasn't dead, but the inhumaneness with which he was treated had erupted a community weighed down by years of police brutality and racial profiling and suppressed by redlining, crippling unemployment, and rising poverty. On the nights of July 12 to July 17, 1967, unrest jolted the city. Torched buildings cast Newark under a red glow, disintegrating whole blocks into charred ruins and causing about $10 million in damages. Violence left twenty-six people dead—most of them Black—and injured more than seven hundred others.

Whitney was four when the riots broke out. She was aware of the violence that was raging near the projects her family called home, even if she didn't quite yet grasp the divide from which it was born. "I remember lying on the floor and eating off the floor . . . for the bullets, you know, the bullets would fly and go through you," she told a reporter who asked about her memory of the unrest. The chaos of the Newark uprising drove Cissy and John—and much of the city's Black middle class—out of the housing projects to neighboring East Orange, an aspirational town that was predominately Black. They took what they saved from Cissy's touring and background work and John's numerous hustles and purchased a cute little Cape Cod on a tree-lined street like in the movies. East Orange was the kind of place where everybody knew everybody. The schools were better there (one Whitney attended would eventually bear her name) and the houses were nicer. Leaving the projects for a house with a pool and a backyard in which the kids could play—isn't that the foundation upon which the Black American dream was born? *Moving on up and finally getting a piece of the pie.* The Houstons had gotten their piece.

***

After Cissy left the Sweet Inspirations in 1970, she signed a solo deal and put out her debut album, *Presenting Cissy Houston*. It didn't give her the break she deserved, a cut made deeper after her label failed to put the money into promoting her surefire reworking of Jim Weatherly's "Midnight Plane to Houston" (revamped into "Midnight Train to Georgia")—instead, Gladys Knight and the Pips would see success as their version went platinum. Though Cissy's solo career struggled to take flight the way her niece Dionne's had a decade prior, her powerhouse soprano was well in demand as a backing vocalist. Cissy's voice was vital to an era of gospel and rhythm and blues, even if she didn't have the worldwide recognition that should have come with it. And years of touring, and the fickleness of the recording industry, had hardened her. She missed being with her kids. She missed singing with her siblings, and she missed directing the choir at New Hope, the church her family called home after transferring from St. Luke's African Methodist Episcopal. Even though the Houstons had left Newark, New Hope was still home—it always would be.

Now that she had a daughter, Cissy was delighted to dote on a baby girl. Whitney was a leggy little girl with elegant good looks. She was smart, sweet, sensitive, and shy—a good girl who minded her manners and had class, as her mother would remind anyone who asked. She loved playing rough with her older brothers and running track. Cissy would dress her in frilly clothes and adorn her hair with ribbons. Whitney hated it. She was a tomboy at heart who preferred the comfort and simplicity of T-shirts and jeans. Her mother's style made the little girl a target for other girls in the neighborhood. She was bullied for the way she dressed and the refined etiquette her mother taught her to carry herself with. She was seen as a prissy princess—too good for anyone, even though she desperately wanted to be accepted by everyone. It made her retreat. She shrank into herself, her self-esteem rattled by the rejection of her peers. Where Whitney felt most at ease, most at home, was at New Hope. It was inevitable that she would gravitate toward the music of the church. She was born into it. Whitney's singing aspirations brought her and Cissy closer. She was a daddy's girl, and Cissy's tight rule was a thorn between mother and daughter. But Cissy knew Whitney had a gift, that her voice could take her far if she took the time to develop it. Her daughter was destined for greatness, and Cissy knew that if anybody could get Whitney there, it was her. She rode her daughter hard at church and harder at home. Cissy was like a lot of Black mamas—she didn't take no shit and didn't play about her kids. When the bullying got to the point where Whitney was running home from school terrified, Cissy scolded her girl and demanded she stand up for herself. She marched her right back outside and told the meanest girl of the bunch to step up and fight her daughter. Many of us have been here before, pushed into a fight to prove a point. Whitney let the frustrations of her frequent taunting flow through her body, and she slugged the bully. Still, John and Cissy pulled her out of public school and sent her to Mount Saint Dominic Academy, an all-girls Catholic school. Gone was the daily taunting from classmates who hated the fancy way she dressed and the prim and proper way she carried herself. She was now taught by strict nuns, wore a uniform, and was the rare Black face in a sea of white girls. It was a lonely existence, surely, for a girl from the hood, to go from running away from her bullies to sticking out at a parochial academy. Girls in their early teens were hanging out with friends and plotting their first dates, but Whitney was finding her fulfillment, joy, and community at church.

Whitney sang with the choir every Sunday and advanced enough to Cissy's satisfaction that she allowed her daughter to assist with directing the members. At age twelve, she had decided, rather emphatically, that she wanted to sing professionally. Cissy tried to talk her daughter out of it, as she was worried that her sweet, sensitive girl would never be ready for the harshness of the music business. But sensing how serious Whitney was about pursuing music, Cissy sat her down. She had one question: "Do you want to sing, or do you want to be in the business?" Cissy's solo career was languishing, and she had no interest in hiding the realities of the industry from her daughter. If Whitney wanted to do this, she needed to know what was ahead. The business could be fickle, and it ate up talent. The road was lonely. There were snakes in the grass, and success was hard to come by—and even harder to sustain. Cissy had decades of experience under her belt, but she had also felt the disappointment of not achieving the level of commercial success that was all around her. She had worked the gospel circuit and broken ground in the genre and adapted to the whims of the secular world, dabbling across soul, pop, rock, and disco, but there was an ugliness to the business that Cissy didn't want her daughter to experience.

With the exception of schoolyard bullying, we were told Whitney's childhood was idyllic, supported by a loving, two-parent home. The Houstons were classically American. Three kids and a dog. John worked for the city of Newark's Central Planning Board, and Cissy's blessed voice helped move them into a middle-class home in the suburbs, out of the ghetto. Church was their foundation, and it kept them connected to the community. But that was the curated image they used to sell Whitney as a transcendent star. The Houstons had their shit, just as every family does. Whitney's parents' relationship was fractured by extramarital affairs and bitterness, and their separation deeply hurt Whitney. She felt betrayed by her mother's affair with the church's pastor and was angry when her father began living with another woman. Her brothers were both her support system and an influence. They both were already messing with drugs. Gary was ten when he tried heroin for the first time, and it would be a failed drug test that dashed his NBA dreams after a season with the Denver Nuggets. It was Whitney's other brother, Michael, who was the one to introduce her to marijuana when she was a teenager, and one of the many revelations in 2018's *Whitney* came from an old friend recounting the time he gave Whitney a baggie of weed and a bump of cocaine for her sweet sixteen.

And there was the darkness that would come to light years after Whitney was gone: that she and Gary were allegedly sexually molested by their cousin Dee Dee while Cissy and John were away working. Whitney left home at eighteen, driven away by resentment and her mother's suffocating grip, which had grown tighter after she started bringing her friend Robyn Crawford around and the whispers of a romantic relationship between the two reached Cissy. Whitney was in search of freedom and in search of herself. She was at that age where she wanted to do as she pleased. "Her mother made her decisions. She guided her, she chose the people that were around her . . . Cissy was everything,"

Frances Grill, the late founder of Click Model Management, an inclusive modeling agency that represented Whitney, recalled in *Whitney: Can I Be Me*. These tensions were all tucked away, of course, when Whitney broke into the industry. And understandably so. All families have their secrets—and there was no room for them where Whitney was headed. She was the anointed one, the one who would take her family the furthest. All their shit would have to stay buried, for that didn't fit the classically American vision that was carved out for Whitney.

***

Even if Whitney never dreamed of musical ambitions, wouldn't there have been some expectation of her to succeed, given the lineage she came from? The hope that a child would follow their parents is an assumption that's especially magnified for those in the public eye. We expect the kids of entertainers or athletes or politicians to take up the family business. There's that old saying "It's in their blood." And Whitney's bloodline was mighty. You couldn't say you knew anything about gospel and not know Cissy Houston. And then there were her cousins Dionne and Dee Dee Warwick and the aunts and uncles who performed with her mom as the Drinkard Singers. And the family she inherited through her mother: Aretha Franklin as an "auntie," Darlene Love as a godmother, Chaka Khan as a role model. Not to mention the voices she was constantly around at New Hope. Whitney wasn't from an ordinary family, where her brilliant talent was a surprise—or a ticket out of poverty. Singing was in her blood. Her birthright. There was no choice but to be great when your mother has toured with Mahalia Jackson and sang with Elvis and Aretha. Showbiz was in Whitney's veins, her career preordained by all who came before her. "Some children are born into show-business families; some leave their families behind to enter show business. Either way, only the rare and lucky ones have sensible parents who are reasonably satisfied with their own lives. The many less fortunate have parents who need the money and crave the reflected glory but still resent being overshadowed by the children they have pushed onstage," Margo Jefferson wrote in *On Michael Jackson*. Jefferson was interrogating the perverse appeal of child stars and the role it played in the fame Michael and his brothers found. But Jefferson was also confronting the ugly shrewdness required of showbiz parents. Papa Joe Jackson ruled with an iron fist and pushed his boys to the brink. Six-hour rehearsals. Missed dance steps met with whippings and stinging words. Joseph didn't offer warmth or tenderness. The children had to get that from Mama Katherine, who found comfort in Jehovah's Witness theology and carried the kindness and empathy Joseph couldn't show their nine kids. He wanted out of Gary, Indiana, a hard steel town about thirty miles away from Chicago, and he knew his boys would be able to accomplish what he couldn't with his own rhythm and blues band. And so, he would get them there, by any means necessary. Joseph was right about his kids' talent, of course. His cruel ways would ultimately result in a dynasty of pop stars that changed the world and symbolize the Black American dream—a family that came from the ghetto and got their piece of the pie. Joseph and Cissy were one and the same when it came to the hubris that filled them. They were born into a time when Black

Americans were fighting to move up in a country that controlled where they lived, how they learned, and who they could become. Their children, undeniably touched with God-given talent, had no choice but to go further than they did and achieve what they could not—for it was in their blood.

Cissy was fiercely meticulous about how she groomed Whitney. Although the music of the church—the Lord's music—was her pride and joy, and the foundation on which she wanted her daughter to cultivate the power of her voice, Cissy exposed her daughter to the secular music she once felt so guilty about singing. She would take Whitney into Manhattan with her when she had to cut background vocals. Whitney got a crash course on the ins and outs of the recording studio before she could even tie her own shoes. By the time she was fourteen, she was singing background with her mother on a disco record for producer Michael Zager. It was Cissy's suggestion that Whitney fill in for a background singer who called in sick. Zager thought Cissy was messing with him. She certainly was not, and Whitney sauntered right into the studio wearing her school uniform and knocked her take out of the park. Zager's zippy "Life's a Party" is the earliest recording we have of Whitney's voice. Listening to it now, it's almost impossible to discern fourteen-year-old Nippy from the woman who would emerge eight or so years later. Her voice was immaculate. Cissy's tireless scrutiny taught Whitney how to use her gift, and her natural, effortless belting is crystal clear on the record. *"Lift your head up when life looks dreary, let your wishes climb to the sky,"* she sings, her voice soaring above her mother's. Whitney's range was something else, pure and bursting with power. Zager was eager to sign her, as was Elektra Records, but Cissy declined them both. Whitney still wasn't out of high school yet, and that wasn't going to fly with Cissy. She wanted her daughter to finish school before getting into the music business. Cissy could have pushed Whitney into the spotlight the second she realized her phenomenal talent the way Joseph Jackson did his boys. But Cissy had the firsthand experience to know that the glitz of showbiz wasn't all glamorous. If she was going to get behind her daughter entering the business, the least Whitney could do was wait until Cissy thought she was ready. That was the deal mother and daughter made, and that slow and steady master-class approach to grooming her daughter's vocal prowess gave Whitney the chance to cut her teeth backing others the way her mother had without the strain of navigating the industry in her youth. Lou Rawls, Alvin Fields, the Neville Brothers, Herbie Mann, Janis Siegel, Chaka Khan, and, of course, Cissy all put out records with Whitney's teenage voice floating in the background. Cissy graduated her baby girl from performing at New Hope to accompanying her onstage at gigs she had booked in the city at clubs like Sweetwater's. Whitney had a small solo set, where she'd cover "Home" from *The Wiz* and "Tomorrow" from *Annie* and astound the crowd with a colossal, gospel-trained voice delivered with unbelievable self-control and a cool self-assurance. Hubris told Cissy that her baby girl was special. How could it not? Whitney came *from* her, and she taught her how to use her voice the way she too had been taught. Cissy knew it was only a matter of time before the world would know how special Whitney's voice was. She was right, of course.

***

In the summer of 1980, Whitney was performing in her mother's cabaret act at the Bottom Line in Greenwich Village. Her older brother Gary—Cissy's firstborn—was also part of the act. He had a stellar voice of his own: deep, rich, and pure like his mother's. Funnily enough, one of Whitney's old principals believed it would be Gary who made it big as a singer and not his sister. But that's the curse of showbiz families—someone makes it and someone doesn't. This particular night at the Bottom Line, Gerry Griffith was in the audience. He was the A&R director at Arista Records, and the buzz on Whitney was spreading around the industry. Of course it was. She had the kind of pedigree that arouses the industry and would have probably taken her far even if she didn't have the talent to support it. Whitney didn't just have a voice; she was blessed with statuesque looks that brought on a teenage modeling career. She was all of five feet, eight inches, with almond-shaped eyes, peachy brown skin, and high cheekbones. Cissy taught her daughter how to grace the stage with elegant poise befitting her regal voice. It all came so easy for Whitney at New Hope, where she felt most comfortable—the most at ease with herself and with her gift. Performing in the clubs was a different beast, though. And Whitney had an off night at the Bottom Line, right in front of the record executive, who left unimpressed by her stoic cover of "Home," the soaring standard from *The Wiz* that she had sung flawlessly so many times before.

Two years would go by before Gerry Griffith circled back around to Whitney. She was being courted by Elektra Records, and Gerry wanted to see her again, so he caught a club gig Whitney had with her mother and her brother Gary. She sang the two numbers that were now the centerpiece of her act: "Tomorrow" and "Home." This time, she knocked it out of the park, the self-assured confidence Cissy instilled in her on full display. Gerry wanted the head of the label, Clive Davis, to hear for himself. Clive *needed* to hear her, Gerry reasoned. Clive had already built a sterling reputation as the man with a golden ear. He'd made stars out of Janis Joplin and Barry Manilow and breathed fresh life into Dionne Warwick's and Aretha Franklin's careers after founding Arista in late 1974. A showcase was set up at Gerry's behest. Over the years Gerry and Clive have disagreed on how the label head reacted to hearing Whitney sing for the first time. She performed "Home" and George Benson's "The Greatest Love of All," a record Clive had commissioned a few years earlier for a film about Muhammad Ali that yielded Arista its first Top 10 R&B hit. Gerry says his boss was unenthused, bored even. If you let Clive tell it, though, he was completely blown away—floored by the "innocent-looking, yet soulful" young woman who blew the roof off Sweetwater's with a voice unlike anyone he had ever heard before. Love at first note is far more conducive to the mythmaking that comes with packaging a new pop star for the masses. And Whitney was primed for packaging: model looks, a knockout voice, effortless charisma, and a rich family history that cut across gospel, soul, and pop. It was a no-brainer to sign her, and Clive knew it.

Just two weeks after signing Whitney to Arista, Clive whisked her away to Hollywood to make her national television debut on *The Merv Griffin Show*. Clive wasn't just the man with the golden ear, he was also a master when it came to the art of promoting talent. He had the spark of a politician, the charisma of a salesman, and always spoke with the conviction of a pastor preaching on Sunday morning. The wheels spun quickly when it came to shaping the narrative around Whitney. There are a few expectations that seem to burden all showbiz children. We all want them to be as good a talent, or better, than their famous kin, and we expect them to be great enough to carry the legacy or, at the very least, stay relevant enough to keep our attention. And Clive used that to hype up his new artist. Whitney hadn't seen the inside of a studio to cut her own stuff yet, but that didn't matter. Clive had the story to sell, and Whitney's was a great one. She had been painstakingly groomed by a showbiz mother, but she was also a blank canvas on which Clive could imprint any brushstrokes needed to create his perfect vision of a modern pop diva—someone who transcended race, age, and whatever else divided us. He believed Whitney could become the voice of a generation. He saw her as the embodiment of the classic American dream, a princess who could be sewn into sequined gowns and presented as a shy ingénue who captured the hearts of millions with just her voice and her smile.

It was decided that Whitney would sing "Home" for her debut on *Merv Griffin*. It had been the part of the set she did with her mother for the longest and to push the mother-and-daughter hook, Cissy joined Whitney on the program to perform a medley that included "Ain't No Way," the Aretha record Cissy had sung background on years earlier, further nodding to the mythology of Whitney's upbringing. It was plum marketing, and Clive knew it was a surefire way to drum up hype—massive hype—for his protégé. "There was Lena Horne. There's Dionne Warwick, but if the mantle is to pass to somebody who's nineteen, who's elegant, who's sensuous, who's innocent, who's got an incredible range of talent—but guts and soul at the same time—it will be Whitney Houston," Clive said with much gusto during his impassioned introduction. "She's a beautiful girl. And her poise doesn't hurt, but it's her natural charm," he continued. "I mean, you either got it, or you don't have it." And ever since little Nippy found her voice at New Hope, it was clear that she had *it*. The rest could come later.

***

Let's go back to *The Wiz* for a second. Back in 1972, New York disc jockey Ken Harper envisioned a Black retelling of L. Frank Baum's classic children's fantasy *The Wonderful Wizard of Oz*. The idea was to take the beloved tale of Dorothy finding her way back home from the Land of Oz and wrap it around the spirited soul of the Motown sound. Basically, *The Wizard of Oz*, but make it Black. Fox backed the project, in exchange for film, publishing, and album rights, and in 1974, *The Wiz: The Super Soul Musical "Wonderful Wizard of Oz"* opened in Baltimore. It survived middling reviews, technical issues, a spiraling budget, and weak ticket sales to become a Broadway sensation. The production won seven Tony Awards, including Best Musical, and Motown and Universal grabbed the rights from Fox and poured $24 million into the film adaptation. What made *The Wiz* radical was its songbook. Gospel, blues, soul, and R&B—all music derived from Black people—hadn't gotten the Broadway or Hollywood treatment in this way. *The Wiz* took a universally beloved tale and retold it as one fundamentally about the perseverance of the Black American dream—dreams complicated by the history of slavery, emancipation, the Great Migration, and civil rights. Even when Black people were freed of those bonds, the battle for liberation continued in a country that denied Blacks access to education, employment, political power, and other basic privileges; a country where ambition was viewed as a threat to white society; and the act of surviving oppression, getting out of the ghetto, and not falling victim to state-sanctioned violence became the Black American dream.

Sidney Lumet's take on *The Wiz* updates the era to post–civil rights America. Turn-of-the-century Kansas is now Harlem, and Emerald City is a glitzy metropolis where the poor working class are stuck under the thumb of a slave-driving tyrant, their aspirations of freedom and upward mobility restricted by evil powers keeping them oppressed. Take away the sorcery and the sci-fi fantasy, and *The Wiz* is a story about the decline of a Black American city. The cast was literal Black excellence—Diana Ross, Michael Jackson, Lena Horne, Nipsey Russell, and Richard Pryor—and jazz savant Quincy Jones reimagined the music. An astonishing sampling of Black talent also contributed to the film in uncredited roles. Roberta Flack, Patti Austin, and Luther Vandross, who composed the jubilant spiritual "Everybody

Rejoice," all sang in the choir that rounded out the film's sound. As did Cissy, who became friends with Luther while working with Aretha. *The Wiz* bombed when it was released to theaters in 1978. We mostly think of the film as the catalyst for Michael's transition into pop domination. He was, after all, the one who had the most at stake, and so he donned a latex nose modeled after a Reese's Peanut Butter Cup wrapper and a tattered clown costume and showed us how desperately he wanted to be a star, without the weight of his brothers or the burden of his brutish father. Michael poured all his anxieties, and the torment of a childhood robbed of innocence, into his anguished Scarecrow. But his smartest move was getting Quincy to take him under his wing after the film wrapped. What could have been an embarrassing failure became a creative opportunity, one that bore *Off the Wall*, of all albums. Michael became a supernova and burned brighter than anyone in his orbit. But he always longed for home. We watched him collect a family of exotic animals, mannequins, cartoon characters, and children. He engineered his marriages and his offspring; altered his face; relished his fantasies—and undid himself with his self-indulgences and paranoia before devastating accusations of child sexual abuse altered how we saw and judged him. But before all of that, he was a boy from Gary, Indiana, whose father's dream was to get his kids out of the ghetto. The Jackson 5 did that, but Michael wanted to go even further. And in May 1983, at the *Motown 25* special, he "moonwalked" across the stage for the first time, showing the world he was leaving behind Motown—and his brothers—in search of a new identity. Michael moonwalked to inconceivable heights, and while he never came back down, he was always "ours" the way Whitney would always be "ours." We wanted them to win because they gave us hope that if somebody from Gary or Newark could make it, any of us could.

A month before Michael's transcendent performance on *Motown 25*, Clive Davis excitedly announced he had signed a fresh new talent who had all the right stuff to go to heights no other woman, Black or otherwise, had gone. That these defining milestones happened so close in proximity was just one of the myriad ways Michael's and Whitney's lives would parallel until their tragic demises—just three years apart—as they experienced similar victories and stumbles after becoming defining pop stars of the 1980s. Whitney didn't have her own sound, or style, or anything that was truly *hers* when she made her debut on *The Merv Griffin Show*. What she did have was a dream and a compelling story: partially her own, but mostly inherited by osmosis of being born last into a showbiz family. It's almost poetic then that the first time we saw Whitney perform, she sang "Home." It's quite likely that Cissy, having performed in the groundbreaking film adaptation, introduced her daughter to the standard that had become an early signature for her at their club shows. After Clive's enthusiastic sales pitch, Whitney emerges onstage in a lavender shoulderless top, black skirt, and simple gold chain. Her nerves are obvious, understandable given that she's just been thrust into the national spotlight. She's timid at first, nearly whispering the first verse of the song. *"When I think of home, I think of a place where there's love overflowing,"* she sings. Cissy, ever the stage mom, takes control and guides the band from behind the curtains. It allows Whitney to find her footing, and by the second verse, she's gearing up to take flight. For the final lines of the song, Whitney unleashes the full power of her voice, pulling out each syllable and vowel and doing a dance with them in the way that would become her calling card. *"I've learned that we must look inside our hearts, to find . . . a world full of looooove, like yours, like miiiiine, like hooooommme."* Whitney's performance on *Merv Griffin* certainly didn't have the cultural impact of "moonwalking," but it is our earliest example of a young woman from Newark with a big voice lifting herself and soaring into orbit, on her way to heights unseen.

STUFF THAT YOU WANT, THING THAT YOU NEED

The Brilliance and Influence of Whitney's Voice

The first image of Whitney Houston and Clive Davis together says it all. They are seated on a couch, arms stretched over the recording contract Clive offered Whitney, their faces wide with cheery smiles. She's dressed in her typical casual flair—jeans and a baggy crewneck—and Clive looks the part of a suave record executive in the 1980s. There's a breezy, nonchalant attitude about Whitney as she peers directly into the camera. She couldn't have known what was next. The records, and ceilings, she would break. The songs she would sing that became embedded in the fabric of pop music and established her voice as the gold standard for decades to come. The reach she would have beyond Newark. The dizzying heights and the dark lows. She couldn't have known the cost that came with signing on the dotted line and being primed for mass marketing as a young Black woman in Ronald Reagan's America.

Clive, however, was already thinking of what should come next. Before the ink even dried, he was plotting the right strategy for Whitney, which was why just two weeks after that photo was snapped he paraded his new discovery in front of the cameras at *The Merv Griffin Show*. The root of Clive's success in the record business was that famous ear of his. He grew up in Crown Heights, the youngest of his lower-middle-class Jewish family. Clive's father, Herman, was an electrician, and then a traveling tie salesman, and his mother, Florence, was a salesclerk at a women's clothing store. A fascination with Broadway musicals was as close to music as Clive got as a kid. Instead, his ambitions showed themselves through academics. He graduated high school at the top of his class and earned a full scholarship to New York University. During his freshman year he lost both his parents and moved in with his sister. After graduating NYU magna cum laude, Clive went on to Harvard Law School (again finishing at the top of his class) and landed a job at a law firm that represented CBS. Clive joined the legal team of CBS subsidiary Columbia Records and in 1965 was appointed as the label's administrative vice president and general manager. By 1967, Clive was head of Columbia, and a trip to the Monterey Pop Festival that year led him to Janis Joplin. Clive was transfixed by Janis and her fiery psychedelic rock band Big Brother and the Holding Company. "I had gotten, for the first time in my life, the almost cliché tingle up your spine," he said of the "electrifying, charismatic white soul sister" who wowed him. Clive had never signed an artist before Janis Joplin and her band. Much of Clive's mythmaking over the years is bound to his ability to sniff out a sure hit. The earliest proof of this is with Janis. In 1968, Janis and the band were finishing their first album for Columbia, *Cheap Thrills*. Clive thought the album's single, a cover of Erma Franklin's funky love song "Piece of My Heart," was much too long and the hook didn't repeat enough. The hook is where much of a song's catchiness lies, and "Piece of My Heart" has a killer hook. Clive went into the studio and reedited a take for radio. He took the new version to Janis, and with some gentle nudging, he got her to agree to the label releasing it. The song went gold, and the record sold more than a million copies. Right in that moment, Clive, someone with zero music training, became the man with the golden—or rather, platinum—ear.

Clive turned Columbia Records into a powerhouse. Aerosmith. Chicago. Santana. Bruce Springsteen. Billy Joel. The Electric Flag. Earth, Wind & Fire. Pink Floyd. Laura Nyro. All signed by Clive. But his reign at Columbia would end in scandal when he was summoned to CBS headquarters in 1973 and told to clear out his desk. Clive had been accused of using company funds to bankroll a Plaza Hotel bar mitzvah for his son, airfare for his pet beagles, and a West Coast rental property, claims he insisted were part of a smear campaign triggered by a federal payola investigation. Payola was never proven, but Clive ended up indicted on tax-evasion charges, and his license to practice law was suspended by the New York State bar. He pleaded guilty to a single count, paid a fine, and a year after his derailment he had been hired by Columbia Pictures to reorganize its failing Bell Records. Clive called the new label Arista—its name taken from the honor society he belonged to in high school—and focused his efforts on finding material for the few acts that stayed on at Bell, including a young singer-songwriter named Barry Manilow. As it goes, Clive found the upbeat Scott English/Richard Kerr ditty "Brandy" and had the idea to slow it down a beat and rename it "Mandy"—largely to avoid confusion with Looking Glass's smash "Brandy (You're a Fine Girl)." Clive's instinct resulted in a number one hit that made Manilow a star and added to Clive's lore as a mighty kingmaker.

Arista's early years saw the signing of the Grateful Dead, Lou Reed, Eric Carmen, Outlaws, the Kinks, and Graham Parker, and the label was the launching pad for Patti Smith. Clive used that famous ear of his to revitalize Dionne Warwick's career after a dry spell on the charts. "You may be ready to give the business up," Clive told her, "but the business is not ready to give you up." Clive tasked Barry Manilow with producing her Arista debut, and 1979's *Dionne* was a platinum seller that introduced a new run of hits from Dionne. A similar reinvention was pulled off when Aretha Franklin arrived to Arista in 1980. Aretha had spent the past dozen years at Jerry Wexler's Atlantic Records, and her move to Arista, where Clive was known to push artists toward their most commercial sound, was derided by critics who felt she traded in her soul and political edge for consumerist pop sap. Aretha and Clive's union proved commercially fruitful after she landed her first gold record in seven years with 1982's *Jump to It*. The album was produced by Aretha's good friend Luther Vandross, by then a big R&B star of his own after his 1980 debut *Never Too Much* went double platinum. *Jump to It*, along with the platinum success of 1985's *Who's Zoomin' Who?*, ushered in a new era for the Queen of Soul. Aretha showed off a fresh, upbeat side and turned out smashes like "Freeway of Love," "I Knew You

Were Waiting (For Me)," and her cover of the Rolling Stones' "Jumpin' Jack Flash."

For all the success Clive found with Dionne and Aretha, they were not artists in his mold. Though Aretha was flirting with younger pop sounds, her DNA was still quite rooted in soul and gospel, and Dionne had already found her niche before she started working with Clive. In Whitney, Clive could do what he couldn't with Dionne or Aretha. She had elegant looks, a church-raised voice, one hell of a backstory, and wasn't yet established. Even though he'd quickly hyped her to a national audience on the *Merv Griffin Show*, the plan was to slowly build Whitney toward her debut album. She continued to develop her voice through background work and recording commercial jingles, and her confidence was built by further exploiting her modeling opportunities. Cissy and John trusted Clive implicitly. They had seen what he'd done for Aretha and Dionne, and they valued his judgment to the point where Whitney's managers and her lawyer demanded a "key man" clause in her contract. Clive would be the one personally selecting the records Whitney sang and the producers and songwriters who contributed to her albums. And if Clive ever left Arista, she would be free to exit with him too.

***

Just after midnight on August 1, 1981, MTV went live. "Ladies and gentlemen, rock and roll," one of the network's founders, John Lack, announced over footage from earlier that year of the first space shuttle countdown of *Columbia* and of Apollo 11's launch in 1969. MTV was a new frontier. Twenty-four-hour music television—"video radio," as it was pitched—before music videos were widely mainstream was certainly a gamble. The Buggles' ironic "Video Killed the Radio Star" was the first video MTV broadcast. The network's identity was rooted almost exclusively in adult contemporary, rock, new pop, and the electronic music emerging at the dawn of the eighties. MTV jammed its airwaves with artists like Pat Benatar, the Who, Styx, REO Speedwagon, Iron Maiden, Rod Stewart, and Phil Collins, and within eighteen months the network was in homes everywhere.

There was little interest in Black artists during MTV's infancy. Fewer than two dozen of the 750 videos MTV played during its first year and a half on-air came from Black acts. Freestyle music and hip-hop were on the rise, but MTV didn't want to touch either. In our days of stringent cultural conservatism, rap was either dismissed as a fad or branded dangerous by critics moralizing over brash lyrics. The music was too loud, too violent, too Black, and MTV executives passed over Black acts they didn't think its young, white audience would like—which was ironic considering many of the artists getting airplay found influence from the music MTV kept off its network. It's hard to picture MTV—a brand synonymous with youth, music, and pop culture—engaging in blatant discrimination, especially when considering hip-hop's global dominance since the turn of the millennium and how blurred genre lines have become, largely under the influence of Black musicians. MTV's position to exclude Black artists that didn't fit into its narrow parameters of rock didn't go unnoticed. David Bowie interrogated an MTV host about it in the middle of an interview. *Rolling Stone* wrote about it. But MTV wasn't alone in this practice. Pop radio was doing the exact same, and often still does. Although hip-hop now accounts for much of the Billboard Hot 100 based on sales and digital streams, that command is rarely reflected on Top 40 radio, with white pop artists making derivatives of R&B, soul, and rap widely outnumbering Black artists from those same genres. That representation is *even worse* when it comes to the representation of Black women on Top 40 radio.

MTV's rise to prominence happened right as Hollywood was in the midst of transformative change as Black entertainers increasingly crossed over to wider audiences. In the civil rights and Black Power era, the idea of being Black and attempting to appeal to all demographics and getting popular with white audiences was viewed as selling out for many Black folks who believed doing so was futile. But those attitudes softened in the eighties, which led to a new vanguard breaking ground across all facets of American culture. Black Entertainment Television went live—a year before MTV, actually. Jesse Jackson ran for president, twice. Eddie Murphy leveraged his *Saturday Night Live* fame to become a massive movie star. Spike Lee emerged as a visionary auteur with innovative films that unflinchingly inter-rogated race relations, colorism, and poverty. Oprah Winfrey was laying the foundation of her TV empire. The highest-rated show on television for much of the decade was about an afflu-ent Black family blissfully living the American dream. Michael Jordan and Magic Johnson were the kings of basketball. Prince was pulling from new wave, disco, punk, soul, funk, and R&B to make provocative pop music that pushed the boundaries of race, gender, sexuality, and religion. Lionel Richie found international stardom with widely accessible adult contemporary hits. Tina

Turner reinvented herself with *Private Dancer*. The Pointer Sisters put out their biggest album. Michael Jackson and his baby sister, Janet, shed their youthful charm and created masterpiece albums that upended pop music. And it was Michael who blew MTV wide open after he and Quincy Jones followed *Off the Wall* with *Thriller*, a sonic boom of an album that turned MJ into a deity. The world was clamoring for *Thriller*, snapping up what felt like a zillion copies, and yet MTV still needed to be pushed into playing "Billie Jean." There was pressure from Quincy, but the threat from the head of Michael's label to expose the network's position on Black artists is what ultimately moved the needle. In the end, everyone won—*Thriller* sold an additional ten million copies, MTV's viewership surged, and the door was burst open for Black artists to become mainstays on the network. Video didn't kill the radio star. It created new ones. And Whitney would be among its biggest creations.

***

On October 31, 1984, Madonna released "Like a Virgin." Like Prince and Michael Jackson before her, she arrived full of big ideas, youthful chutzpah, and music that craved our devotion. She was a wildly different pop heroine—one of sex, glamour, materialism, and Blonde Ambition. Madonna mastered the art of role-play from the start, changing personas and sounds like wigs. The music was exhilarating—perfectly crafted, brazen floor-fillers from hotshot producers like John "Jellybean" Benitez, Nile Rodgers, and Stephen Bray. MTV's quick ascent made image matter more than ever. In our current era, when

MTV is *Teen Mom* and *Catfish* and hours-long stretches of a clip show hosted by a skateboarder, it's strange to fathom that there was ever a time when the network mattered as a vehicle into pop stardom, as we've become so accustomed to artists breaking from a single going viral on SoundCloud or TikTok. But before social media and streaming platforms displaced the vitalness of MTV, the network was a beacon of promotion that did what radio simply couldn't by being a visual medium. There was now a platform that centered the music video, which would quickly become a powerful form of promotion at a time when fans actually went to the store and dropped $15 on an album. Labels and artists got savvier. And pop became shinier and sleeker, and there was now an audience growing ravenous for more. *"I Want My MTV! I Want My MTV!"* In Madonna we had a visual artist who knew not only how to merchandize her image but how to meet the demands of the MTV era. Her greatest talent was, perhaps, her ability to appropriate sounds and styles and make them feel wholly original. The first time we heard her, on 1982's "Everybody," she was channeling Teena Marie on a track that had *just* enough of an R&B groove that it was marketed to Black listeners—and because the single's cover art primarily had Black folks on it, there was an assumption among many that this new artist was a Black woman. By no means is Madonna a showstopper of a singer. Her voice is feather light, but it's elastic enough to manipulate however she desires. Her first records—"Everybody," "Burning Up," "Holiday," "Lucky Star," and "Borderline"—were irresistible dance sensations that showed an artist making a strong case for pop ubiquity. And then she dropped "Like a Virgin" and "Material Girl." Madonna played to the cameras better than most anyone, and she made outrage and rebellion her brand. She baited Catholics, sang of teenage pregnancy, was unashamed of her sexual freedom, and burst with arrogance. At the inaugural MTV Music Video Awards in 1984, Madonna opened the show with a performance of "Like a Virgin." She writhed around the floor in a bustier wedding gown and lacy stockings, the words "Boy Toy" etched on her belt. America blushed, and pop's first alpha woman was born.

Exactly five months to the date after Madonna's MTV coronation, Whitney's self-titled debut album was released. For two years, Clive worked on curating the album and prepping its arrival. Though he believed Whitney was an easy sell, producers weren't so eager to record with her. Clive was told she was too unremarkable, that her voice wasn't enough, and that she was too showy of a singer to be palatable to the masses. The budget swelled as Clive spared no expense in making sure the songs that made the album were surefire hits. But a collection of great records doesn't matter if they can't be marketed and sold, and Clive knew this. He was promoting a woman—a Black woman at that—to MTV right as Madonna was hitting her stride. Whitney was the church-raised, fairly wholesome, prodigious talent from a formidable legacy. She was the literal All-American image. Though Prince, Michael, and Madonna presented radically different ideas of pop, Clive was a man of tradition. He saw Whitney in the vein of Dionne and Lena and Barbra and Diana, whose voices *were* the spectacle. That was what Clive was after. He searched for records that combined the soul, pop, jazz, and gospel vocal traditions of the greats he revered, but he also wanted her to appeal to the MTV demo that craved stylish pop and slick soul. Anything that was "too Black sounding" was sent back to the studio, including an early pass of her take on Marilyn McCoo and Billy Davis Jr.'s "Saving All My Love for You" after Clive felt it showed *too* much of Whitney's gospel roots. " 'We want Joni Mitchell. We want Barbra Streisand' . . . 'We don't want a female James Brown,' " the late former Arista publicist Kenneth Reynolds remembered Clive saying. It was a fine line to walk: have just enough gospel edge to be seen as an authentically Black vocalist, but not too much that she could only be marketed as R&B. MTV might have modernized pop, but the battle lines that had been drawn after disco died were still in place: R&B was "Black music," and "Black music" didn't go pop. Clive wanted Whitney to be universal and not read as explicitly Black, which would have made her less likely to break onto the pop chart. He once told Whitney after a performance that punctuating the end of songs with soulful improvisation was okay so long as it doesn't "go on and on just aimlessly," but that knack for call-and-response was the flavor she learned from church—the Black church—and it was integral to who Whitney was as a singer. But it didn't always work for pop audiences, Clive reasoned. The same applied to her image. Clive complained about the portrait intended for the cover—an elegant close-up of Whitney looking radiant in a peachy cream sari, her hair slicked back and a single string of pearls draped over her neck. She looked "too ethnic," Clive said, and grumbled to staffers that he wanted her to look like *everyone else*. And so her cropped Afro was covered with blond wigs and her peachy-colored skin was made brighter with bursts of makeup. In the memoir he put out a year after Whitney's death, Clive wrote that he was both color-blind and naive to the complications of marketing Whitney as a pop singer who was also Black—which completely contradicts much of what Clive told the press around the launch of her first album and over the years. As he put it in his book, he heard from numerous Black artists frustrated over not being able to recoup the recording and video costs of their albums because they were limited to just R&B airplay, but Clive was around long enough to know of this *before* even signing Whitney. He had launched enough artists to understand the mechanics of pop radio and what an artist needed to do to cut through. Claiming naivete around Whitney's Blackness and how that impacted the approach that was taken with her early records is one of the many revisionist liberties Clive has taken with how he framed his role in Whitney's life and career for reasons only he knows.

The first song on *Whitney Houston* is "You Give Good Love." It was originally intended for jazzy R&B singer Roberta Flack, but her assistant snubbed the demo writer. The song's producer, Kashif Saleem, thought it could be a good fit for Whitney. He'd originally seen her sing at a club gig at Clive's request and was not impressed with her lounge act, but when his friend La La sent him a demo of the ballad she had written, Kashif, who was signed to Arista as a solo act, thought the tender record could be a knockout for her. There's a breezy sensuousness to Kashif's arrangement. Kashif was known for his experimental, spacious productions, which favored drum machines and synthesizers over horns and percussionists, and the effervescent records Kashif cut with Evelyn "Champagne" King helped set a tone, sonically, as the sound found its position in a post-disco pop landscape. "You Give Good Love" sounds like the innocence of a teenage romance. Whitney sings of a love that is romanticized with the syrupy sweetness of a fairy tale—that "perfect love" that girls dream of, as the lyric goes. The way Clive saw it, Whitney needed to establish herself in the Black marketplace first. "Otherwise, you can fall between cracks, where Top 40 won't play you and R&B won't consider you their own," he explained to the *Los Angeles Times* in 1986. "You Give Good Love" would top the R&B charts and surprise the label by crossing over to the pop chart and rising to number three.

After introducing Whitney to core R&B listeners, "Saving All My Love for You" was released to court adult contemporary listeners. There was some hand-wringing from Cissy over the adulterous theme at the center of record, but the smoky jazz ballad is a whopper of a vocal performance from Whitney, and it shot to number one on the pop charts, knocking Aretha Franklin's spunky "Freeway of Love" from the top, to the delight of everyone (minus Auntie Ree). Clive and Whitney had made good on the hype, and they were just getting started. "How Will I Know" shifted everything for Whitney. The record was originally intended for Janet Jackson, who made a play at getting out of her brother's shadow with a pair of albums packed with bubblegum soul and slick disco rhythms. She passed on the record in favor of going to Minneapolis to work with Jimmy Jam and Terry Lewis to make an album that would fundamentally redefine R&B. Arista's Gerry Griffith thought "How Will I Know" was the perfect pop crossover smash when he heard the demo. Clive felt the same, and he approached Narada Michael Walden to produce it. Narada was overseeing Aretha's *Who's Zoomin'*

Who?, taking her from the middle-of-the-road adult contemporary she was doing with Luther Vandross into the dance- and synth-pop-influenced R&B that was invading the pop charts. Narada was struck by the power of Whitney's voice—how she could sing with a supple sweetness one moment, then pull from the depths of her gut and send a mighty growl out of her chest like Aretha the next. He retooled "How Will I Know," changing the lyrics and chord progressions. Inspired by Prince's sonic experimentations, Narada stacked the drum machine over his playing on the drum pads. Then he stacked Cissy's backing vocals with Whitney's. The high intro that opens the song—"There's a *booooy*"—was recorded in just a single take, a skill that made recording sessions with Whitney a breeze.

"How Will I Know" is our first real glimpse into precisely the type of artist Clive was in search of. Youthful and vivacious, Whitney was the graceful girl-next-door in mile-high crimp locks and a metallic minidress delivering a candy-colored fantasy in the video for the euphoric dance track. The visual is quintessential eighties-era MTV, with its quirky choreography, vibrantly painted set, camera trickery, and nonsensical plot. Unlike Madonna, Whitney is no natural dancer; that much is obvious from her awkward flailing. But her years of modeling and her graceful beauty paid off in her visual presentation. She exuded a confidence that was sexy and effortless. Whitney didn't take herself seriously as she bopped around the dancers, and she didn't need to. Not with that voice. The world had yet to hear anything like Whitney, a singer who took the intense conviction of gospel singing and imprinted it on bubbly Top 40 pop arrangements. It was her second consecutive number one.

Whitney Houston became the first debut album—and the first by any woman—to have three number one singles after her pop-gospel power ballad "Greatest Love of All" hit the top of the charts (where it stayed for three weeks straight). The criticism of Whitney and the album was mixed. Her material was dismissed as too formulaic and devoid of any artistic risk-taking for a voice as substantial as hers. Critics bemoaned the fact that four producers shaped the album, and that three of its ten tracks were duets—two of which were with Jermaine Jackson, one of the album's producers. *Rolling Stone* lauded Whitney as "one of the most exciting new voices in years," but a critic for the *New York Times* groused that she had yet to find a distinctive style in the way her role models had. "She lacks Aretha Franklin's jazzy sass, Gladys Knight's embracing warmth, Tina Turner's raw energy, Diana Ross's kittenish sleekness, Deniece Williams's delicacy, and the endless dramatic reserves of Patti La Belle and Jennifer Holliday. Rather she is a composite of all these singers," one of the sharper lines of the review reads. The consensus was that the album captured but a small fraction of the gospel power that made Whitney worthy of all the hype her label spent hundreds of thousands of dollars to manufacture.

But critics are just that. Critics. Whitney's music struck a chord with the masses, and a year after its release, *Whitney Houston* was the number one album in the country—where it remained for fourteen nonconsecutive weeks, surpassing Tina Turner's *Private Dancer* to become the best-selling album by a Black female vocalist in pop history at the time. Whitney frenzy swept America and much of the world. She was on fire out the gate, much to her and the label's surprise—even Clive, in all his arrogance, was shocked by how she took off. With her first album, Whitney landed atop multiple Billboard year-end lists, won seven American Music Awards and a Video Music Award, and nabbed multiple nominations at the 1986 Grammy Awards, including Album of the Year—though Clive was angry that she was ineligible for Best New Artist because of a duet she had done with Teddy Pendergrass for his album that was a minor R&B hit. Whitney was awarded her first Grammy, winning Best Pop Vocal Performance, Female, for "Saving All My Love for You," and her spellbinding performance of the torch ballad during the Grammys telecast would earn her an Emmy. That was what she did with just her *first* album.

The idea that Whitney was a mere vessel carefully programmed by a Svengali took hold almost instantly. Who was Whitney anyway? Prince and Michael and Madonna were dominating eighties pop with grandiose personal statements and constantly toying with innovations and reinvention. Because she was at the top of the charts, and everywhere else, those questions were asked, often. Critics couldn't deny the power of her voice and the way she used her instrument. She was a peerless vocalist. But who was the woman singing these great love songs that didn't come from her heart and weren't even selected by her? The image of a young, beautiful ingénue under the thumb of a powerful man in a suit is as old a showbiz tale as they come. And then there's the complicated history between Jewish record executives and producers, who have played a tremendous role in building the entertainment industry, and the Black talent they have worked with—and at times exploited—which gave way to the bigoted stereotype that the entire industry is controlled by Jews looking to take advantage of Black artists. It's a touchpoint that added another layer of complications to how Whitney and Clive were perceived by critics and the public. It came up in the interview for the only *Rolling Stone* cover she got in her lifetime. It was 1993, and by then she had racked up an astonishing ten number-one singles and her first three albums and the soundtrack to *The Bodyguard* had sold twenty-six million copies—and that was just in the United States. Whitney already knew the thorny side of fame by this point and had grown increasingly unrestrained with the press. She was asked, rather forwardly, if it bothered her that people saw Clive as the mastermind behind her. "I don't like it when they see me as this little person who doesn't know what to do with herself—like I have no idea what I want, like I'm just a puppet and Clive's got the strings," Whitney said. "That's bullshit. That's demeaning to me, because that ain't how it is, and it never was. And never will be. I wouldn't be with anybody who didn't respect my opinion. *Nobody* makes me do anything I don't want to do. You can't make me sing something I don't want to sing." She'd spend the rest of her career biting back at that idea.

But back in 1986, there was a great deal of pressure on Whitney, on Clive, on the label, to replicate the success of that first album. And so, the ol' "if it ain't broke, don't fix it" approach was applied to Whitney's sophomore project, right down to its title—it would simply be called *Whitney*, following a tradition of women at Arista: Dionne. Aretha. Carly. Three of the producers from her debut, Narada Michael Walden, Michael Masser, and Kashif, were tapped for the project and Jellybean Benitez was added to the stable. Narada Michael Walden handled the bulk of the project, which helped make the album a more cohesive listen than its predecessor. The success of her debut set the formula that was followed: bouncy pop R&B and lush power ballads about heartbreak and empowerment that showcased her vocal range. Where Whitney's first album painted her as young and shy, the collection of records on her second album showed a woman experienced with love and desire. The album opens with "I Wanna Dance with Somebody (Who Loves Me)," an exhilarating track that's brazen in its attempt at re-creating the flavor of "How Will I Know." Narada Michael Walden, unenthused by the original western-flavored demo, worked to make it funkier and feel more like a dance-R&B number. The end result was an amalgamation of the irresistible danceability of "How Will I Know" with the peppiness of Cyndi Lauper's "Girls Just Want to Have Fun." The team behind the "How Will I Know" video was also hired to direct and choregraph a vibrant visual for "I Wanna Dance with Somebody." Whitney burst onto the screen, her blond crimps taller than ever. She slunk and flirted with the camera. Grace and charisma seeped out of her pores. If you didn't see her as a star before, you had to now. The record was undeniable, even if it didn't feel any different from what she just put out. "I Wanna Dance with Somebody" skyrocketed to number one. So did two more contributions from Narada: the anthemic rock-dance number "So Emotional" and the power ballad "Where Do Broken Hearts Go," which brought her tally to seven consecutive number ones, a feat that pushed her over the Beatles and the Bee Gees.

We have been reminded so much of the records Whitney broke that the actual weight of what she was doing is often lost in the grandiosity of her accomplishments. She was pulling all this

off before streaming simplified—and complicated—our relationship with music. It was the late eighties, a time where you had to
physically go to a record store and part with fifteen bucks for an
album—before technology made it possible to pay $9.99 a month
and have access to millions of albums on your cell phone, smart
TV, and on pretty much every digital gadget in existence today.
Even though MTV made pop music more image-conscious,
that didn't change the fact that an artist's commercial success
largely depended upon record sales and touring. There wasn't
the brand-forward artistry or viral-based pop stardom that we
see now. Artists topped the charts by selling millions and millions of *physical* records without blogs or Twitter hype or being
featured on the right Spotify playlist or in the right ad.

Released June 2, 1987, *Whitney* was the first album by a
female artist to debut at number one on the pop chart. Whitney
kicked down the wall for Black women in the industry with
her first two albums. She and Sade were able to cut through
the notoriously segregated MTV, creating an opening for Janet
Jackson and Anita Baker. Whitney had reached that Michael
Jackson *Thriller* level of fame. Her sales were through the roof,
and the records she broke were too dizzying to comprehend.
She was chipping away at cultural barriers that would liberate
generations of Black women artists to come, but critics still
didn't know what to think of America's sweetheart. Some of the
reviews for *Whitney* were rough. Critics thought the album was
too safe, too similar to her debut. *Rolling Stone* called it a "mess
of an album that succeeds in spite of itself" and noted it was
"easy to dismiss as overcalculated, hollowed-out pop product,
so suffocated by professionalism that only the faintest pulse of

soul remains." The *Los Angeles Times* brandished it a "consider-able disappointment," and the *New York Times* review said the album had little heart.

Snide titles like "yuppie icon" or "crossover queen" were bestowed upon Whitney, and Black radio stations made it a point to not play her music. The growing ire over her straitlaced image reached a tipping point at the 1989 Soul Train Awards, where her name was met with scattered boos among the audience. Black critics felt she wasn't Black enough, while white critics applauded her album for being "bolder, blacker, badder"—that was actually a line a white critic wrote about her in *Time* magazine. All this chatter rattled her. Whitney sniped at journalists who pressed her on the criticisms of the music and her roots, as did Cissy, who rarely left her daughter's side. She couldn't understand why she was being persecuted for singing the music she enjoyed or why her music was seen as defining her Blackness. Her emergence as a poised princess who projected grandeur and elegance played against the typical image of Black women, particularly those who came from cities transformed by upris-ings. Before Whitney, the country hadn't collectively christened a Black girl as America's Sweetheart. But what had she given up to get there? What had she shed? For a time at the beginning of her career she wasn't engaging with press directly. Some of it was Clive's mythmaking at play—an elusive chanteuse was certainly more titillating than an overexposed one. But we also know now that some of what kept Whitney at bay from the press was the fact that she could be a loose cannon. She knew she was walking between two worlds: the royal debutante who spoke in the prissy mid-Atlantic accent whom she was media trained into being and the chain-smoking, around-the-way girl who let curses fly freely and, as she boasted to *Time*, could "get down, really freakin' dirty with you."

The conversation around Whitney's Blackness—and what she shed for mainstream acceptance—echoes that of Diana Ross. Though the world was much different in the late eighties than it was when Berry Gordy founded Motown Records at the twilight of the civil rights movement, there's a throughline between Whitney and Diana that's important to understand when considering what Whitney was up against when she made her debut. Motown was driven, in part, by the idea of assimilation, and Berry Gordy was promoting the idea of Black middle-class mobility as much as he was marketing soul music. A former auto worker, Berry imprinted the principals he learned on the assembly line to his label. The product was sophisticated soul music that appealed to the masses. "The Sound of Young America" was the slogan. Reaching across color lines and demographics required a palatable image. Motown was plucking acts out of the projects, but that's not what Berry was trying to sell. He wanted to sell polished, refined Blackness divorced of the ghetto and its poorness. Berry wanted to give Black folks another vision of Blackness, and he figured the best way for white America to start seeing Black people as whole was to infiltrate their households with music that appealed to them. This strategy seems retrograde now, but at the time it was subversive. And so the Supremes, Stevie Wonder, Marvin Gaye, Smokey Robinson, the Jackson 5, the Four Tops, Martha Reeves, Tammi Terrell, and the Marvelettes all went through the finishing school Berry had in-house at the label to help them assimilate. Grooming, poise, and social graces were instilled in Motown artists as they were molded into polished versions of themselves—and stripped of any signifiers of the Black ghettos they came from. In keeping with the image of Black middle-class aspiration, Berry Gordy uprooted Motown's headquarters from Detroit to the West Coast after the long, hot summer of 1967 had transformed the city. Motown, as music scholar Mark Anthony Neal posits, sought to showcase "Black progress in terms of the integration of mainstream and elite American institutions by Blacks with highly textured middle-class sensibilities."

Motown became the largest Black-owned company in America by marketing soul music, and Blackness by extension, to audiences across color lines and demographics at a time when the idea of "soul" was intrinsically connected to Black Power and communal pride—concepts that were inherently threatening to white America. It was Berry's belief that Black women would be at the center of desegregating pop music. As he saw it, white America would find Black women less intimidating than the male performers whose sensuality and sexuality frightened them. Diana Ross is a direct result of Berry's philosophy. She was fresh out of high school when he agreed to sign her and the Supremes (then called the Primettes). The grooming was immediate. The Supremes' immature rough edges were smoothed and shaped until they became regal, bourgeois women. They were taught how to stand and how to hold posture. Attention couldn't be drawn to their bodies, particularly their derrieres, for the curves of Black women made them haughty and not docile in the way Berry wanted them to appear. They were taught to be mindful of their facial

expressions while performing: singing with too much conviction the way they'd been taught in church resulted in faces that
could be read as angry, and they were instead instructed to sing
with a smile and their eyes frozen on a fixed point. From the
start, Berry saw the undeniable charisma and crossover appeal
of Diane, which became the more regal Diana (like Dionne
Warwick, whose last name was really spelled Warrick, a typo
informed her stage name). Berry worked hard to shape her
into a superstar, and their relationship would blur the lines
between professional and romantic until they decided to end
their personal relationship. But for all her success, Diana was
seen only as a hollow vessel. The same as Whitney. Both were
looked at as women controlled and exploited by a powerful
man who stripped them of their fullness, their Blackness, in
exchange for mass-market appeal. Whitney bristled at the
comparisons, which followed her through the entirety of her
career, the same way she hedged against the belief that she
was merely the creation of a man and had no autonomy over
her voice or her image.

Determined to push back against the questions over her identity and her music, Whitney was eager to branch out when she
started working on her third album in 1989. She wanted to dig
deeper into her gospel roots and explore conceptual projects.
A few years earlier, Janet Jackson had dropped *Control*, an
aggressive assertion of independence that helped birth the New
Jack Swing era. And there was Madonna, who followed up her
monstrous *Like a Virgin* with *True Blue*, an even bigger and more

acclaimed album. Watching Janet and Madonna write and produce their own music made Whitney wonder if she too should be doing the same. Clive reminded her that she was of the great tradition of Billie Holiday, Ella Fitzgerald, Barbra Streisand, and Frank Sinatra—talents whose genius lay in their voice and how they interpreted the songs they sang.

Controversy around Whitney's image and the music she was making was too loud to ignore by the end of the eighties, and Clive honored his protégé's wish to shift sonic direction for her third album. Kenneth "Babyface" Edmonds and Antonio "L.A." Reid were brought on board to write and produce, along with past collaborators Narada Michael Walden, Michael Masser, and Gerry Goffin. Babyface and L.A. Reid arose from funk-R&B outfit the Deele to become hotshot producers with slick R&B sounds that merged the candescent Black pop of the Motown era with the muscular funk and dance grooves Prince brought to the center. Babyface and L.A. Reid, along with Teddy Riley, Jimmy Jam, and Terry Lewis, were rewriting contemporary R&B. The Black vocalizing inherent in gospel now had a hip-hop edge, on top of being deeply informed by dance-pop productions. A new language had been created, one that bridged the gap between R&B and hip-hop—redefining both genres. Janet Jackson's *Control* is ground zero for New Jack's explosion as a pop force, with its fusion of R&B, rap, funk, disco, and synthesized percussion, but Teddy Riley was its innovator. Teddy grew up singing in church and took to the keyboards, studying the way the preacher pounded on the organ. Gospel was the foundation, like most R&B. But he was a young Black kid coming of age in Harlem during the birth of hip-hop, and rap was as much of his core as gospel was. Teddy took those influences and merged them with jazz and electro for the music he made with Wreckx-N-Effect, Guy, and BLACKstreet. It was in a *Village Voice* profile of Teddy in 1987 that writer Barry Michael Cooper gave this new language being created its name: New Jack Swing.

Babyface and L.A. Reid really toed the line between edge and mainstream pop accessibility. The duo moved between R&B-flavored contemporary pop to hard-knocking New Jack Swing. They pushed Bobby Brown away from the fluffy bubble-gum pop he was known for in New Edition with their work on *Don't Be Cruel*—another landmark album of the New Jack era—and created hits for the Whispers, Perri "Pebbles" Reid, Karyn White, Sheena Easton, and Paula Abdul. Clive gave them funding to launch LaFace Records in 1989 under Arista. The label would put Atlanta on the map as a Black music mecca—similar to what Motown did for Detroit—by launching TLC, Usher, Toni Braxton, and Outkast. LaFace, Andre Harrell's Uptown Records, and Puff's Bad Boy Records aggressively moved R&B to the center of the pop conversation as it blurred the lines between soul and hip-hop. At the dawn of the 1990s, New Jack Swing was the pulse of Black pop music. Tasked with widening Whitney's reach to Black listeners that felt her sound was too pop, Babyface and L.A. Reid invited her to Atlanta to work on music. They played Whitney the demo of "I'm Your Baby Tonight," a fiery track with a throbbing kick that would push her out of her shell. It was the first song they recorded together. "I'm Your Baby Tonight" excels by leaning heavily on Whitney's knack for marrying the call-and-response of the Black church with the percussiveness of dance music while also reintroducing her as a woman with far more edge than her sappier ballads allowed. The hook said it all: *"Whatever you want from me, I'm giving you everything / I'm your baby tonight."*

Babyface and L.A. Reid took the framework that made Whitney a sensation and sharpened it with their work on *I'm Your Baby Tonight*. The title track and "My Name Is Not Susan" are sassy anthems bursting with the sort of brash hip-hop energy that became a staple of Whitney's later work, but the dance-pop and extravagant balladry that were her signature remained the centerpiece of the album. "Miracle," "All the Man That I Need," and "After We Make Love" are classic Whitney ballads—supple, soaring, her voice in its full belting majesty. *I'm Your Baby Tonight* isn't necessarily about innovation. The fluffy, Luther Vandross–produced dance jam "Who Do You Love" and L.A. Reid and Babyface's upbeat banger "Anymore" could have easily fit into Whitney's earlier albums. But that's not important here.

I'm Your Baby Tonight is Whitney's first attempt at career autonomy. We think of it as her trying to be edgy, showing off a harder street persona shaped by hip-hop to snipe back at critics who thought she lacked flavor. Those bits are true, but the album is far more interesting when reassessing it as Whitney's first creative breakthrough. It's here where we see her write and produce her own music for once. Clive's philosophy around his protégé penning her own lyrics was simple. He didn't discourage Whitney, instead telling her if she could write a song better than the seven back-to-back number ones she made, then she should go for it—which certainly wasn't the most encouraging thing he could have told an artist. But Whitney was determined to express herself creatively beyond simply singing. She co-produced the

funky New Jack stomper "I'm Knockin'" with her musical director Ricky Minor and co-wrote a gospel-influenced dance record
with BeBe Winans and Keith Thomas called "Takin' a Chance"
that was included on the Japanese edition of the album. This
was also the first time she experimented with her voice. We
know the thrill when she belts. It's what we associate most with
Whitney—those great, soaring high notes that feel light and airy,
as if you're flying with her. But she's just as powerful when she
sits in her lower register and coasts on a record. *I'm Your Baby
Tonight* has fewer power ballads, which made room for records
like the flirty "Lover for Life" and the hard-grooving "I Belong
to You"—two of the more straightforward R&B records on the
album not produced by Babyface and L.A. Reid. But she's possibly
at her best vocally on "We Didn't Know," a breezy R&B-pop romp
with Stevie Wonder that's one of the more interesting records on
the album, with its ability to marry the soaring chorus of a pop
ballad with dense R&B harmonies and the zigzag of dance-pop
rhythms. Though Whitney was at her most elastic on *I'm Your
Baby Tonight* and the album was a hit when it was released in
November 1990, it didn't silence critics who saw her as trying
too hard to compete with the spitfire pop of Janet, Paula, and
Madonna—women with music that had distinct points of view
and sharp aesthetics and was presented in highly energetic performances stuffed with high-octane choreography and theatrics.

A natural progression in music superstardom is crossing
over to film after establishing your music chops. Berry Gordy's
obsession with turning his love Diana Ross into a Hollywood
leading lady led to *Lady Sings the Blues*, *Mahogany*, and *The
Wiz*. Prince made *Purple Rain* and became an even bigger rock

star. Madonna's brilliance at absorbing characters and personas allowed her to live in both worlds comfortably and merge the two to sensational success. Naturally, Whitney made the leap. She was Kevin Costner's first, and only, choice for *The Bodyguard*. The script had sat around for years. Lawrence Kasdan wrote the screenplay back in 1975 and landed an agent from it. A Warner Bros. executive bought the script as a vehicle for Steve McQueen and Diana Ross before that pairing fell apart and the project was reworked with Diana and Ryan O'Neal, which also collapsed. After reading the script while shooting *Silverado* with Lawrence Kasdan in 1985, Kevin Costner committed to getting the film made. Inspired by a Japanese samurai film, Kasdan's script was a classic romantic drama. Set in the world of showbiz, *The Bodyguard* tells the story of pop star and Oscar-nominated actress Rachel Marron, who falls in love with the gruff bodyguard she's hired to protect herself after a series of death threats. Whitney wasn't initially enthusiastic about the film, which would incorporate new music she'd perform as part of the soundtrack. She kept stalling even as rewrites were made to the script, until Costner called her and made his pitch. *The Bodyguard* did a couple of things: it showed an interracial romance in a mainstream film, a rather big deal then; and it proved Whitney's screen presence was enough to anchor a film. Whitney's natural charisma made her believable as a tough yet vulnerable diva, but the film goes far out of the way to not reckon with the realities of its own premise. Costner specifically wanted Whitney for the role, partially because she was already one of the biggest pop stars on the planet, but *The Bodyguard* shies away from the realities of the challenges for women like Whitney, or her onscreen character, to become mainstream stars. Because the film is devoid of any substantive acknowledgment of its heroine's race, it's jarring to see an entire film about a relationship portrayed without addressing any of the taboo-ness that made Whitney's casting remarkable in the first place. Ultimately the film was panned by critics, mostly because it was overly saccharine and lacked any real nuance on the race or fame aspects that were central to its story. But the soundtrack pushed what would have been a flop into a box office sensation. Clive Davis, ever the savvy business-man, had brokered the deal for Arista to handle the soundtrack that he would co-produce with Whitney, who was now exert-ing more creative control over her music. Having found a new groove with Babyface and L.A. Reid on *I'm Your Baby Tonight*, Whitney teamed up with the duo to co-write and co-produce the ferocious New Jack Swing rocker "Queen of the Night." She had the idea of rerecording her favorite Chaka Khan hit "I'm Every Woman," which longtime collaborator Narada Michael Walden updated, and Whitney worked with her friend BeBe Winans to record the classic gospel hymn "Jesus Loves Me." Costner had suggested David Foster as a contributor to the soundtrack, and he'd go on to produce the three pop ballads Whitney sang on the soundtrack, including "I Will Always Love You."

The *Bodyguard* soundtrack topped the pop charts, a posi-tion it stayed in for twenty nonconsecutive weeks on its way toward becoming the highest-selling soundtrack in history, in large part due to the earth-shattering success of "I Will Always Love You"—which at one point boosted the soundtrack to move over a million copies in one week, breaking a record for Nielsen SoundScan. Whitney's work on *The Bodyguard* yielded three Grammys, including Album and Record of the Year, and a mantelful of almost every music award imaginable. She set records that are still in the history books, and the film opened the door to a fruitful Hollywood career that rarely strayed away from her identity as a vocalist.

***

With Whitney, it was all in her voice. Powerful and pure, her voice was a marvel. She could deliver a euphoric wail or stretch a note remarkably far, so that each syllable softly floated on its own. There was magic in the way she manipulated and controlled notes. It's what made her live performances more thrilling than her studio recordings, which is a skill not every singer possesses. Whitney sang with a calm, poised clarity that made the sheer wizardry of how she belted all the more spectacular. Her mother, Cissy, and Aretha came from an old style of the church, where they wailed with unrestrained passion. That's what you do with God's music—you sing from your whole being—and Whitney brought that conviction to everything she sang. Her voice, and its power, gave the bright, romantic anthems an emotional heft that belied any fluffy lyrics or rigid production. At the height of her prowess, her vocal performances were spine-tingling. She sang with such a fury it seemed as though her lungs could sprout out of her back like wings and lift her into flight. Had she solely been marketed as a soul singer who occasionally dabbled in dance-pop up-tempos, critics might have been more forgiving. Her voice, in all its gospel-soaked glory, brought the soul to whatever it was she sang. Take the marketing and the Clive

Davis–orchestrated hype out of the picture and what's left is music that was very much in step with what R&B sounded like in the years after disco lost its command and before hip-hop gave it the sharper edges that would bend and reshape its sound over the next two decades.

Because Whitney was engineered for pop audiences there was this expectation that she needed to be all things to all people—expectations heightened by the fact that Whitney was a Black woman clamoring for airplay and MTV spins alongside mostly white acts. To be a woman in pop meant exhaustive comparisons to any other woman in the industry, defined by what qualities they did or didn't have. Here was a graceful singer with an extraordinary pedigree making sweet, romantic soul music and joyous dance anthems, but it was who she *wasn't* that became the fascination of critics unconvinced that a Black woman *wanted* to sing these tunes. The praise heaped on her in the beginning almost always snuck in questions around *who* she was and *what* she lacked in comparison to other Black women in the industry. How could she have the fury and histrionics of Aretha Franklin's voice—but not the soul? Why couldn't she have the erotic funk of Chaka Khan and Donna Summer or the sensual groove of Anita Baker? Her stage performances were a marvel, yes, but why didn't she move with the electricity of Tina Turner?

Whitney was a Black woman laying the groundwork to becoming a pop monolith in a system that never sought to make space for her, and we ridiculed her for not navigating those spaces the way we thought she could, or should, as a Black woman. Instead of celebrating the glass ceiling she was chipping away at, we wanted Whitney to fit more squarely into our idea of Blackness, an idea she wasn't meeting because she made light pop fare that didn't mine the depths of sorrow and pain the way soul singers typically did. In dismissing Whitney as a glamorous showgirl shaped by a Svengali, we ignored the simple truth that her voice, and how we heard it, was of her own doing. She didn't write most of her songs, but she produced her voice on them. How she sang the records, the runs she did, the meaning she placed throughout the lyrics were of her choosing. Everyone who worked with Whitney has told stories of how she could kill a song in a single take or how she'd listen to an arrangement once and immediately know how she wanted to interpret the lyrics. Those licks and flourishes that we try to imitate when we listen to her music were of her own creation. That ability to imprint the passion of gospel vocalizing on tender love songs and exhilarating dance anthems that have been flipped and remixed a million times over by club DJs is what helped her win over mainstream audiences. Whitney brought an unrivaled dexterity to her performances. From the naivete of "Saving All My Love for You" and "So Emotional" to the sass and vigor of "My Name Is Not Susan" and "It's Not Right but It's Okay," and all the shades in between, she sang with the conviction of a preacher at the pulpit. She was the rare voice that cut across the masses, across age groups and racial groups. A lot of it was marketing, yes, but her voice did the work.

When we consider our love of Whitney Houston or our connection to her voice, there's most certainly always a mention of her rendition of "The Star-Spangled Banner" or "I Will Always Love You." These are the untouchable moments that have vocally cemented Whitney as one of the greatest to ever stand in front of a microphone, and "I Will Always Love You" is her crown jewel.

But the record almost didn't happen, actually. As the music for *The Bodyguard* was coming together in 1992, Kevin Costner had circled Jimmy Ruffin's "What Becomes of the Broken-hearted" as the song Whitney would sing for the film's climax. There was little excitement around the prospect of Whitney covering the Motown hit, and the idea was thwarted after Paul Young covered it for *Fried Green Tomatoes*. Costner, who was a music buff, then suggested "I Will Always Love You." Dolly Parton had written the mournful tune back in 1973 about severing ties with her mentor and creative partner Porter Wagoner. It went to number one on the country charts and was one of the best-selling singles of 1974. Its success interested Elvis Presley, who wanted to cover it but demanded half of Parton's publishing in exchange—which she obviously refused. Instead, Linda Ronstadt covered it in 1975, and that was the version producer David Foster sent to Whitney after Costner told him it was the perfect song (unaware that it was a Dolly Parton song). Costner had his own vision for the arrangement. This was to be the showstopper of the film, and he thought the ballad would be more affecting with an a cappella intro. Whitney's voice, languid and searing, unaccompanied for nearly a minute. It was a tough sell. Neither Clive nor Foster thought it would work. How would radio respond to a pop ballad that had no music behind the first verse? Foster agreed to try it Costner's way but planned on adding instruments later. He flew down to Miami, where Whitney was wrapping up filming, to record the new version. The performance in the scene needed to feel authentic, so Whitney would be singing it live instead of lip-synching the track. After hearing that Ronstadt's version was what Whitney had learned, Dolly Parton made a call to David Foster and told him about the third verse left off Ronstadt's cover. She read the lyrics to him over the phone, and he ran into rehearsal and taught Whitney the rest, while working with the recording musicians hidden offstage.

The intro succeeds in its mission to create drama. Just the sound of Whitney's voice, crisp and immaculate, was, on its own, a wink at the fact that she was a peerless singer. Those first forty-five seconds are tender and full of restraint, allowing the melancholy of Dolly's lyrics to land on the listener. *"If I should stay, I would only be in your way / So I'll go but I know, I'll think of you every step of the way,"* she sings before lifting off with the chorus. Taking her time with the first verse and allowing the words to gently unfurl is straight out of the church. She's not stretching out any of the words yet, but she's slowly building toward it. She's hooking you in and taking you on an emotional journey that climaxes with a complete knockout of runs and a melodramatic sax solo from Kirk Whalum, further driving home the song's bittersweet lyrics. "When she opened her mouth, I realized that Kevin Costner had come up with one of the greatest ideas in the history of movie music," David Foster wrote in his memoir, *Hitman*. "[Her mother, Cissy,] was standing right beside me in the ballroom, and she realized it, too. At one point, she turned to me and said: 'You know, you're witnessing greatness right now.' She was right."

It's really in the way Whitney manipulates her voice. There's a moment during "I Will Always Love You" where she stretches "I" for nearly six seconds. One letter, slowly dragged out far enough that her voice is able to move through multiple notes at her highest ranges. We know the technique as melisma, and the four minutes and thirty-one seconds of "I Will Always Love You" is a master class in its usage. The core of her DNA as a singer was control, but melisma was the secret sauce. She had an ability to swoop and dive and zig and zag with unflappable dexterity. Her manipulation of words is what brought meaning to her music. We *felt* every syllable Whitney sang because of the way she enunciated and added dramatic flair to words. It was especially impactful, of course, in her balladry. As gloriously over-the-top as "Greatest Love of All" is, we believe Whitney when she declares, "I decided long ago, never to walk in anyone's shadows," because of the way she wraps her voice around the words and syllables. It's in the way she extends the "I" and "you" and the swelling inflections she places throughout "I Will Always Love You" or the floating runs in the last minute of "You Give Good Love" or the crescendo bridges and hooks that were the signature of her power ballads and what gave dance records like "If I Told You That," "I Wanna Dance with Somebody (Who Loves Me)," and "How Will I Know" their euphoric rush. When she brags, "I've got the stuff that you want, I've got the thing that you need," on "Queen of the Night," we believe her the very same way we believe her when she's delivering an inspirational Olympic theme song like "One Moment in Time" or belting the anthem or assuring an old lover that she wishes them joy and happiness.

Whitney knew her voice was an instrument, and she was intentional in how she played it. Cissy teaching her how to access the depths of her vocal power was just half the battle. Breath control was key, especially when singing across multiple ranges with crystal-clear clarity and force. She learned how to use her body to control her voice. "Heart. Mind. Guts," her mother taught her. This is best heard whenever she dipped in and out of melismatic singing like an acrobat tumbling across the mat. Her trick was zeroing in on particular syllables and vowels that allowed her to conserve the air she needed to sustain those colossal notes from her upper register. Whitney was most at ease when she was belting or in her midrange, where her prowess came most naturally. She harnessed a warm, velvety tone, and one of her hallmarks was mixing the piercing belts of her head voice with the lush softness of her chest voice. Melismatic singing the way we heard it from Whitney is most responsible for shaping the central thesis of contemporary pop. It's a style that inspired Mariah Carey and Adele and Beyoncé and Ariana Grande, and countless *American Idol* and *Voice* contestants have tried to mimic it. Though Whitney is credited for the mainstream popularity of melismatic singing, it's not a technique she relied on exclusively. Whitney was an improvisational singer, something she took from singing songs of worship and praise in church. The choices she made vocally always came from her spirit, and she was always so intentional in the way she sang, which is why we typically revere her live showings more than her recordings, because she rarely performed a song the same way twice.

And yet, so much of our reading of Whitney's voice is informed by her struggles to maintain her full range after her *Bodyguard* peak. Whitney lost the ability to access her higher registers with the ease we were used to—the years of chain-smoking and drug use would be damaging enough, but it didn't help that she wasn't as disciplined when it came to maintaining her voice amid the grueling demands required by live singing. She also got older, and the voice is like any muscle; you have to condition it. The power you have at twenty-five won't be as easy to harness at thirty-five or forty-five, especially if you aren't taking care of yourself. Over time, as she struggled to access all the textures of her voice, both from the normal wear and tear that comes with time and from her own doing, Whitney grew more comfortable staying inside her lower ranges, which meant power ballads like "I Will Always Love You" or "Greatest Love of All" didn't have the same majestic feeling, as she continuously failed to deliver them with the soaring gusto the world was used to.

And that's the downfall of a voice like Whitney's. Because she was such a remarkably gifted vocalist, the appreciation of her voice is intrinsically tied to its command. There wasn't consideration for it outside of the highs she could reach. And that's a shame, given how intriguing the deeper, huskier parts of her voice can be. The mature, raspier voice on display in the twilight of her career didn't have the stratospheric range or the sparkling sheen of her youth. It was the voice of a woman who had lived—often with wild abandon, as we'd learn after *The Bodyguard.* There are plenty of artists who have lost some of their voice from age or injury—Elton John, Bob Dylan, Joni Mitchell, and Mick Jagger come to mind—but we embrace them for the way their voices have evolved over the years, because of their artistry. Since Whitney didn't always put pen to paper and write the lyrics she sang, or have a hand in producing the music, or have any real substantive dialogue with the public about what was going on with her, it was easy to paint her as an empty vessel: a one-of-a-kind singer wrapped in corporate gloss who made formulaic pop and lacked any artistic rigor or real connection to the music she made. No matter what she sang, one question always accompanied Whitney's music: Who *was* she? Who was the woman who made the candescent love songs that made us *feel*? But Whitney's voice was always revealing who she was—the pain she felt, the faith she had, the redemption she deeply yearned for, the love she was in search of. Whitney always sounded *alive*. She had a voice that was so full of the soul and meaning we searched for in her lyrics. Too bad we just didn't listen closely enough the first time around.

MY LONELY HEART CALLS

On Sex, Desire, and Sexuality

In a matter of seconds—fifty-three, to be exact—the expression on Whitney's face goes from cheerful to horrified. It was 1986, and a twenty-two-year-old Whitney was making the rounds promoting her debut album overseas and booked an appearance on the popular French variety show *Champs-Élysées*. Whitney knew the routine. Smile for the cameras, graciously answer the softball questions with pep, and, most importantly, sell yourself and the product with a knockout performance. Whitney was a natural in those early days. Her effervescence and sweet charm took her far with interviewers already enamored of her effortless performances or dishing on her famous relatives. *Champs-Élysées* should have just been another innocuous stop on the promo trail. Fifty-three seconds was all it took. The show's host, Michel Drucker, hadn't even gotten his first question out when guest Serge Gainsbourg hijacked the interview. In the late

1980s, the legendary musician and singer-songwriter was a bit more famous for his provocative and unhinged appearances on French TV, which proved true the moment Whitney sat down next to him. There was lust in his eyes. And Serge couldn't control the urge to fawn over her. Whitney played the good media darling. She knew a radiant smile and a giggle were currency, and she deployed both as he drew closer to her personal space. She had been around enough men in interviews to know how to rein in the flirty ones. At first Serge was charming, standing to kiss her hand. Then he got grabby, sliding a hand across her neck and working his way to stroke her earlobe. He was clearly intoxicated, and the compliments spilling out of his mouth were a jumbled mess of fractured words the embarrassed host attempted to clean up. Serge grew more agitated by the second, by the host and by Whitney's unflappable charm, and it sent him on an incoherent rant before he turned to Whitney and blurted out, *"I want to fuck her."*

Fifty-three seconds was all it took for a television appearance to turn into blatant sexual harassment. It was the sort of crass, predatory behavior that wouldn't possibly be tolerated in a world altered by the #MeToo movement, but this was the late 1980s and men like Serge Gainsbourg were regarded as cheeky, drunken messes who meant no harm. It's appalling to watch. He was aggressive in invading her personal space, reaching to stroke her face and pet her hair as if she were an animal at the zoo—and kept going even as Whitney physically restrained his hands from further violating her body. Right then, Whitney was every woman who had ever seen her talents, or her work, ignored by a man who only regarded her as a piece of meat. A sex toy for his pleasure. Whitney brushed it off, the way too many women have had to in order to move through the day when they encounter men like Serge Gainsbourg in the workplace or out in the world. But his brutish behavior wasn't just an indictment of the era, it was a reminder of how women in pop were constantly and easily objectified—a treatment that was particularly amplified as Whitney's star rose.

For all the prickly opinions of her music and the questions surrounding Whitney's poised debutante image, there was a near obsession with her beauty. Granted, some of it was fanned by Arista, who made sure to promote her past as a teenage model to the press. In a sense, it became the center of her image. It was certainly the one thing about Whitney that wasn't up for debate. She was strikingly gorgeous, with peachy brown skin and sandy hair that framed a bright, blemish-free face. Of course Whitney broke into modeling and graced the cover of *Seventeen*—she had it going on. But many of her early interviews were framed around the notion that she had it tough growing up as a girl who was teased and bullied for having lighter skin than the girls in her neighborhood and a mother who dolled her up like a princess. It's a framing that would have certainly received closer interrogation had it happened now, given where our conversations around colorism within the Black community have evolved in the twenty-first century. Not to negate the insecurities of her childhood teasing, but Whitney was in an industry where her light skin benefited her tremendously. She had a privilege that only women of certain complexions were afforded. Would she have been able to open the same doors if she was a few shades darker? The history of Black women in America points to a harsh reality that makes it implausible to believe Whitney would have been as beloved or even embraced in the music and film industries if her skin was the color of dark chocolate or if her Afro curls were any kinkier.

With the infatuation over Whitney's beauty came a curiosity about who she was laying with. Here was this beautiful young woman singing songs of romance and yearning without ever divulging to the public who had her heart. It's standard interest that follows all celebrities, but there was something about Whitney's reticence to discuss her private life that quickly drew the ire of the press. And who could blame them? There's not much space for enigma around a public persona when the narrative promoting it was crafted around famous family connections and being groomed for pop audiences. Whitney understood the game, so she ducked and dived around the increased prying into her private life with cute but curt retorts. And the curiosity only intensified as her star rose. Who was she hanging out with? Who was she dating? Who was she fucking? The press and the public wanted to know *everything*. This was pop music in the eighties, and she was coming up alongside Madonna and Prince and Michael and Janet, artists who commanded the press with titillating images and provocative interviews. These were artists who mastered the art of the public persona and created immersive universes with their albums, and Whitney's approach was far less thrilling. She didn't wield sex or shock or complexity the way her contemporaries did. They were letting the public in either through the worlds they were presenting in their music and performances or the way they manipulated the press to their advantage. And Whitney was the opposite. She became more resentful toward the media, which only agitated them further. The red-hot success of her first two albums made her a global superstar, but she grew increasingly hostile toward the media, who asked her to respond to the critics who didn't take to her music or answer to the mounting speculation that her reluctance to divulge her personal life meant she was possibly hiding something. The tabloids would link her to someone, and it would spread through radio jockeys, talk show hosts, and journalists, which Whitney would respond to with either perky rebuttals or downright snarling. And with the absence of any other intimate details around her life, who Whitney was dating became of primary interest. The idea that she was singing beautifully convincing songs about matters of the heart without wanting to ever discuss matters of the heart was egregious to the media, who seemed to not know what was the graver offense—the possibility that Whitney was not a complex person, or the reality of her being one and actively choosing to not let the public in.

***

In the summer of 1980, Robyn Crawford was working at the East Orange Community Development Center as a youth counselor when she was stopped in her tracks by an unfamiliar face. The young woman was wearing a silk plaid blouse, slim-fitting shorts, red-striped Adidas Gazelles, and a visor with the Red Cross logo stitched on it. She introduced herself by her whole name—Whitney Elizabeth Houston—which tickled Robyn. They both had taken jobs as youth counselors and got to know each other while working with kids in Columbian Park near Whitney's family house in Doddtown. It was a bond that formed almost immediately, and they were inseparable that summer. If you saw one, you saw the other. Robyn was nineteen at the time. She was a stunning beauty—slim and tall, with light caramel skin—and two years older than Whitney, but Robyn was enamored of her sweetness, grace, and maturity. Whitney, in turn, was grateful to finally have a close friend in her life. For years she lacked true companionship outside of her brothers. The Black girls in her neighborhood bullied her for being prissy and neat, the way her mother implored her to be, and the white girls at her private school ignored her for not being one of them. She had the choir at New Hope, which was her first love, but her parents' separation and Cissy's affair had scandalized the church. Robyn was an escape from all that. There was comfort and freedom in their friendship. In Robyn, Whitney found a confidant to whom she could divulge her ambitions, her fears, and her desires. She also found a protector, someone who was unyieldingly loyal and had her back—which she became aware of rather quickly when rumors began to spread about their closeness. "I remember thinking: 'I've known this person seems like all my life,'" Whitney recalled. They spent hours laughing and sharing secrets. With Robyn, she could be Nippy, the tomboy who loved Jesus and singing in church and preferred to wear blue jeans and T-shirts and smoked Newports and got high and cursed. With Robyn, she didn't have to be the Whitney she needed to present in order to appease a mother who was foremost a woman of faith. With Robyn, she could just *be*.

Whitney and Robyn's first kiss came in those first weeks of getting to know each other during their summer together. It happened the way first kisses tend to between two people who realize they might have feelings beyond friendship. They were hanging out in Whitney's living room, after a long walk in the neighborhood, when they found themselves face-to-face. Their lips met, bound by all that had been unspoken between the two. That first kiss was long, warm like honey, and would have led to more had Whitney not been so worried about her brothers coming home. Robyn's nerves were racing. She had been with girls before, but for all she knew, Whitney hadn't. They crossed a line. But had *she* crossed a line? They didn't talk about whatever it was that was happening between them, but the closeness deepened. Whitney regaled Robyn with stories of singing with Chaka Khan in the studio, and of Cissy's work with her cousin Dionne and her "auntie" Aretha Franklin. They listened to Cissy's recordings with Elvis Presley and the Sweet Inspirations. She'd pick apart Aretha's records and school Robyn on her mother's runs and the licks she did that made whatever track they listened to special. Whitney invited her to come to New Hope to hear her sing, and Robyn was knocked out by the power and majesty of the big voice that came out of her little body. They made love after that church service, their bodies connecting for the first time. "Whatever energy we had between us all that time was expressed though our bodies that night. It was free and honest. It was tender and loving," Robyn revealed in her exquisite 2019 memoir detailing her life with Whitney after decades of silence. "We both wanted to touch and explore each other, and we did until we fell asleep in each other's arms."

Robyn and Whitney lost themselves in each other that summer, entangled in a deep bond that existed in a space without definition. Afternoons were spent sunbathing at the Jersey Shore, where Whitney found solace in rushing into the ocean for a dip, or curled up at the park. Their first experience going to a gay club was that summer, the night ending with them making love in their rental car before a cop busted them and told the ladies to move along. On occasion Robyn and Whitney made the trek to Harlem to buy a dime bag of weed and try to score a bit of cocaine. They'd get high as Whitney offered her latest music lesson. Robyn shuttled Whitney to her modeling gigs and to the club shows she did with her mother at Sweetwater's, and Whitney went to see Robyn at her college basketball games. They were partners in a traditional sense but never had a real conversation about labels. "Lesbian." "Gay." "Bisexual." "Girlfriend." Those words didn't ever come up. Both had been with men, and what was happening between them remained unspoken. Their affection had fully blossomed, but they hid that part of their relationship from everyone—even those who suspected something. "We were friends. We were lovers. We were everything to each other," Robyn wrote in her book. "We weren't falling in love. We just were. We had each other. We were one: That's how it felt." The ways of the church taught them that what was between them was wrong, a sin that damned them to hell. Guilt or judgment never lingered in the air after their flesh touched, but they still didn't want anyone to know. Cissy surely would have had a fit, though Robyn suspected her own mother knew her relationship with Whitney went beyond friendship.

They lived in their bubble, sneaking in lovemaking and partying when their mothers weren't at home or when they had enough cash to get a hotel or take a little getaway to Asbury Park. It worked for them. As Whitney was laying the groundwork for her singing career, Robyn was right there with her. She was her audience and a sounding board when Whitney wanted to toss around ideas about the songs she hoped to one day record. Laying around in bed together is where Whitney first got the idea to cover Chaka Khan's "I'm Every Woman," jotting it down in a notebook Robyn reminded her about years later. In those moments alone, they plotted their future together. Whitney knew where she was headed, and she was bringing Robyn along. "Stick with me, I'll take you around the world," she promised. However, they knew the final destination—pop stardom—didn't hold space for their kind of love, and shortly after Whitney signed her record deal with Clive Davis, she gifted Robyn with a slate-blue Bible and said they should end the physical side of their relationship. It would make her journey more difficult, Whitney reasoned. In her book, Robyn explained that Whitney told her that she wanted to have children one day and that living that kind of life—the life they were living—meant they would go to hell. Though Robyn also shared a similar understanding of religion to Whitney's, gifting her with a Bible as a reminder of why their bond couldn't exist in a particular way felt like a cruel cover for the true reason why their bond couldn't continue. Whitney was a woman diving into the music business. There were already the baked-in barriers of trying to break into the biz—and even though her legacy gave her an opening,

Whitney was still a Black woman being groomed for a record deal. Making it was going to be hard enough on its own. God forbid you were Black *and* gay or bisexual.

But Whitney was also a woman of the church. Yeah, she had plans for pop fame, but she was sneaking around with Robyn because she didn't want her mother to know. She didn't want her brothers to know. And she most definitely didn't want the congregation at New Hope to know. There was no space, period, for the sin she and Robyn were indulging in. Black religiosity has historically grappled with its shame regarding sex, and even though it still does, there's been some progress from leaders making efforts to evolve their theology and ethics regarding sex and sexuality. It took the suffering of untold generations and years of sex scandals outing some of the Black church's most high-profile men for there to be some real cultural shift, and it's still a conversation that's met with polarizing hysterics despite how progressive we have become as a society. Even if Whitney didn't end up taking off the way she would, she knew her and Robyn's public relationship couldn't appear as anything other than platonic friendship, for there was church on one side and the music business on the other. They had already had conversations about how their relationship—as undefined as it was—would impact Whitney's recording career. People around them were already gossiping about their closeness, and where they were headed, there would only be more eyes, and more judgment, on them. "You know what we shared. You know how I feel about you and we will always have that," Whitney told her. Even if there wasn't the fear of damnation, there was the reality that the music industry, like much of the world in the 1980s, was an intolerant place where homophobia openly thrived.

***

I've always thought it was perfect that Whitney's debut album opens with "You Give Good Love." It's a lavish morsel of bright eighties R&B that her voice gracefully flutters over. You might have locked lips with a crush for the first time while "You Give Good Love" played on the radio, or you might have slow-danced to it at senior prom. It's that kind of song—sweet, romantic, made for slow grinding under the soft spin of a disco ball or fogging up the car with your sweetheart. "You Give Good Love" was released as Whitney's first single in order to establish a core fan base through Black radio, a savvy, no-brainer move on Clive's part, since the record is a straightforward R&B love ballad that sweeps you off your feet.

"You Give Good Love" also firmly framed our image of Whitney and how we believed she saw love and sex. She was twenty-two when her much-hyped debut arrived, but there was a youthful innocence permeating her music that played as juvenile, particularly when paired with her princess image. "You Give Good Love" romanticizes a fairy tale–like love story while the next two records on the album ("Thinking About You" and "Someone for Me") have Whitney singing about being a lovesick fool who needs to be scolded by her mama to get out of the house and have some fun. Both records play over fluffy dance-R&B beats tailor-made for whirling around a skating rink on a Saturday night. It's not until "Saving All My Love," Whitney's cover of Marilyn McCoo and Billy Davis Jr.'s minor 1978 hit, that she seduces. The slow burner, with its jazzy flourishes and smoldering vocals, sees her singing about being the other woman in a torrid love affair. By the second time Whitney sings, "*'Cause tonight is the night that I'm feeling all right / We'll be making love the whole night through,*" she lets the line about making love until morning linger, stretching out the lyrics after assuring her taken paramour that "no other woman is gonna love you more." She caught some heat for putting out a tune about being a mistress, but it was a moment of vulnerability on an album that was largely devoid of emotional depth, despite being stuffed with soft ballads about relationships.

Whitney's presentation as a naive young woman who saw love through doe eyes remained on her next album. Though she was then twenty-four, she didn't stray too far from music that sounded like it could soundtrack a teen drama. Clive had found a winning formula, and Whitney's sophomore album played it safe, even down to it being named after her again—dropping her last name in a bid to push Whitney toward singular fame as a pop diva. *Whitney* is evenly split between bright dance records and big ballads, the two moods she operated in. The upbeat records are aggressively formulaic: "I Wanna Dance with Somebody (Who Loves Me)" succeeds so greatly at replicating the sugary high of "How Will I Know" that it still sounds like a shot of dopamine today, and "Love Will Save the Day" and "Love Is a Contact Sport" are indistinguishable from the zippy dance-pop numbers of her debut. Whitney does a bit more heavy lifting emotionally this time around. "Didn't We Almost Have It All," "Where Do Broken Hearts Go," and "You're Still My Man" are potent torch songs capturing the throes of heartbreak. The album is at its most interesting when Whitney is reinterpreting "For the Love of You" and "Just the Lonely Talking Again," R&B numbers originally made by the Isley Brothers and the Manhattans, respectively. These were songs created from the male gaze, which typically veered toward more amatory matters. While her cover of "For the Love of You" doesn't venture from the honeyed groove the Isleys brought to the record, "Just the Lonely Talking Again" is completely different from the original. Where the Manhattans steeped their yearning ballad with an erotic edge by grounding the record with a funky bass line, Whitney's version built in a languid strings arrangement and had Kenny G on the sax. Her version is sensual foreplay in comparison to the original's bump-and-grind vibe. It's the sexiest song in her catalog next to "Oh Yes," and that record came over a decade later, once Whitney started working with hip-hop producers and recording music with a bit more bass and bite than her earlier pop froth.

After her first two albums Whitney was christened the "Prom Queen of Soul" by *Time*. It was their way to mint her as the heir apparent to Aretha Franklin's throne, but the statement also spoke to the perception of Whitney. She was the young deity with coquettish flair but no real substance. She didn't *sell* sex through her music or her visual aesthetic the way her contemporaries did, and without music that fully mined the depths of the human experience, Whitney was seen as a wholesome Cosby kid with a gigantic voice. And her seeming lack of interest in expressing any sexuality or desire in her work was a red flag for critics and pop audiences hungry for the titillation the MTV era ushered in.

Whitney and Madonna and Janet Jackson were all competing for the same space on MTV and pop radio, and though Whitney had a *voice* neither could match, what Madonna and Janet
made emphatically clear in their records, music videos, aesthetic, and ever-changing personas was fearlessness. They were
unafraid to push boundaries and aimed to provoke. Madonna and
Janet pushed new ideas of sexual freedom and liberation through
lenses centering female pleasure—and did it with an agency we
hadn't yet seen from women operating in an industry that loves
to sexualize them but rejects their power. In her 2017 book, *Good
Booty*, music critic Ann Powers posited that Madonna "came to
stand for a style of liberal, sex-positive feminism that was less
idealistic and openly radical than 1970s women's liberation but
better served the tastes of women entering the corporate sphere
or trying to bring awareness into their otherwise conventional
marriages." Madonna writhed and orgasmed to her delight in
her videos and performances for all to see, and Janet offered
clear instruction on how she wanted to please and be pleased
on records that altered the framework of R&B. Madonna and
Janet embraced eroticism—long before it was mainstream—and
didn't shy away from making the type of sexually explicit funk
Prince dominated MTV with. Sexuality and gender were interrogated in their music just as much as matters of the heart and
their worldviews. But Whitney did none of this. There was no
real sense through her early music that sexual pleasure was ever
on her mind. Who knows if that would have been any different if
she had more agency over the records she sang in the beginning,
but her arrival as a young ingénue at a time when Madonna and
Janet were exploding on the pop charts with music that explored

female desire contributed to the idea that she lacked not just emotional depth but any real sex appeal outside of her looks.

Whitney attempted to shed that wholesome image on 1990's *I'm Your Baby Tonight,* an album that leaned into the funkier edge of New Jack Swing. Gone was the young lady who navigated love like she was the lead in a John Hughes flick. In her place was a grown woman who sat in the thick of love and embraced all its pleasures, and its tensions. *I'm Your Baby Tonight* is looked at as Whitney trying to "own" her Blackness by leaning into the contemporary R&B sounds of her peers at the time. But the consensus among Black music fans and critics was that her records didn't match all the hype lobbed on her from Clive and the label. Her music lacked the edge and attitude that came with Prince and Janet, lacked the sensuality of Anita Baker and Chaka, and lacked the excitement that came with Tina Turner, and it was being marketed aggressively to pop radio. Although her cousin Dionne had easily made the leap from the church to pop balladry, she didn't come up in the MTV age, where pop music was as much about shock and gimmick as it was about raw talent.

I'm Your Baby Tonight sought to dismantle the image of Whitney the debutante prom queen who dreamed of dancing with somebody for whom she saved all her love. This was the album where Whitney finally offered her perspective on love and sex. To her, sex didn't matter much without commitment, and she had no interest in one without the other. "*I believe in one love, baby, true monogamy,*" she sings on "Anymore." The fantasy of love that permeated her early work always presented her as the princess waiting to be swept away by a prince. Whitney's music almost exclusively lived in the realm of fantasy. There was no real tension, no real stakes, or any of the emotional complexities that come with loving another human and building a life together. The songs on *I'm Your Baby Tonight* pushed her framing of love beyond the sweet fairy tale. She seethed at being mistaken for a previous girlfriend on the funky "My Name Is Not Susan"; basked in the afterglow of lovemaking on "After We Make Love"; pledged submission to a man who took her to ecstasy on the title track; and she sang about falling in love with a friend on the light "We Didn't Know."

Whitney's work on *I'm Your Baby Tonight* happened right as she began a romance with Bobby Brown, who was born Robert Barisford Brown on February 5, 1969, in Roxbury, Massachusetts. Growing up in the projects as a young Black boy meant you grew up so much quicker—out of necessity, out of survival—and like far too many of our boys and men, Bobby's childhood was informed by a constant threat of violence. Bobby was into basketball and boxing (which his mother quickly nixed), but he discovered early that his voice was special. Bobby's mother, a grade-school teacher, introduced her son to the music of Sam Cooke and Donny Hathaway and his father, a blue-collar man, put him on to the blues. The whole Brown family sang in church, but it was the funk of James Brown and groups like Parliament-Funkadelic and Earth, Wind & Fire that captivated young Bobby most and pushed him toward wanting to be an entertainer.

When Bobby was nine, he met Michael Bivins at the neighborhood Boys and Girls Club. They both played basketball, danced, and sang (briefly joining a dance troupe with some older guys who called themselves Transitions). Wanting to sing and dance, Bobby and Michael formed a vocal group with Ricky

Bell and two other homeboys from their projects, Travis Pettus
and Corey Rackley, who'd leave and be replaced by two other
friends, Ralph Tresvant and Ronnie DeVoe, the latter of whom
was the nephew of choreographer Brooke Payne. It was Payne
who christened the group, as legend goes, after watching them
at a talent competition. "The new edition of the Jackson 5," he
thought. *Lightbulb.* A group was born. It was promoter/producer/
Svengali Maurice Starr that had the savvy to market the five
rapping and singing young Black teenagers from the projects as
a teeny-bop act when he signed them to his Streetwise imprint
in 1982. Bobby was barely fourteen when New Edition's debut
album, *Candy Girl*, was released in 1983. The record is sweet as
bubblegum, with about as much edge as a butter knife. It wasn't
just slick marketing. The War on Drugs that had begun a decade
earlier under Nixon had added to White America's perception of
Black men as virile threats to society, and though the members
of New Edition were between the ages of thirteen and sixteen,
Starr knew they wouldn't be excluded from the criminalization
that beset rap music, so he merged hip-hop aesthetics with the
sweet-faced, docile respectability Berry Gordy sent out of the
Motown factory.

New Edition served as the definitive model for the modern
boy band: soulful harmonies, a smidge of edge, sharp choreography, distinct personalities within the group (the shy one, the bad
boy, the baby face, the heartthrob, the cool one). New Edition's
bubbly earworms took off. But the boys got their first taste of the
ugliness of the business when they were dropped right back off
at the projects after their first tour with a check for $1.87 each.
The boys had been signed to a production deal, not a record

contract. "Legalized slavery," their tour manager called it. They broke free from Starr (who then assembled the white version of New Edition that he called New Kids on the Block), only to get into another bad management deal that left them in debt with their label. The spoils of fame got Bobby in trouble. Imagine coming from where he came from and before you've really hit puberty, you're famous and getting showered with panties at your concert. Bobby was living young, wild, and free after seeing so much shit in the hood. And he'd be the first to tell you he got caught up. Saddled with debt, New Edition quickly recorded a third album as tensions between Bobby and the group started to simmer. R&B heads remember the beef between Bobby and his brothers in the group. The backstage brawls. The egos. The years of drama. No one was surprised that the group got tired of all his shit and voted him out, but everyone was surprised to see Bobby blow up the way he did on his own. And that's really the beauty of a hit, and Bobby hit the biggest lick with 1988's *Don't Be Cruel*, an album that helped establish the New Jack Swing genre and christen him an R&B king.

Bobby was big, but Whitney was a supernova. Even if there wasn't any of the speculative chatter around their union, Whitney was a massive pop star at that point, and any relationship she entered into was going to be intensely scrutinized by the media and the public. Bobby represented all the parts of Whitney that she couldn't freely put on display as a Black woman playing the role of All-American pop princess. Bobby was loud. He didn't censor himself. He was ghetto fabulous and didn't care to code-switch for the media. And he made the kind of music that made you want to grind your hips, music that equally owed a debt to rap and R&B—music that was unquestionably *Black*.

Whitney met Bobby in 1989 at the Soul Train Music Awards, when she bumped against the back of his head while chatting with BeBe and CeCe Winans in the row behind him. It was a playful flirtation on Whitney's part, completely antithetical to the immature girl waiting for a man she presented on her records. She saw what she wanted, and she went for it. The Soul Train Awards are a turning point in the way we looked at Whitney—both as an artist and as a Black woman. Bobby was one of the hottest young Black men in America the night he met Whitney. The crowd ate up his gyrating performance of "My Prerogative," and his breakout album *Don't Be Cruel* took the trophy for Album of the Year by a male vocalist. Whitney's reception, however, was far frostier. She was booed when her name was called among the female nominees for Best R&B/Urban Contemporary single. "Where Do Broken Hearts Go" was up against Karyn White's "Superwoman"—one of the finest ballads Babyface and L.A. Reid ever produced—"The Right Stuff" by Vanessa Williams, and Anita Baker's smoldering "Giving You the Best That I Got." It was a stacked category, and Anita Baker would be the victor, but the mention of Whitney's name eliciting a chorus of boos was the confirmation that her community didn't love her as universally as the rest of the world. Black radio and its listeners were tired of the fluffy records Whitney put out and the persona she sold to the press—one that was colorless and clandestine. She was a sellout, an Oreo: white on the inside, Black on the outside. *Whitey Houston*, she was called. Getting jeered at an awards show celebrating Black artists was a huge blow to her ego, but the fact that Whitney came out on the other side of her humiliation with a bold, brash album and an even brasher man created the illusion that it was all an orchestrated act. Whitney and Bobby's courtship, and much of their marriage, was seen as a PR move to silence the noise around her. A thesis was established and universally accepted as fact. This was a marriage of convenience, a win-win for all. Bobby needed to class up his bad-boy image, and he provided Whitney with some street cred—and a reprieve from the rumors around her and Robyn, who remained by Whitney's side throughout much of her career.

***

The speculation about Whitney and Robyn had come swiftly. There had been whispers when they were teens working together at summer camp, since everyone could see how inseparable they were. And the gossip about their closeness carried over to the music industry, as they both knew it would before Whitney cut off their physical relationship. Whitney's instinct that people wouldn't leave them alone if they found out about them was rooted in the reality that the entertainment industry, like the Black church community she came from, was incredibly homophobic. Speculating over someone's queerness was a sport for radio jockeys and tabloids in those days, but the pace at which the public learned information about celebrities gave radio jockeys and hosts on MTV and BET the biggest advantage. They all had a direct line to their audience in a more immediate way compared to print journalists. In the late eighties and early nineties, you weren't aware something happened with an artist unless you heard it on the radio, MTV, BET, or it hit the tabloids. Today, artists can just jump online and speak directly to their audience. Artists can break their own news, dispel rumors, or atone for their transgressions without engaging the press. But this was the eighties. There was no Internet. No Twitter. No Instagram. There was no Perez Hilton or *Us Weekly* or Oh No They Didn't or DeuxMoi. Our culture of celebrity gossip depended on the access that radio jocks, journalists, and hosts on MTV or *Entertainment Tonight* got. In those days it was much easier to keep things under wraps—like Whitney's affair with Jermaine Jackson, who was married to Hazel Gordy and nearly ten years older, as they worked on her debut album. But when things *did* go from open industry secret to news, it was all the more sensationalized. So even though Whitney and Robyn's romantic relationship ended when the ink dried on her contract with Arista, their closeness drew immediate intrigue. They had an apartment together, and Whitney had appointed Robyn as her executive assistant, a role that expanded over time. In those halcyon days of Whitney's career, the press was presented with an emphatic image of the church girl from a wholesome family with deep ties to the music industry. But she was still a Black woman making a play for crossover stardom in the music video age. Pop music was sexier and glossier by then, and Whitney's image was so carefully crafted, down to her parents presenting as a united pair despite a tense separation. At first, the press indulged Whitney's reluctance to divulge her personal life. It intensified the intrigue and her sex appeal. After the red-hot success of her first two albums, Whitney was the biggest thing in pop music. But the press had grown exhausted by her image.

She was singing these sweet love songs that made the world fall in love with her, but who was she giving her love to? And why was she so angry that anyone wanted to know?

Whitney's refusal to discuss her personal life just fanned the flames. MTV didn't only make pop music more image-conscious, it was ground zero for a new kind of fan culture. Audiences felt closer to pop stars, and that proximity in the pre–social media era was almost exclusively reliant upon media access. Fans learned about their artists through their engagement with magazines and music journalists, radio jockeys, and talk shows. Before Google arrived to give us unlimited access to information, there were only a handful of ways a fan could get close to an artist. The public's interest in Whitney's love life wasn't abnormal for a celebrity of her stature, but her reticent demeanor and growing hostility raised red flags. She indulged the media when they asked about her courtships with Eddie Murphy and Randall Cunningham, but until Bobby came in the picture, when you saw Whitney in public, you most likely only saw Robyn standing next to her.

In *A Song for You*, Robyn wrote that the first time she met Whitney's father, he suggested they go out to the movies with a couple of guys on a double date, to be seen in public. Robyn cringed. *"He actually wants us to stage fake-boyfriend scenarios,"* she thought to herself. This was the way it was then. The liberation of queer Americans was only in its infancy. Decades of suppression and erasure hit a tipping point with Stonewall, and a new era of queer openness and pride was upon us. But the gay liberation hadn't yet disrupted mainstream music, and it certainly wouldn't have extended to a Black woman riding the top of the pop charts. The glitter and gold of the disco era had long rusted, and queer folks were under constant attack in Reagan's America. AIDS came, and the world's homophobia turned into a war against queers. Generations would pass before the world shifted, and we wouldn't have real confirmation of Whitney's sexual fluidity until long after she was dead and Robyn broke a nearly forty-year silence to write *A Song for You* out of a desire to free Whitney, and certainly herself, from the shame that came with their commitment to silence that they made out of necessity—and out of survival. In the 1980s, if you were queer and navigating Hollywood or the music industry, a shot at mainstream success often came at the expense of hiding parts of yourself. Going into the shadows of the closet, for many, was the only option. Even the Village People shied away from their queer origins when they hit it big with their deliciously gay anthem "YMCA." Whitney and Robyn were on the precipice of adulthood when their lives intertwined that summer in 1980. Whitney was already grinding toward her career, but take that off the table and you have a teenage girl experiencing a same-sex romance right at the onset of AIDS, an epidemic that would be met not just with blatant homophobia disguised as moral panic but messaging rooted in shame. Whitney and Robyn were teenagers with connections to the Black church, so their experience with same-sex love was hearing how it would send them to hell or give them AIDS and kill them. We hadn't moved toward harm reduction yet, so all we had was abstinence messaging, which allowed sex that wasn't heterosexual to be seen as an evil sin that would ruin you—a moral failure shared with the War on Drugs, which used initiatives like Just Say No and Drug

Abuse Resistance Education (D.A.R.E.) to color the perception of the same drugs that were at the center of the hedonism and free-spirited counterculture of the sixties and seventies. At seventeen, Whitney knew that no one could find out about the sex she was having with Robyn—just as much as she knew that no one could find out that they were getting high.

A quarter century removed from Whitney's ascent, Black queer creatives are at the forefront of music and film and television, in part because of a cultural shift that has allowed a generation to break through and be embraced in the mainstream—and also because we've finally come around and confronted the ways in which the shame and judgment within our communities were instrumental in keeping some of our greatest Black talents in the closet. Now we have Frank Ocean, Kehlani, and Janelle Monáe progressing R&B with their sounds while centering their sexuality; Lil Nas X was able to become the first gay rapper to top the pop charts; shows like *Empire* and *Pose* and queer creators like Lena Waithe and Janet Mock have shifted the way Black queer characters are represented in film and television. But none of this framework existed in 1985 when Whitney made her debut. She had no path forward that allowed her the space, or the grace, to figure out herself—and especially not in front of the world. There was no Ellen DeGeneres or k.d. lang or Melissa Etheridge or Rosie O'Donnell. And even though their coming-outs were historic moments in the movement, these were white women who didn't carry the burden Whitney would have had on her shoulders as a Black woman from a famous gospel family.

If Whitney was of the Jazz Age, her relationship with Robyn would have barely raised an eyebrow. Under the smoky lights of speakeasies and cabarets, blues singers freely sang about exploring their sexuality. The genre wasn't yet mainstream, so there wasn't much pressure to play it straight for conservative white Americans who feared Black sexuality as much as they fetishized it. The blues scene thrived during the Harlem Renaissance. Black queer artists lived openly, even as they risked persecution for engaging in homosexual acts. *"I went out last night with a crowd of my friends / It must've been women, 'cause I don't like no men . . . Talk to the gals just like any old man . . . ,"* Ma Rainey sang on 1928's "Prove It on Me," a record the Mother of the Blues wrote in response to gossip about her sexuality after she was arrested for partaking in an orgy with several women. Ma Rainey is our earliest example of a Black woman explicitly embracing lesbianism in her music. She set the mold for Black divas by trotting out onstage in sequined gowns, false lashes, and high heels—her teeth capped in gold, a diamond tiara above her head, and her clavicle laced with a necklace made of gold teeth. Ma Rainey wasn't alone. Her protégé, and rumored paramour, Bessie Smith, sang about sexual freedom much to the ire of her abusive husband and became the highest-paid Black entertainer of her time; Gladys Bentley gained popularity for her cross-dressing performances before later claiming to be "cured" of her homosexuality; and in 1935, Lucille Bogan recorded "B.D. Woman's Blues," where she longed of a time when "bull dykes" didn't need to deal with men—and that's one of her cleaner records.

The freedom queer Black women felt in their music vanished on the other side of the Great Depression as Black upward mobility and the civil rights movement focused on preserving the Black nuclear family. Anything that didn't fit into a traditional heterosexual construct was seen as subversive and a threat toward the assimilation to white norms that was critical for integration. Gospel and blues merged into R&B and soul, genres that romanticized heterosexual desire. The Motown era presented Black women as docile romantics in order to achieve crossover success, but the sexual freeness percolating across funk, disco, and glam rock allowed Black women to present different ideas of female sensuality. Donna Summer, Patti LaBelle, Tina Turner, Chaka Khan, and Diana Ross all centered female pleasure, and their music is essential to the radical ways Black women in music explored their sexuality after the respectability of the 1950s and 1960s. The liberation they found in their bodies and their embracement of queer fans made them all gay icons at a time when even allyship from mainstream artists was considered risky. Whitney closing the chapter on the physical intimacy she shared with Robyn after she signed her deal can only be seen as an act of survival. The tolerance extended to queer artists was still few and far between as pop music was rife with homophobic gatekeepers. After Whitney asked her label to fly Robyn out to meet her during a Black radio convention in 1985, her appearance made the straight radio jocks and program directors perk up, and they spent the weekend buzzing about the pair. The chatter made its way to print journalists, who eventually started asking in every interview, *Is Whitney gay? Are Whitney and Robyn a couple?* Long before Robyn ever broke her silence, the public arrived at the conclusion that Whitney was a closeted lesbian and she and Robyn were star-crossed lovers doomed by the oppression of society and Whitney's religious family. Could things have been different for Whitney if she had come from a different background? Perhaps, but I have a hard time believing she would have presented any differently considering where we were in the late eighties and in the nineties.

When Whitney was christened the Prom Queen of Soul in 1987 by *Time*, she was asked about the tabloid chatter on her sexuality. Specifically, the nature of her relationship with Robyn. Whitney took her usual stance—some variance of a nonchalant dismissal—and called Robyn over to directly address the reporter. But there was also a flippant denial: "Anyway, whose business is it if you're gay or like dogs?" It was meant to shut down the conversation, but Whitney had a habit of reacting to press in ways that at times could be curiously defensive. She could flip the debutante act on and off, and it was typically those moments of being asked about Robyn or about Bobby or about the drugs where code-switching went off and she slipped into Nippy, who was tougher and brasher than the *Whitney Houston* who pertly smiled for the cameras. Maybe it was the fear of having to explain what she herself didn't yet understand, or maybe it was her commitment to survival and preserving her image, or maybe it was the desire to not be defined as one thing, but the inquiries around her sexuality typically provoked Whitney's nastier side. She grew more irritated that we questioned her when she didn't say the things we wanted to hear in interviews, and her trust in the press was irrevocably tarnished in 1990, after a reporter spun Whitney and Robyn's enthusiasm for how they were running the Whitney Houston empire into a faux exposé. Whitney saw the media as "blood-sucking demons" and vowed to never engage the press again, a threat that was impossible to sustain before the advent of social media gave celebrities the ability to promote themselves without taking a single question from a journalist.

And so the question persisted, and she continued to push back. When her denials weren't dressed in offhand language, she sometimes disparaged the role Robyn played in her life as she tried to assert her heterosexuality or defend her union with Bobby after they got together and the questions didn't stop. She even once made a comment in jest to the *Washington Post* in response to gossip that Bobby and Robyn had come to physical blows that he would have knocked Robyn out if it was true and that she and Robyn had had "enough time together" and the "relationship had changed from friendship to more of an employer-employee arrangement," a sentiment she repeated often. "People want to know if there is a relationship: Our relationship is that we're friends. We've been friends since we were kids. She now is my employee. I'm her employer. And we're still best of friends," Whitney said in her 1993 *Rolling Stone* cover story. "You mean to tell me that if I have a woman friend, I have to have a lesbian relationship with her? That's bullshit. There are so many, so many female artists who have women as their confidantes, and nobody questions that. So I realize that it's like 'Whitney Houston—she's popular, let's fuck with her.' I have denied it over and over again, and nobody's accepted it. Or the media hasn't." Surely Whitney didn't intend on linking homosexuality with bestiality in *Time* magazine or to downplay her closest friend as the help or the years of aggressive denials that were sometimes wrapped in bigoted language. We can't know what was in Whitney's heart back then, but the way she sometimes spoke of Robyn's role in her life could be read

as bitter deflection by those who haven't felt confined to loving in the shadows, afraid of what their family would think or
ashamed to embrace their truth. This isn't to exonerate the harm
that came with the bigoted things she said, but Whitney was a
young woman, a Black one, rising to the top during a time when
state-sanctioned homophobia was the norm. She didn't see
herself as gay, and we didn't talk about sexual fluidity with the
ease we do now. This was very much a time when you were gay if
you had sex with the same sex, period. That's where our thinking
was—and for some, it's where their thinking still remains. That
rigid thinking would have challenged Whitney's career, and she
and Robyn knew it. And Clive knew it. It wasn't until the world
had shifted that he came out as bisexual, and that was in 2013,
when he was eighty and Whitney had been dead a year.

Even if Whitney and Robyn wanted to continue anything
before Bobby came into the picture, they were staring down the
righteousness of Cissy and the church *and* the oppression of the
music industry. "When the question was asked about her being
gay, she automatically said no," her sister-in-law and manager
Pat Houston told me. "How do you dispute that?" Cissy definitely
made it no secret that she would have not been okay with her
daughter having a same-sex relationship. It didn't go without
noticing that the Houston family selected Donnie McClurkin,
T. D. Jakes, and Marvin Winans—powerful leaders of the Black
church community who have been open about their anti-gay
views—to be among the voices eulogizing Whitney at her funeral
compared with what Aretha did the night before the homegoing, when she paid tribute to her honorary niece during a show
at Radio City Music Hall alongside Bishop Carlton Pearson, a

minister who has been celebrated for his inclusiveness. And just a year after Whitney's tragic death, Oprah Winfrey pressed Cissy on her position about her daughter and Robyn. First Oprah asked Cissy if she believed Whitney and Robyn were in a relationship: "I don't really know about that, you know," she says, which is essentially what Cissy wrote in the memoir she was promoting with this Oprah interview (it was her second memoir, after 1998's *How Sweet the Sound*, which barely mentioned Bobby and completely ignored Robyn). When Oprah asked Cissy if it would have bothered her if her daughter *was* gay, Cissy's response was terse: "Absolutely." She didn't need to say another word about the subject, and she hasn't since.

We have done enough excavations of the Black church and the trauma it has inflicted on its queer congregants to imagine what Whitney and Robyn were up against at home. Cissy was an elder in the church, as well as a trustee. Any talk about her daughter being involved with another woman—famous or not—would be unfathomable. We were so far away from any real cultural breakthrough as it related to female sexuality in the Black community and what that looked like when not subscribed to heterosexual standards. And there certainly hadn't been the reckonings among the homophobic, closeted men of the cloth who have exposed the hypocrisies that divided the Black church community for decades. When whispers about Whitney and Robyn reached Cissy's ear, she had a fit. The great length she went to erase Robyn's importance in Whitney's life when writing about her daughter's rise in her book says a lot about Cissy's orientation around the closeness shared between her daughter and Robyn. And once the noise grew louder in the media, Cissy tried to forbid Robyn from walking next to Whitney in public or sitting next to her at awards shows. Cissy's influence was mighty. Mighty enough that Robyn christened her "Big Cuda." Everyone knew to straighten up whenever Cissy was around. But Whitney was steadfast on keeping Robyn by her side in a powerful role on her team, much to the chagrin of her parents and her brothers. And Cissy made Robyn's life hellish because of it. She thought their closeness was "unnatural" and even slapped Robyn across the face once, angry that she couldn't reach Whitney the moment she wanted. It was so tense between Robyn and the Houstons that John considered paying a goon to have her kneecaps broken. But Robyn was a safe place for Whitney. Fame came with a massive toll. The criticism when she didn't perform at her best, the chatter about not being *Black* enough, the speculation around her sexuality and her marriage. It all wore Whitney down—the drugs and drinking would do the rest—and Robyn was there through it all. She took the punches for both of them and showed a fierce level of loyalty and protection that only comes from loving someone purely with the fullness of your heart. In Robyn, Whitney found solace and safety away from the spotlight. It was an established fact that you couldn't get to Whitney without going through Robyn—a rule that ruffled her family, all of whom were dependent upon Whitney financially.

In the years since Whitney's death, the Houstons have confronted their treatment of Robyn and reflected on their role and complicity in Whitney's addiction. Their anger toward Robyn has long been perceived as deep-rooted homophobia, given their ties to the church, but the truth is their resentment was also about control. Robyn had Whitney's trust. She had her ear.

She quickly went from assistant to creative director as Whitney leaned on her friend more and more when it came to her career. "Whitney was the only girl, and the baby, and you're looking at a family that is extremely protective. It wouldn't have mattered who it was. It was about her not being around them," Whitney's sister-in-law/manager Pat Houston told me ahead of the 2018 premiere of the estate-sanctioned documentary *Whitney*. It was the second intimate portrait to come out, following 2017's *Whitney: Can I Be Me*, which documented the tension between Robyn and Whitney's family and with Bobby before Robyn reached her breaking point and left the Houston camp for good. Both films showed parts of Whitney that were hidden from public view—and the immense pressure she was under. The weight of providing for those around her, how often they took advantage of her kindness, how deeply unhappy she was—how incredibly different she was around Robyn. It was a brutal reminder that family and money hardly ever mix, and certainly not on the level of the millions of dollars Whitney was raking in. Everyone was on payroll, and Robyn was often the only one looking out for Whitney's interests. As much as Cissy disliked Robyn, she is the first to admit that it was Robyn, and not Whitney's brothers, who came to her and voiced concerns that the recreational drug habit they all indulged in appeared to be spiraling out of control for Whitney. "We were all using her. Even our mother," her brother Gary told me. "Robyn loved Nippy for who she was, it didn't matter that she sang. That she was *Whitney Houston*." But Gary's tone in *Whitney* was much different. He seethes when discussing Robyn. To him, she was a nobody: "An opportunist. She was a wannabe . . . And she happened to involve herself with Nippy, for whatever reasons. I knew that she was, uh . . . something that I didn't want my sister to be involved with. It was evil. It was wicked. I knew what she was. And I tried to tell my sister to leave her alone." Gary later lamented his choice of words in the film and admitted it was out of hurt feelings, but that was the attitude that was perceived to run rampant throughout a family that was more concerned about Whitney's relationship with another woman than with her growing dependency on substances.

The image of Whitney literally closing the book on her romantic relationship with Robyn by gifting her a Bible is the most searing image in *A Song for You*. Whitney opted to deny a part of herself because it would make her life, and her career, easier. Less complicated. If only that turned out to be the reality, though. Robyn held on to what they shared for nearly forty years before speaking in detail about their brief romantic history or the fifteen years she spent at Whitney's side as her friend and trusted advisor, which is perhaps the clearest statement we have about her love and respect for Whitney. Our cultural understanding of the spectrum on which human sexuality lies has shifted so greatly in the last decade, but we're still not in a place where queer pop stars are reaching the heights that Whitney had while living openly. Maybe one day we will be.

I've often gone back to one interview Whitney did with Katie Couric in 1996. *The Bodyguard* and "The Star-Spangled Banner" were well in the rearview by then, and Whitney was straddling Hollywood and music with *Waiting to Exhale* and *The Preacher's Wife*, projects that fully transitioned her into making the most authentic music of her life. She was more than a decade into her career, and while the contradictions she lived offstage were starting to reveal cracks in the façade—performances were getting shaky, and the stories about her and Bobby were disconcerting—the full extent of her troubles still weren't fully apparent to the public beyond tabloid fodder. She and Bobby had gotten married four years earlier, and Whitney was a mother to Bobbi Kristina, who was three or so at the time, but that question of the nature of her relationship with Robyn still hung in the air. The rumors and assumptions continued to persist, as did the narrative from industry gossips that her relationship with Bobby was one of convenience. It was all fuel for the tabloids and would be the source of trashy, unauthorized biographies—one of which was written by the scorned boyfriend of Whitney's former publicist—and Couric asked Whitney about the speculation. All of it. The *"Black enough"* critique, the attention on her marriage, and her feelings around why there had been nonstop gossip about her and Robyn. The viewer didn't get to hear Couric's question, only Whitney's response: "This wasn't her world. I brought her into this madness. She goes, 'Why am I the target? What did I do?' I said, 'You're my friend . . . You play basketball. They think you're a man, I don't know!' She's a damn good basketball player. She can beat any guy there is, I love it," Houston told Couric before a nervous laugh fell out of her mouth. Couric, her head slightly tilted to the right, was clearly reading Whitney's nervous energy and prodded her. "Because she plays basketball, people think she's a lesbian?" Couric wondered. In Whitney's dismissal of the speculation, she played up the stereotypes of butch women—muscular, athletic, masculine—while overstressing her own femininity at the expense of Robyn's humanity. "I'm a mother, I'm a wife, I'm a daughter," she responded, as if those qualities couldn't be true of queer women. There were other less graceful interviews, particularly in the latter stretch in her career, but there was something about the absurdity of the speculation around whether Whitney was in the closet getting the attention of a primetime *Dateline* interview that shows us exactly *why* she felt the need to stay there. Why she felt the need to defend *and* protect herself and Robyn. I do wonder what would have been different had Whitney come out and said, "I was once with a woman," or confirmed the brief romance she shared with Robyn. What would have shifted for the world if when Katie Couric asked her about the rumors or how she felt about the constant speculation, Whitney put the conversation to bed and simply said, "This is who I am, love me or leave me"?

MISS AMERICA, THE BEAUTIFUL

The Burden of the National Anthem and the Politics of Whitney's Blackness

Who other than Whitney Houston could stand in triumph on a winter night in Tampa and sing "The Star-Spangled Banner" better than it had ever been sung before? When Whitney stepped on that stage at Super Bowl XXV and brought the world to a hush with the all-time greatest rendition of "The Star-Spangled Banner," she was amid a hot streak most pop stars only dream of. She was the only artist to have seven consecutive number one Billboard Hot 100 hits, and she was the first woman to debut atop the Billboard 200 album chart. Whitney's sensational rise was as much a part of her narrative as her miraculous voice and her famous kin. Clive Davis made sure of it, with his perfectly orchestrated rollout of her first two albums. *Billboard* called her "the pop equivalent of a De Mille extravaganza—epic and expensive." She was Clive's most perfect creation. Of course, Whitney was made for this moment, she *was* the moment. Whitney had broken ground on MTV and in pop music, and her meteoric rise and streak of crossover singles made her the de facto voice of the post–civil rights era. Whitney was marketed as proudly All-American, Miss Beautiful with a voice that transcended all that divided us in this great country. So who else but Whitney could meet the moment? Who else had a voice that could touch everyone in that stadium and everyone watching from their living room?

It could have only been Whitney. She and all the other babies who straddled the Boomer and Gen X generations had seen society become more integrated. It was the era that cultural critic Touré pegged "cultural biraciality," where a generation of kids were embracing cultures outside their own. Think about how many little Black boys who loved punk and rock and funk saw themselves in Prince's chameleon-like approach to pop. Or how it wasn't just young Black kids across the five boroughs or in Compton bumping LL Cool J and N.W.A. If the concerts didn't tell you that, the war white women raged on rap most certainly did. The "tough on crime" policies from the Reagan administration that inspired much of the "dangerous" hip-hop that sent white folks into hysterics were still ravaging Black American dreams in communities across the nation. Black men and women were either victims or villains, depending on who was asked. The tension of uncertainty already hanging thick in the Black neighborhoods was intensified by the Gulf War. Putting your body on the line for a nation that too often showed you how little it valued you and yours was heavy. For Black folks, the land of the free brimmed with oppression, even for our brave brothers and sisters who fought for the freedom of their country. Even if Whitney caught flack for her peppy pop tunes, she was still a Black girl from Newark with that voice, a voice that could inspire us all by singing the anthem like no one had sung it before—and like no one has sung it since.

"If you were there, you could feel the intensity," Whitney said in a 2000 interview. But even if you weren't there, you could *feel* it. Millions watched the sound of her voice explode like bombs bursting in air—astonished that a voice that mighty came out of one person. Think about the moment. Madonna and Janet Jackson were volleying number one hits. Mariah Carey was the new pop queen then. Prince was taking us on orgasmic sonic adventures and reinventing himself time and time again. And Michael Jackson had entered his *Dangerous* era. We worshipped MJ, but he had all but evaporated into the image of whiteness. Michael had shed his Blackness in a physical sense the way we believed Whitney shed hers in her music and public personas. The victorious feeling Whitney Houston baked into the anthem is why we thumb our nose at those who are unable to make us feel like we are basking in victory after they've sung "The Star-Spangled Banner." When Fergie turned the anthem into a burlesque romp or Christina Aguilera forgot the words or some moderately famous singer in over their head hit a sharp note, we turn their failure into our entertainment—sending them into the ether of the Internet for our forever judgment and ridicule. Six months before Whitney sang the anthem, Roseanne Barr screeched her way through it before a San Diego Padres game. It was a trainwreck. And to make it worse, Roseanne spit and grabbed her crotch during the performance. Death threats and anti-Semitic rhetoric followed, because there's nothing more

American than destroying celebrities who do stupid shit. Her Saturday cartoon got nixed. The president called her a disgrace. Hell, Roseanne went viral before it was a thing—and got canceled before that was a thing too.

No one but Whitney could have met the moment. She had dropped "You Give Good Love" and "Saving All My Love for You" and "How Will I Know" and "Greatest Love of All" and—*now, take a deep breath*—"I Wanna Dance with Somebody (Who Loves Me)" and "So Emotional" and "Where Do Broken Hearts Go" and "I'm Your Baby Tonight." Whitney was still a year away from ruling the world with "I Will Always Love You," but she was already at the top when she stood on that winter night in Tampa with jets roaring in the air above her. No one but Whitney could have taken the anthem and breathed so much life and meaning into it. In Tony Kushner's landmark play *Angels in America*, there's a snarky line about how the word "free" in the song's lyric is set to a note so high, nobody can reach it. But there wasn't a note too high for Whitney. Certainly not 1991 Whitney. Oh, the places her voice could go, and Whitney showed us just how far she could take her voice that night.

She was inspired by Marvin Gaye's smooth rendition of "The Star-Spangled Banner" at the NBA All-Star Game in '83. Marvin took the anthem and stretched it from its familiar 3/4 waltz into a smoldering soul record by grounding the hymn in a drum and keyboard track. But it was his swagger—effortlessly charismatic, yet sensuous—that sold it. The same way Whitney sold it when she stretched the anthem just as wide, filling the space with gospel flourishes and those money notes, those big runs that went sky-high, while dressed like an Olympic athlete.

The sheer magnitude of Whitney's voice and her transcendent performance turned the anthem into a moment of pure elation and pride for country. But she was a Black artist singing an anthem that was built on the horrific oppressions of her people, and there's a burden that comes with that—even if Whitney didn't think about it when she stood on that stage and did what she did best.

See, we tend to forget—or ignore—the roots from which "The Star-Spangled Banner" sprouted. We don't pass along the truths of which these lyrics were born—how white supremacy was at the foundation of these words we sing to pledge our undying patriotism. How could we? When we're standing at ballgames dressed in jerseys to cheer on sports heroes, our hands on our hearts, these are the words we are asked to sing to evoke the pride of being in the land of the free and the home of the brave. What are we to do with the ugliness that comes with loving a country with soil rich from the bloodshed of those who shoulder the trauma of its creation—from the pillaging of the land to the enslaved bodies that toiled atop it? The answer for Black people was to make their own anthem, and that's why for the last century "Lift Every Voice and Sing" has been our rallying cry for liberation and a lasting symbol of Black pride. In the battle over Colin Kaepernick's right to peacefully protest the injustices of Black Americans by taking a knee during the national anthem, it was conveniently forgotten—or perhaps intentionally ignored—that the anthem is a product of Black injustice and continues to remain a symbol for it. This has always been a country that has benefited from the oppression and degradation of Black people—from the unconscionable terrors of chattel slavery to the hunting of our Black men and boys by white lynch mobs or the KKK or the police or whatever group of "very fine people" former president Trump told to stand back and stand by rather than explicitly condemn before some of those very people showed their allegiance to him by storming the Capitol in his name. The fact that there was still a contentious election *after* four years of Trump's unrestrained racism and attempts at fascism forced those with the privilege to stop feigning ignorance over how deep-seated racism is in this country. But even after the summer of unrest in 2020 pushed people into the streets during a global pandemic to march and put their bodies on the line to make the Black Lives Matter movement the most impactful racial movement in modern history, white conservatives were more up in arms about stores being looted and athletes continuing Kaepernick's mission than they were about the loss of Black lives at the center of it all. But for Trump and his cult, or the conservatives who have bashed Kaepernick's cause and trash BLM with their All Lives Matter rhetoric, it was never about defending patriotism. This was about upholding supremacy. A biracial man had dared to use the ugly history of the anthem and its complications for Black people in America to shine a light on the continued mistreatment of his people, and he was called unpatriotic. He was labeled anti-cop, anti-military, anti-American. A football quarterback was painted as a traitor for using his fame to force the white folks who loved to watch him throw that ball down the field to confront the oppressions of Black men and women in this country. Kaepernick got death threats and was essentially stripped of his football career. All for taking a knee during "The Star-Spangled Banner."

I once had a white conservative friend tearfully explain to me why it was so awful that Kaepernick was distracting from games and why he needed to be more grateful about his wealth. *Distracting. Grateful for his wealth.* That's what she fixed her white mouth to say to a Black man. I asked her about the anthem's history. She couldn't tell me a single detail. I asked her about the song's third verse, which we don't talk much about. She couldn't recite a line. I mentioned doing away with the ritual altogether, or replacing it with "America the Beautiful" or "God Bless America." She hated the idea but had no actual reasoning as to why. She was committed to her anger. A Black athlete didn't just shut up and throw the ball for *her* entertainment and collect his millions. He was ungrateful. He was a distraction. Funny how that works.

It's important we go back to 1814, when Francis Scott Key wrote those lyrics as the flag waved majestically after battle. Key was a lawyer and an amateur poet. Born into slaveholding wealth, he fought to uphold the practice. Key became an advisor to President Andrew Jackson (himself a wealthy slaveholder), who nominated him as the U.S. district attorney for the nation's capital. During his time in office, Key worked to suppress the abolitionists who founded the anti-slavery movement, and he aggressively prosecuted slavery laws, even seeking the death penalty for an enslaved nineteen-year-old man accused of trying to murder his enslaver. Because of Key's influence, Jackson named Roger Taney (Key's best friend and brother-in-law) to be chief justice of the United States, and he went on to author the *Dred Scott* decision in 1857, which upheld enslavers' power, even in free states, and denied citizenship to free Black people. Key, like Jackson and like Taney, didn't believe Black people were entitled to any rights. To Key, Black people were untrustworthy and lazy. A nuisance to white folks. As he put it, Blacks—free or not—were "a distinct and inferior race of people, which all experience proves to be the greatest evil that afflicts a community."

That gets lost when we allow the history of the anthem to be divorced from the man who penned its lyrics while relishing in the victorious sight of the battle flag still standing after the British bombardment. The rush of victory and the pride of country, of the men who fought for it, is the crux of patriotism. Of Americanism. "The Star-Spangled Banner" promotes that to the point where *not* standing for it has riled up enough people that it's unlikely Colin Kaepernick will ever play in the NFL again. But those people almost never mention the song's origins, or can even tell you anything about the third verse, which has been lost to time and shame in the hundred years since it stopped being sung. Before the refrain we know so well—"*And the star-spangled banner in triumph doth wave / O'er the land of the free and the home of the brave*"—Key derided the thousands of former slaves who joined the British in exchange for a passage to freedom in Canada: "*No refuge could save the hireling and slave / From the terror of flight or the gloom of the grave,*" the lyrics go. Holding the contradictions of patriotism and oppression that sit at the core of these lyrics makes performing the anthem while Black so deeply complicated—and makes what Whitney accomplished on that night in the winter of 1991 all the more remarkable.

It's one of those moments in time that is seared into our minds: Whitney standing in the fullness of her power, dressed down in that white tracksuit with red and blue accents and white Nike Cortezes—her arms stretched wide, head tilted back as she belted the high note like a gold medalist clutching victory. Picture it. Remember the beauty of her voice? *That voice.* The sweat dotting her face as she sang with all her might on top of the prerecorded track. *That feeling.* The emotion of it all. Whitney sang like she was at the pulpit giving glory to God. I can still see the flashes of faces caught by the camera, tears freely staining people's cheeks as they waved tiny American flags. She made it look so easy, while making us *feel* so much. In that moment, Whitney offered the pride and joy of country while easing the fear over the Gulf War, which had started ten days prior and cast a shadow of anxiety—and extra security—over the Super Bowl. The focus in her eyes, the warmth coming from her soul when she hits her peak, the cymbals punctuating the ferocity in her voice as she worked toward that extraordinary climax. It felt like she held those big notes for an eternity: *"Ooooo'er the land of the freeeeeeeeeeeee and the hooooooome of theeeeeeeeeee braaaaaaaaaaaave."* Think about her standing there, sweaty, arms stretched out in triumph, dressed like she's running track for Team USA. Doesn't it fill you with pride? The physicality of it all. Her voice, pouring into the microphone at full power despite the security of a prerecording blasting out the loudspeakers. This was a live sporting event, not a concert. Whitney was the sideshow, barely even the opening act when you think of all the pomp that comes with a Super Bowl. But what she did on that dais? Nothing else about that night in Tampa even mattered. Most people can't tell you who played in the big game, but they can tell you precisely where they were when they saw Whitney stand there and sing the anthem with all her might. The night she stole America's heart and became a hero. There's Whitney *before* the anthem and Whitney after—that's just how big this thing got. An anthem born from the hands of a man who wanted to continue chattel slavery redefined by a Black woman whose majestic interpretation turned these lyrics into a Top 20 pop hit.

Try to remember the moment. For two minutes Whitney stood in the absolute peak of her brilliance. There was no chatter of her music not being "Black enough"; there was no sneering about who she was; there was no discussion about how she lacked the edge of Madonna and the moves of Janet or how she lacked enough singularity outside of her voice. In that moment all that mattered was *that voice* and its power. In those two minutes, Whitney became the embodiment of the ultimate American dream. She had reached the mountaintop, and the sheer magic of her voice moved the country to fall in love with itself a little deeper. And that is Blackness at its core. Whitney took the anthem, and all the darkness it casts down on Black folks, and transformed it into something that moved the world. In some ways, that night in Tampa was the Blackest thing Whitney has ever done—even if she, or any of us, didn't realize it then.

***

The victory of "The Star-Spangled Banner" and its dizzying success wouldn't deliver Whitney from the interrogation and policing of her Blackness. *I'm Your Baby Tonight* was viewed as a much too self-aware attempt at silencing the chatter—and there was so much chatter around Whitney. So much speculation. We gossiped about whether she was gay. We derided her for getting with Bobby—some of you reading this might have even had an office pool going on how long they'd last. We dismissed her music as not "Black enough" for years, and then we chided her for being too ghetto after she dropped the princess act and stopped hiding the Newports. Just a few months after her transcendent performance of the national anthem, she was back to being prodded about it all. "I know what my color is," she was pushed to declare in a 1991 *Ebony* profile. Whitney spent a large stretch of her career saying something of the sort in interviews. Regardless of the ceilings Whitney shattered, there was always someone out there thinking she wasn't *"Black enough"* because of the path she took to kick those barriers in; or because of the music she made; or because, despite the great lineage she came from, it was a white man steering the ship of her career.

Black cultural identity, as it relates to music, can be most linked to the genres of music pioneered by Black folks. Blues and soul and gospel measured the human condition. Motown centered on conventional upward mobility—love and marriage and *movin' on up*. Rap was about bearing witness to lives broken by the realities of being Black in America. Jazz and country and rock were in our blood and part of our contributions to music, but where did pop fit in? We were arguing about this long before Whitney, and we still are long after the day she left this earth. Even following the success of the anthem she was being raked over the coals for what we believed she had given up in order to take over the pop world. We looked at Whitney and thought she was being forced to sing those records because she wasn't writing or choosing them, a belief that was confirmed in those moments she stopped being so polite and got a little too real in front of the camera. Whitney had come up in a time when genre lines were as rigid as our thoughts around them. To be a "Black musician" in 1985 or 1995 or 2005 or 2020 often meant fitting perfectly into the genre lines expected of Black acts. "Pop music" meant "white music," and being Black and attempting to paint outside the lines meant you were thumbing your nose at *your* audience—alienating them in a bid to cross over and be accepted by whites. You were a sellout. It's not just music. Black artists and filmmakers and writers have all had to confront the expectations, or the demands, from their people to speak directly to them through their art.

Those boos Whitney received at the Soul Train Awards in 1989 confirmed what the critics had been saying about her from the start: Black folks believed she was a fraud. They were tired of the *act*. They were tired of the music that didn't naturally sound like the R&B and soul they got from those who came before her. *I'm Your Baby Tonight* had enough funky New Jack Swing bangers on it to show Whitney was listening to the gossip and wanted to show she had creative autonomy. And she wanted to shut us up. But it was all too calculated for people. She was trying too hard to *be* hard. And then she got with Bobby Brown? It all felt too calculated for some. It didn't help that this was happening at the same time Uptown and Bad Boy Records were ushering in the ghetto-fabulous era that would introduce us to Mary J. Blige. *"What's the 411, hun? / I got it goin' on, hun."* Mary dripped in so much swag. From the start, Mary's music was undeniable in the way it spoke directly, and exclusively, to Black womanhood. She was singing the blues for the hip-hop generation. There were no airs to Mary. She was born in the Bronx and raised in Yonkers and had grit, attitude, glamour, and none of the overly polished refinement that made Whitney and Diana feel inaccessible. She cut herself open on records and sang about the sorrows of heartbreak and the painful betrayal of abuse and the glory of sisterhood and the sweetness of new beginnings. Mary was that round-the-way girl who spoke to us the way we wanted Whitney to speak to us—the way we wanted her to show us the parts of herself we knew she was hiding in order to appeal to all demographics. Eventually Black folks got tired of waiting. "Sometimes it gets down to that, you know? You're not Black enough for them," Whitney told Katie Couric in 1996. "You're not R&B enough. You're very, very pop. The white audience have taken you away from them."

There's an expectation of our Black women in music to assimilate in order to take up space, particularly in pop music, where European beauty standards are exalted. Fair skin, slender figures, and windswept hair was more marketable than chocolatey skin and Afro hair and wide nostrils and wider hips. Prince and Michael could glide between whatever genres and aesthetics fit their mood, but Black women barely enjoyed that kind of freedom. Even now, Black women are rarely afforded the space to subvert stereotypical identities without being met with pushback. Those who don't try to fit squarely into R&B or hip-hop are criticized far more than their male counterparts. They are dismissed as inauthentic and accused of pandering to white audiences if they color too far outside genre lines. This is an industry powered by Black music but largely run by white record executives. So much of the contemporary pop music of the last quarter century is simply variations of music with Black roots done by white musicians. From Elvis to the Beatles to the Rolling Stones to Teena Marie to Madonna to New Kids on the Block all the way up to the boom of teenage dreams ruling *Total Request Live* through Justin Bieber and Adele and Ariana Grande and Sam Smith and Post Malone. We are now in an era where cultural appropriation has veered into straight-up cosplay. Much of our criticisms of the Kardashians and Jenners is connected to how we see them—as culturally biracial women who have "borrowed" freely from the physical traits of Black women, traits viewed as desirable so long as they aren't *actually* on Black bodies. They've plumped up their lips and their hips and layered themselves with makeup until they are varying shades of brown. We have watched them give birth to a host of mixed-race children conceived with rappers or athletes while leveraging our fascination and repulsion of them into billon-dollar empires.

And we see it with pop music. It's in the way Miley Cyrus, Justin Bieber, Katy Perry, Billie Eilish—and Madonna before all of them—have imprinted their music with AAVE or co-opted rap sounds and hip-hop fashion trends, and it's in the way Ariana's deepened complexion has gotten her accused of Blackfishing. Shifting appearances to make music pulled from traditionally Black genres is problematic, certainly, but what is more offensive is how this act of cultural trespassing—as old as it is—seems to only be permissive in one direction. Pop music, the way we tend to define it today, isn't really anything more than a mishmash of cultures and sounds, so of course R&B's and hip-hop's widening prominence at the turn of the century would inspire white artists. But we seem to only allow white artists the freedom to explore disparate sounds. Look at Beyoncé, Rihanna, and Nicki Minaj—arguably the biggest Black artists to rise since MJ and

Prince and Whitney back in the eighties. Not a single one of them reached their apex without somebody saying their music wasn't "Black enough." Our historically rigid view of pop music has continued along strict genre lines, even as the streaming era has given way to a generation of listeners who categorize music by mood and playlist and don't think much at all about genre. Women in pop already have the expectations to look a certain way, but Black women are shouldering a double burden. They must look and sound a particular way if they want to cross over to pop radio. Their skin can't be too dark, their bodies can't be too thick, and their hair can't be too kinky. And that's just the image. Black women in pop also have to constantly wrestle with the tug-of-war between authenticity and ambition. There has always been a fine line between appealing to white folks and "selling out," and the benchmark seems to move depending on who's being discussed. White artists don't have to worry about that at all. Miley Cyrus and Post Malone can peddle in hip-hop as they please and still be seen as pop stars or rock stars, but we side-eye Lizzo for making music that appeals to white folks. There's a privilege in Justin Bieber being able to voice his frustrations when the Grammys didn't put him in an R&B category while staying silent about the Grammys' historic snubbing of Black artists in major categories or even using his influence to voice outrage over pop radio's continued segregation, which keeps R&B and hip-hop artists from getting the same airplay he regularly enjoys. Beyoncé is the biggest star on the planet, with music releases that are now cultural milestones, and yet she's been MIA from pop radio for the better part of a decade as she moved her music deeper into centering the Black experience.

And it took Rihanna's repudiation of her pop-princess persona on 2016's *Anti* to get the best critical praise of her career. Just imagine what it must have been like for Whitney in 1991. Even after breaking down all those doors and standing in so much triumph, she was told it wasn't enough. *She* wasn't enough.

Eventually Whitney morphed. First, with the music. And then her voice. And on it went until suddenly she was *too* Black. Whitney's embrace of overt Blackness came later in the nineties, when she taught us to *shoop* and her film roles came from a Terry McMillan tome or put her next to Denzel. We'd see it when she dropped the act, when she checked a reporter by letting the Newark in her creep out her mouth. For now she played it safe. And in playing it safe, Whitney was cast as inauthentic. We had Reverend Al Sharpton labeling her "Whitey" Houston and some Black disc jockeys refusing to play her records. This was the price Whitney paid for being marketed to white audiences. Clive and Cissy had worked hard to make Whitney the "kind of Black that white people could accept," which is how Lena Horne described the tightrope she once walked as a Black woman entertaining white audiences she could never socialize with. We might have no longer been segregated by schools or bathrooms when Whitney followed in Lena's tradition of great pop singing, but we weren't removed from the tightrope. Whitney did the dance well—too well for those who thought she had her toes dipped too far in "pop music" because pop equals white, remember? Never mind the R&B records on her album. Never mind the gospel vocalizing she unleashed in big power ballads. It wasn't *enough*. Whitney wasn't accepted in the way she wanted to be. But how does one sing *more* Black? What did we actually want from her that she could have given us without sacrificing her own dreams? That's the conundrum Black artists too often find themselves in. Sammy Davis Jr. was there. Sam Cooke was there. Whitney was there. Mariah was there. Beyoncé was there. Rihanna was there. Lizzo was there. Lil Nas X was there. Some of this is because of the disconnect that remains between the history of Black contributions to popular music and the segregated genre lines the music industry continues to promote. Black artists have had to contend with reductive terms like "race records" or "Black music" or "urban"—all square boxes white radio programmers and record executives have used to denote the music made by Black people. Music made by Black people in this country has influenced white cultural tastes since the beginning of time, but, as we continue to see, music made by Black artists has to grapple with far more boundaries than the same music made by white artists. We know that to be Black in America means living in a state of double-consciousness. The great W. E. B. Du Bois laid it out in *The Souls of Black Folk*. "It is a peculiar sensation," Du Bois wrote of double-consciousness, "this sense of always looking at one's self through the eyes of others, of measuring one's soul by the tape of a world that looks on in amused contempt and pity." The history of the Black man and woman in America, Du Bois theorized, is the struggle with the discord of trying to hold one's Blackness and one's American-ism in equal measure. That shows up in the pressures we place on Black artists, politicians, and athletes and that conflict of the "twoness" and the warring ideals that come with holding both.

And we saw that with Whitney. The mental gymnastics she went through in interviews, adjusting the parts of her that upheld the image that had been crafted. Her look, her tone, the way she held her body—it was all surveyed and judged in real time. She knew this. Black folks knew this. We move through the world in a constant state of reading the rooms we are in. Some of us shave down parts of ourselves depending on what spaces we're in, and some of us don't. That constant code-switching is exhausting, and it wore on Whitney. We saw her on the days when she just didn't have *it* for a reporter and their questions—or their accusations about her Blackness or her sexuality or her music. We heard it when she suppressed the mid-Atlantic accent and let Nippy spill out. And we saw it when she ignored the expectation of the cameras pointed on her and just *was*.

In 1989, the writer Trey Ellis published his famous essay on "The New Black Aesthetic." Ellis grew up in predominately white, middle- and working-class suburbs around New Haven, Connecticut, where "it wasn't unusual to be called 'Oreo' and 'nigger' on the same day." He operated from a place of cultural biraciality—though he called himself a "cultural mulatto," a phrase he used to describe Blacks who possessed the ability to thrive and exist in white society while maintaining all facets of their identity. There were two types of cultural mulattos, Ellis opined: "thriving hybrids" and "neutered mutants." Thriving hybrids have transcended the stereotypes indicative of Blackness, meaning their identity *isn't* indicative of their Blackness, whereas neutered mutants are tragic mulattos who alienate themselves from Black culture as they struggle to fit into white culture. "We no longer need to deny or suppress any part of our complicated and sometimes contradictory cultural baggage to please either white people or Black," Ellis wrote in the essay, which marked the growing cultural dominance of Black creatives in mainstream spaces at the dawn of the nineties. Ellis lauded Spike Lee and Prince and hip-hop and Eddie Murphy but reviled Whitney Houston and Lionel Richie for the way he interpreted their presentation of Blackness. They were two of the biggest Black pop stars at the time, but Ellis saw them as "cultural-mulatto, assimilationist nightmares; neutered mutations instead of thriving hybrids. Trying to please both worlds instead of themselves, they end up truly pleasing neither." Ellis wrote that Lionel's frothy "Dancing on the Ceiling" and Whitney's frothier "I Wanna Dance with Somebody" were lifeless "precisely because they have applied Porcelana fade cream to their once extremely soulful throats." It's interesting that Michael was out of the conversation. His Blackness was at the core of his music, which made what appeared to be a very clear repellence of his Black features and his Black skin feel like a bewildering contradiction. But Michael somehow managed to top *Thriller* with 1987's *Bad*, an album packed with ferocious funk and rock and slick R&B and dance. His exterior had completely morphed into literal whiteness, but he was in the studio churning out records like "The Way You Make Me Feel" and "Smooth Criminal" and "I Just Can't Stop Loving You." The way Ellis saw it, Whitney and Lionel were the worst kind of sellout. Ellis couldn't see why a Whitney or a Lionel needed to occupy the spaces they did. Rhythm and blues had been the root of so much that white artists needed to borrow from it. Not the other way around. Because blues was the root. Because soul was the root. Because gospel was the root. Because jazz was the root. Because rock was the root. The thought of Black artists taking the gifts cultivated from these roots and making music that overtly reached for audiences outside of their communities was obscene to some. But the racially mixed pop of Whitney, of Lionel, of Prince, and of Michael spoke to our hope for a post-racial America, even if it was one that could somehow exist without dismantling the racism that built our country and informed the worldviews Black artists did—or didn't—build around their music and their personas.

Three decades later, and we have yet to really move past this conversation. We're still not beyond this idea of judging one's Blackness in proximity to the stereotypical identifiers they do and don't exhibit. The way one speaks. The music one makes. The way one dresses—and who they date, and what their politics are, and on and on. We expect Black folks to represent more than themselves. Because of the deep-rooted history of oppression and racism rooted in the land of the "free," Black folks have no choice but to be more than themselves. We have to hold the history of our culture, of our people, of our past. Ta-Nehisi Coates interrogated those expectations, and how they have historically impacted Black cultural icons, in a 2018 essay for the *Atlantic*. Coates wrote that the gift of Black music, of Black art was unlike any other in this country "because it is not simply a matter of singular talent, or even of tradition, or lineage, but of something more grand and monstrous . . . The gift can never wholly belong to a singular artist, free of expectation and scrutiny, because the gift is no more solely theirs than the suffering that produced it." Heavy is the head that wears the crown. And there's a twisted irony in the fact that those who wore the heaviest crowns—Whitney, Prince, and Michael—are all gone now. They all collapsed under the weight of the crown, one way or another. Coates wrote those words in response to growing frustrations over Kanye West. We've been watching him slowly crumble under the weight of his crown for years. Before the MAGA hat and the bizarre ramblings and the run for president and the self-aggrandizing and the cultish positioning of his choir and his apparel and shoes, Kanye was showing us through visionary music and boundless ambition that he wanted to shed all expectations of a rapper. Those expectations can become stifling to artists. Even Beyoncé grew tired of stretching herself to appease both sides with her Diana Ross approach to pop stardom. Though she never directly pandered to white audiences, her carefully crafted image was similar to that of Whitney's, and her apolitical stance allowed her to become the most famous entertainer on the planet. It wasn't until she stopped caring about chasing pop charts and airplay on Top 40 radio that Beyoncé began making the most socially ambitious artistic statements of her career. That it happened through work that also centered her point of view as a Black woman in America was no surprise to those who had followed her since she was a teenager from Houston singing fiery Black girl magic anthems with her sisterfriends in Destiny's Child. But a different Beyoncé emerged at Super Bowl 50. A quarter century after Whitney stood in power, Beyoncé used the Super Bowl to usher herself into the next phase of her career. She had already had her own victories at the Super Bowl—singing a lovely, Whitney-inspired rendition of the "The Star-Spangled Banner" at Super Bowl XXXVIII and shutting down Super Bowl XLVII with a spectacular halftime concert. But there was Beyoncé *before* she performed "Formation" at Super Bowl 50 and Beyoncé *after*. Since releasing "Formation," the first single from 2016's *Lemonade,* Beyoncé has pursued projects that have allowed her to place her Blackness squarely at the center of her work. She made a conscious choice to do what felt good to her artistic vision, but she is proof that cultural dominance still doesn't translate to album sales or radio play or Grammys in major categories. She's one of the most decorated artists of our time and has been making the best music of her career, but it's no coincidence that Beyoncé crosses over far less than she did when she was calling to *all the single ladies!* Even after Whitney, there's still a price to pay for the freedom of thriving *because* of your Blackness and not in spite of it.

Whitney's post–Super Bowl dominance came right as Mariah Carey was breaking through, and we did what we always did with two women who made similar music: we pitted them against each other. Mariah was six years younger than Whitney, but both had the same question lingering over their heads: Were they Black *enough*? With Mariah it was more about her outward appearance, and not always the music she made. Because she was a biracial girl with very light skin and curly tresses, her heritage was either questioned or overlooked by critics. A 1990 review in the *Los Angeles Times* raved about the gospel flour-ishes of her voice and how she was the real deal while describing Mariah as a "white singer who has a Black vocal style." Mariah was widely cast by the media as a white girl who sang Black—a "white Whitney Houston"—or there was an insinuation that she was purposely channeling racial ambiguity to appeal to wider

demographics. Also like Whitney, Mariah was seen as an ingénue who was being controlled by a powerful older man—which,
in Mariah's case, was Tommy Mottola, the head of her label,
who would become her husband and keep her under his thumb
personally and professionally for years before she divorced
him. Where Mariah differed from Whitney, though, was her
commitment to moving her music toward hip-hop as the genre
grew more popular. Though she dabbled in pop ballads and
synth-heavy dance joints, her core was always R&B. And that was
never up for question, even if the world needed to be reminded
time and time again that Mariah was a Black woman. Years later,
she'd let it slip that Mottola had her music scrubbed of its gospel inflections, removing the vocal licks we love from our soul
singers in a bid to keep her music safe for crossover success. It
was Mariah who popularized the pop/hip-hop crossover with
indelible earworms like "Fantasy" and "Honey." It's pop standard
now to sandwich rap verses on a melodic tune, but Mariah helped
normalize it, and she did so without any of the stigmas that
ensnared Whitney. Not that Mariah was exempt from the cruelty
of racism beyond the anti-Blackness of dismissing her biracial
identity. Like the time comedian Sandra Bernhard unleashed
a tirade of racist jokes about Mariah "acting real niggerish" as
she mocked her proximity to hip-hop. Because we tend to fail
our Black women, there was no public outrage and nobody had
Mariah's back until she wrote the NAACP herself to ask for support. Like much of what Whitney endured during her career, it
feels implausible that any of this was allowed given the time we
live in now. But it's not. Beyoncé and Rihanna have had to assert
their Blackness in an industry that often treats Black women as

a monolith. And it comes up in the way Lizzo has had to defend her right to rap and sing and dance and make music that's bubbly and fuses genre lines. For every critic declaring Lizzo the Aretha of a new generation there were twice as many wondering *who* she was making music for and dissecting why so many white women saw themselves in her music. And we see it in the way Tinashe and Kelela and Dawn Richard have struggled to break into the mainstream as Black girls channeling alternative and progressive spins on R&B. Kinda makes you wonder if Whitney ever really stood a chance. What's the point of breaking the barrier if we only want our Black artists to fit snugly into the boxes we draw around them?

None of this mattered, though, on that winter night in Tampa, when Whitney stood in triumph—arms stretched wide, head tilted back as she belted the highest of notes with the precision of an Olympic athlete. For two minutes Whitney pulled off the most spectacular act of code-switching: she took the burden of holding an anthem that was built on the oppression of Black Americans and injected it with hope and love and unrestrained patriotism on the world's biggest stage. We expect Black artists to represent more than just themselves. There's no other choice. Not with the history we stand upon. Whitney had no other choice but to do what she did that night when she put on a white tracksuit and found splendor in lyrics born out of the white supremacy that has powered the land of the free for more than four hundred years. It was her rendition that has become the gold standard, and we've measured everyone who sings it against Whitney's performance. She was *that* good. There have been other brilliant renditions. But only Whitney moved the world with hers. It was her rendition that recirculated in the aftermath of 9/11, shooting back onto the charts—giving her the final Top 10 hit she'd have in her career. When we needed to feel hope and pride again after the attacks, Whitney's voice served as that beacon of hope—even as she was crumbling under the weight of her crown. The day before terrorists slammed planes into the World Trade Center, there were rumors that Whitney had died of a drug overdose. It was nasty gossip, but that's how we were treating Whitney after the turn of the millennium. Her crown had cracked under the pressures of living up to the Whitney the world demanded her to be. It's exceptionally cruel to think about. Once again she had taken the anthem, and all its darkness, and used it to bring comfort to a nation that wasn't even treating her like a human. But isn't that Blackness at its core?

BOLDER, BLACKER, BADDER

The Sisters with Voices That Transformed Whitney

In our era of digitally assisted remembrance, Whitney Houston occupies a space that eluded her in life. A space where her Blackness is admired, never doubted. A glimpse of Whitney frozen in time or on a continuous loop is probably deep in your camera roll or stored among your most used GIFs. And if you don't have Whitney saved to be at your disposal, she's certainly graced your Twitter or Instagram feed or popped up in a group chat with your friends—craning her neck dramatically, or rolling her eyes, or looking exasperated or declaring, "Ahhh, that's history" in the most pleasing manor. In death, through the permanence of memes, Whitney has become an auntie to all of us. It was always there, of course. Beneath the politesse, sequined gowns, and sugary pop confections that made her Whitney Houston was a round-the-way girl. But the diva hunger games that kept us bent on stacking her against Madonna, Janet, Paula, and Mariah as they all climbed the pop ladder made us overlook the idea of sisterhood that was integral to Whitney's position in the music industry throughout her career.

The greatest Whitney GIF of all time—okay, maybe not the greatest, but certainly a Top 5 contender—was born out of the very sisterhood she held so dear. You've seen it. Natalie Cole is clutching the American Music Award she bested Whitney (and Paula Abdul) for as they laugh and point at each other, Natalie from the stage in her black sequined gown and gloves, and Whitney from her seat. "I don't know how many times that Whitney and I have been in the same category together," Natalie says at the beginning of her acceptance speech, locking eyes with her girl Whitney, "but I'm gonna enjoy this one!" It's a beautiful image. This was 1992, and these were two pop powerhouses relishing in their success, but they were also Black women who were good girlfriends very publicly rooting for each other in a hellish industry that endlessly judged women against one another. Whitney and Natalie were entertainers who descended from music royalty, which magnified the pressures that came with their career and contributed to their struggles with drug dependency. They were women trying to make it—and left us far before they should have. I keep the GIF of Whitney and Natalie in my arsenal anytime I want to gas up one of my friends. Anytime I want to punctuate a *"yass"* or give praise to a shady read or a good word, I turn to that moment of Whitney and Natalie joyously showing each other love. Whenever I look at it, my mind tries to place them here now, as if they were still here, competing for awards and giving us more joyful moments like the one they shared at the American Music Awards in 1992.

Sisterhood was so deep at the core of who Whitney was and how she moved in the industry. It's what I've appreciated most about her, outside of any of her talents. As she got older, Whitney's embracement of sisterhood showed an accessibility that her music and public-facing image had lacked in the beginning of her career. The way she uplifted Brandy and Monica in her name; how she embraced Kelly Price and Faith Evans and Deborah Cox; her deep friendships with Mariah and Mary J. Blige and CeCe Winans and Pebbles. The way she allowed herself to be vulnerable with Oprah Winfrey and talk about hitting rock bottom and the worst of her years with Bobby. We came to see Whitney as the quintessential Black auntie. And those GIFs of her being funny and shady that are frozen in our phones or the phrases she's uttered that have embedded themselves in our psyche and become part of our vernacular all come from this period that I like to call the emergence of *Auntie Nippy.*

Before Whitney recorded the boldest (and most undeniably *Black*) music of her career, she filmed *Waiting to Exhale.* The adaptation of Terry McMillan's bestselling tome centers sisterhood in its story of the trials and tribulations of modern Black women navigating romantic and familial relationships. Whitney had reached her zenith after singing the national anthem and followed that with the blockbuster success of *The Bodyguard* and its record-breaking soundtrack. For her next film role, she wanted something more complex. Something more real. Something that allowed her to show up onscreen as more than Whitney Houston, the pop diva. She found that in *Waiting to Exhale.* Terry McMillan writes beautifully and honestly about contemporary Black women. She writes of women who put their pain and desires on display; who live boldly or reck-lessly and are hopelessly looking for love, or at the very least a good lay; women who are trying to have it all in a world that doesn't always have it for them. McMillan spoke directly, and frankly, to Black women looking to get their groove back. She wrote for the women who were sick of trifling-ass men; the women who had been in Sorrow's kitchen and licked out all the pots; and the women who were in search of sexual freedom and personal liberation. *Waiting to Exhale*, her third novel, focused on a quartet of middle-class, thirtysomething Black women in the throes of emotional tumult and the sisterhood that kept them going. These were richly complex women—successful in their careers but deeply frustrated with love and family. The book made McMillan a household name when it became one of the best-selling works of fiction in 1992. Critics railed against her—the same way they rail against Tyler Perry now—for not being imaginative or ambitious enough in her prose and explor-ing subject matter that focused too much on the intersection of class, gender, and Black heterosexual desire without interrogat-ing the racism, sexism, or socioeconomic volatility that impacts the way Black folks live in America. But McMillan, like Perry, was connecting with an audience that rarely saw themselves imprinted in fiction or television or film. We all knew women like Savannah and Robin and Gloria and Bernadine—glamorous, vulnerable, impulsive, passionate, feisty, *human*. These were real women who could have easily been our sisters or our favor-ite aunties. I was seven or eight when I found my mother's copy of *Waiting to Exhale* in her bedroom. I wouldn't read it fully until I was a teenager, but I was captivated by the cover, the brown faceless silhouettes dressed in sharp, vibrant clothes. The cover looked like the contemporary Black art my mama and all her sisterfriends—my *aunties*—had in their apartments. I would lay in bed with her as she read, curled up in her warmth—lost in my own (age-appropriate) adventure.

Given its success, a film adaptation of *Waiting to Exhale* was inevitable. Forest Whitaker made his directorial debut with the film, and Angela Bassett, Lela Rochon, Loretta Devine, and Whitney were cast in the lead roles. At last Whitney had a nuanced role, one that required more of her than *The Bodyguard* and *The Preacher's Wife*—films that were ostensibly built around the marvel of her singing voice. Savannah Jackson wasn't a superstar pop diva being stalked or a neglected wife visited by a debonair angel. She was a weary woman who had reached great heights in her career but was deeply frustrated by her romantic prospects and her meddling mother. Savannah was a woman in search of peace of mind and a love that was meaningful. Like her sisterfriends, she was holding her breath for Mr. Right and tired of entertaining all the Mr. Wrongs who drifted into her life and made her shrink herself and put her needs second. Released around Christmas in 1995, *Waiting to Exhale* made history as the first film with all-Black female leads to open at number one at the box office. The popularity of the book and its blockbuster film adaptation were influential in normalizing middle-class Black women in the popular cultural consciousness. Studios were then eager to greenlight slickly produced soap operas exploring the Black middle class through ensemble family dramas and romantic comedies—far different from the hood films pouring out of Hollywood that coincided with the popularity of hip-hop and confronted the tumult of Black life in inner cities across the country. Whitney, like her onscreen character, was a woman in her early thirties. She had had a few years of marriage and motherhood under her belt, and twice as many as a superstar entertainer. She was worn out from the unkind press, the criticism of her personal life, of her music, and the nagging questions of authenticity.

Waiting to Exhale was pivotal in helping her change the narrative in a way she hadn't been able to before. Whitney melted into the role of Savannah—a woman who had it all but somehow couldn't snag a man who wasn't a trifling dog. Whitney was sharp and funny in her performance, but more than that, she took the weariness her character lived in and merged it with her own pain. We didn't know the depths of her personal sorrows yet. We suspected things were bad between her and Bobby. The tabloids churned out stories of Bobby's infidelity and partying, and there was gossip that Whitney was a standoffish diva on set, chatter her co-stars attempted to silence. Years later, after she was long gone, we learned that Whitney actually overdosed on cocaine while shooting the film in Arizona. Whitney's issues with drugs were still a secret from the general public, which again was only possible because we weren't yet in a time when celebrity news was a twenty-four-hour machine. As far as we knew, Whitney was just a woman who appeared to be in a toxic marriage.

Whitney initially had no interest in recording any new music for *Waiting to Exhale*, but she couldn't resist working with her friend Kenny "Babyface" Edmonds, whom Whitaker brought on to compose the film's score and produce its soundtrack. As work on the movie was underway, Babyface would drop in on the set to absorb the film's scenes, and he built the soundtrack around its subtext. Both he and Whitney had the idea that the soundtrack should be an all-Black female affair to mirror the theme of the film, and the resulting album is a veritable snapshot of the sisters with voices that mattered most in 1995. Aretha Franklin, Patti LaBelle, and Chaka Khan—three of Whitney's foremothers—delivered knockout performances, and Babyface brought out the best of the gaggle of voices that Whitney paved the way for. There's Brandy, whose youthful vibrancy gave the funky banger "Sittin' Up in My Room" a sugary rush akin to early Whitney; TLC, Chanté Moore, Faith Evans, and SWV brought smoldering sex jams to the mix; Toni Braxton's "Let It Flow" is a smooth torch ballad that, along with Mary J. Blige's searing "Not Gon' Cry," became a contemporary anthem for thirtysomething Black women.

The *Waiting to Exhale* soundtrack is bookended by the suite of records Whitney cut with Babyface. Taking on the character of Savannah pushed Whitney away from her good-girl image. Savannah was strong and vulnerable, and she expressed her sexual desire and was vocal about her ambitions and disappointments. Savannah was a regular woman. And though Whitney was a grown-ass woman in her early thirties at this point, her public persona was still tightly positioned as a regal pop vocalist who made sweet love songs without profound substance. Her music wasn't sexy or provocative, but Babyface was a master savant when it came to crafting understated and seductive pop-soul records. He and his former producing partner, L.A. Reid, had taken Whitney away from fluffy, formulaic pop when they injected her with a taste of New Jack Swing funk for *I'm Your Baby Tonight*—an album crammed with bangers that hold up better than most of her pre-*Bodyguard* work but regarded as a half-baked attempt at being edgy. So what if *I'm Your Baby Tonight* was a rebuttal to the "not Black enough" comments, the jokes, and the humiliation of being jeered at the Soul Train Awards the night she met Bobby? Whitney had exerted some control over her artistry—the very thing she was so widely criticized for—and it *still* wasn't good enough to silence the conversation on her authenticity or artistic choices. Hindsight has given us much clarity about how we read Whitney the first time around. Those years between *The Bodyguard* and *Waiting to Exhale* were treacherous. She had the career and the family, but the price of fame meant she also constantly saw her name and face splashed across the tabloids. The rumors about her and Robyn persisted. Her drama with Bobby and his own troubles were under constant scrutiny. And her drug use had crossed the line from recreational to perilous. Though she only recorded three songs for *Waiting to Exhale*, this is where Whitney flips the script on us—for good. Back when she was circling the globe on her *Bodyguard* world tour, Babyface sent the demo for "Why Does It Hurt So Bad." It's one hell of a ballad about a woman finding the strength to leave a poisonous relationship, and the anguish over still loving the man she knows is harmful. Whitney passed on the record when Clive played it for her. She told him she couldn't relate to the emotions and, according to him, it was one of the rare times they disagreed on a song. "I wasn't really in the mood for singing about why it hurts so bad," Whitney admitted while on the promo trail for *Waiting to Exhale*. But enough had happened to her by 1995 that made her, in her words, ready to sing about "not only the joys of things, but the pains of things, also."

Whitney recorded many a lovelorn lament in her lifetime, but "Why Does It Hurt So Bad" hit different, especially since we had read enough of the gossip to suspect she was pulling from her own shit with Bobby. There's a mournfulness in her voice throughout the record. Typical Whitney ballads pulled from her ability to belt, her ability to climb to the sweetness of her top voice and belt those high notes we love. That control, that vibrato, made her love songs so gorgeous and emotive. However, Whitney doesn't lean on the top of her range for "Why Does It Hurt So Bad." The verses are understated, her voice restrained. Even though the bridge is the octave-crushing crescendo we expect from a Whitney Houston ballad, she sounds as if she's singing to *herself*. *"'Never again' that's what I said to myself, I never wanna feel your kind of pain again / Just when I think it's over, just when I think it's through, I find myself right back in love with you,"* she sings before sliding back into mournful restraint—but not without telling her man he makes her wanna shoot him. It's a biting line that reflected the fed-up attitudes Terry McMillan brought to life with her characters while also toying with the domestic turmoil in Whitney's real life that would work itself into her post–*Waiting to Exhale* music.

"Why Does It Hurt So Bad" wasn't the big hit from *Waiting to Exhale*. That distinction goes to the breezy "Exhale (Shoop Shoop)." With its anthemic "shoop shoop" hook and laid-back groove, "Exhale" debuted at number one on the Billboard Hot 100 chart—the third song in history to do so after Michael Jackson's "You Are Not Alone" and Mariah Carey's "Fantasy." *Waiting to Exhale* introduced a new era for Whitney. She had broken the records and barriers required to pave the way for a new generation of young Black girls to come and spin their magic in pop music, and a quick scan of the *Waiting to Exhale* soundtrack album tracklist will show you the depths of the influence Whitney had, just a decade into her career. Since her death, we have come to realize all it took for her to do this—to break the ceiling and open the door for the generations of sisters' voices that have come after her. We watched her shrink the parts of herself that got in the way of the image being sold. Whitney covered her Afro curls with vivacious, honey blonde wigs and spoke with all the measured, delicate grace of the princess Clive Davis packaged her to be. Whitney's public image put her at odds with what we wanted her to be, with *who* we thought she should be as a Black girl from Newark, New Jersey. We wanted more of the Whitney that slipped out when she tired of code-switching. The Whitney who checked you for asking a sharp question, or for pressing her too hard about her man or the music she made. The Whitney who told Oprah to mind her business and reminded Barbara Walters that she didn't know shit about her. *Waiting to Exhale* gave Whitney the space to reset. The space to free herself from the curated image that was now difficult to take seriously and show us something more real, something we could feel. We wanted her to reveal the woman behind *Whitney Houston*, a woman we all knew was in desperate need of exhaling.

***

White America's perception of Black sexuality has always been a peculiar mix of intrigue, obsession, and fear. Black men are seen as endowed, lascivious Mandingos, Black women as jezebels—both with insatiable appetites and reckless indulgences. And sex often sat at the root of the obsession over Whitney and Bobby's relationship from a largely white media industrial complex. People saw a woman whose carnal desires were being questioned saddle up with a man whose raunchy performances and lustful music made White America blush. Bobby came from a school of R&B crooners that knew sex sold profoundly well. There wasn't much that separated Elvis's and Mick Jagger's proclivity for hip swiveling and lip licking onstage from the sweaty performances Bobby put on that teased his sex, but Bobby blew up during a time when musicians were persecuted in parts of the country for indecent performances. In 1989, Bobby was arrested during a concert in Columbus, Georgia, for violating the city's "Lewd Law," which prohibited performers at an event attended by people under the age of eighteen to show nudity or sexual pictures or use "four-letter words" or simulate sex acts. The local city council had passed the ordinance a few years earlier after a Beastie Boys concert ruffled enough feathers. Bobby being arrested mid-show (he finished the concert an hour later after being released with a $652 fine) for grinding on a fan created a thrilling headline that helped frame him as the sexy "Bad Boy of R&B," but the reality is male erotica and desire have never *not* been at the center of pop and rock and R&B and hip-hop. Bobby was no different. Sex was his specialty, and it contributed to the lascivious image he relished after being kicked out of New Edition. And the media ate it up, of course. Depending on who was asked, Bobby was seen as a danger, or a jolt, to Whitney's pure image. The belief spun by disc jockeys and gossips was that Whitney only chose Bobby because his hard edge gave her a needed boost of credibility in the eyes of Black America, and he went along with it because the proximity to Whitney benefited his career. It certainly made for a good angle, especially for those who yearned to know who Whitney was getting down with and had spent years berating her with questions about who she was sharing her bed with. Despite Whitney's insistence that we never get it twisted when it came to who she was and what she wanted for herself, the idea of her and Bobby was met with skepticism by Black folks and horror (and intrigue) by White America. Post-*Exhale* Whitney was fed up—not just with our opinions and our gossip about Bobby and having to defend her marriage to the press whenever they asked (and they *always* asked), but with Bobby and his drama. We read about his other women, and their fights, and wondered why they still were together. Why Whitney Houston, a woman who could have whoever she wanted in the world, *settled* for a man who wasn't good for—or to—her. "I'm like an American princess. White America wanted me to marry someone white," Whitney explained to journalist Jamie Foster Brown in 1996. "They don't understand why I'd want a strong Black man." Whitney's reading spoke to only half of it. In her post-*Exhale* transformation we couldn't understand why she was still sticking around with a man who brought her as much drama as Bobby did. Of course he was the father of her child, but we couldn't grasp why she stayed.

Why she stayed despite the other women, why she stayed despite the constant humiliation. For so long, Whitney's tragic demise was boiled down to Bobby. *It had to be him.* Her family hinted at it. Her post-*Exhale* music hinted at it. Bobby was from the hood. His run-ins with the law felt constant. And he seemed to savor this bad-boy image. Of course Bobby was the source of her problems, we reasoned. He was the reason she slipped so far in those years. That's what we believed to be true. The drugs were Bobby's fault. The bad press and the bad performances were Bobby's fault. It had to have all been Bobby's fault, right? That was the narrative we collectively agreed on. Only after Whitney's death, after her family started being a little more honest with themselves, and with us, did we learn differently. And only after Bobby channeled his guilt and his own shame into personal transformation did we believe differently.

When Whitney and Bobby linked up after the 1989 Soul Train Awards, we side-eyed the whole thing. We never forgot how she was booed by her own people. But we forget that was the same award show where Bobby showed up and showed out with a sweltering performance of "My Prerogative." Run it back online. The brother had it going on. Bobby was hot. Whitney was hot. Could you blame Whitney for shooting her shot with Bobby that night? In the beginning they fought so hard against the speculation that their union was rooted in convenience, and not love. It's brutal no matter how you think about it, but it feels especially twisted given how hard the media was on Whitney for *not* being in a public relationship. But the optics were hard to shake. The same night she's jeered for not having enough "Black" in her—whatever that means, really—she cozies up to Bobby? People didn't buy it, so much so that their first duet together is called "Something in Common." They wanted *us* to believe their love so badly. And she got it from both sides. White America looked at Whitney and Bobby and saw a pop princess and an R&B thug while Black America saw a woman trying to silence the gossip mill by showing how down she was and snagging the fine brotha who left New Edition and gave us *Don't Be Cruel.* The princess and the frog, that's how we talked about their relationship. That's the image that lingered for the entirety of their fifteen-year marriage. We reduced Bobby to "Mr. Whitney Houston" and diminished Whitney for her romantic choices. We judged Whitney for the lengths she went to elevate her man publicly and we put her on trial for his misdeeds. Whitney's constant promotion of Bobby's gift and her brash reminders of his contributions to R&B made her look like a woman shrinking herself to let an envious man have a moment under the sun. Our obsession with the idea of them as an odd couple kept us going, and we never looked away. Even as Whitney revealed more of herself in the years after her struggles became too obvious to hide, we couldn't help but blame Bobby. Her family was doing it, so why couldn't we? *He* was the one with the criminal record, the tabloid drama, the baby mamas, and the drama-filled career. He was a blemish on America's Sweetheart and the reason why her life descended into chaos, we all reasoned. When we saw Whitney leaping into Bobby's arms after his years of run-ins with the law landed him in jail for a month in 2000, she was so very far away from the image we expected of her. In that moment she was every woman who saw their man swallowed into the criminal justice system. But we looked at Whitney, messy-haired and barefoot, and called her ghetto because she held her man down.

Naturally, our voyeuristic obsession with Whitney and Bobby spilled into reality television. What other reason did we have to tune into *Being Bobby Brown* when it premiered in 2005, other than our curiosity about how they lived? Our belief of Bobby being the stain on Whitney's reputation was calcified by his troubles with the law. Bobby had a decade of undignified charges under his belt, including battery against Whitney (he denies any physical violence, and Whitney said her husband was only ever emotionally abusive). His recording career was essentially dead, but he was sustaining his own relevance with a decent enough film career. "We were curious about the frog," filmmaker Tracey Baker-Simmons said of *Being Bobby Brown*'s inspiration. She was, like all of us, captivated by the craziness of it all. This was a romance that felt so unlikely. *Why him, girl? Why not Eddie Murphy or somebody with less drama?* Before the cameras even rolled we had watched, in horror, as Whitney lost her sheen during the halcyon days of the new millennium when she declared "*Crack is wack*" to Diane Sawyer and showed us that her once-marvelous gift was being rusted by Newports and crack cocaine. Of course she would appear on her husband's reality show. There was no other option, she reminded the filmmakers, who certainly were more than eager to have snagged the access. They knew we were all *hoping* she would show up. And they knew we wanted to see if they were just as much a hot mess as the headlines made them out to be.

Being Bobby Brown eviscerated whatever was left of Whitney's regal pop queen image. That persona never emerges onscreen. Who did show up was Nippy, chain-smoking and guzzling apple martinis and shouting phrases like *"Hell to the no"* and *"Kiss my ass."* It was 2005, and the landscape of reality television was swelling with projects anchored by celebrities shamelessly pulling back the veil on the interiors of their lives. It was fun to see Ozzy Osbourne onscreen as the aloof dad and needy husband. It was fun to see Jessica Simpson *be* the ditzy blonde we had assumed her to be. It was fun watching Britney Spears rebel with her own princess-and-the-frog romance that she allowed to play out in a shot-on-the-fly docuseries—before the tabloids and our judgment destroyed her. *Being Bobby Brown* surely had its moments of fun in the eleven episodes that aired before Bravo pulled the plug on it after Whitney refused to continue to film. The way Whitney and Bobby would break into song and dance spontaneously and were the life of the party regardless of who else was around was as fun to watch as their lustful passion for each other and Bobby's commitment to showing himself as an affable family man. What wasn't fun? Seeing Whitney escort Bobby to court and be by his side at a hearing about him physically striking her in the face and threatening to beat her ass during an argument (they had a romantic dinner immediately after court) or sitting through Bobby's crass comments about sex with his wife or casually oversharing to the world about removing excrement from her behind to relieve her constipation. It wasn't fun seeing Whitney show up onscreen as a shell of herself—wild-haired, gaunt, foulmouthed, and erratic. And it wasn't fun watching Bobby so shamelessly clawing his way toward relevance, his wife's tattered image his only foothold.

***

There wasn't a finer time for R&B than the nineties. You can almost taste it. Golden like brown sugar, sweet like honey, nineties R&B is an era stuffed with innovation after innovation, a time when young Black girls and women taught us to be crazy, sexy, and cool and the fellas told us the many, many ways they wanted to give you that *"good lovin', body rockin', knockin' boots"* type of loving. Nineties R&B was Teddy Riley and Babyface and L.A. Reid and Jimmy Jam and Terry Lewis in the deepest of their bags. Nineties R&B was Andre Harrell and Puff Daddy redefining Black commercial pop by making it unapologetically ghetto fabulous. Nineties R&B was Mary J. Blige baring her soul to us and being crowned the Queen of Hip-Hop Soul. Nineties R&B gave us the sonic boom that was Mariah Carey wrapping her honeyed voice around delicious soul samples and gritty rap verses and bulldozing the wall in between the two. Nineties R&B gave us earth goddesses, sex gods, Missy "Misdemeanor" Elliott, the flyest girl groups, the slickest boy bands, and damn near everything in between. Nineties R&B gave us teenage princesses like Brandy, Monica, and Aaliyah delivering the stickiest of hits. Nineties R&B gave us outré producers like Rodney "Darkchild" Jerkins and Timbaland and the Neptunes crafting intoxicating beats. Nineties R&B saw the genre merge deeper and deeper with hip-hop *and* flirt with funk and jazz and house and electronic and music pulled from sub-Saharan African traditions to birth subgenres that widened R&B's influence greatly over the next decade. It's only right—and most definitely okay—that nineties R&B would also give us Whitney's greatest transformation yet.

As R&B morphed under the growing weight of rap, the pop landscape was shifting in an entirely different direction—one that was perfectly calibrated for young ears and directly informed by the hybrid sounds coming out of R&B. Pop was playing catch-up, really. Before Britney Spears put her robotic purr on the coquettish anthem ". . . Baby One More Time," the record was offered to TLC, whose blend of funk, soul, and hip-hop put them on the map in the New Jack Swing era. ". . . Baby One More Time" took the euphoric confection that made "How Will I Know" aggressively catchy and married it with just enough edge that it sounded like a lighter version of the New Jack Swing that TLC was moving away from in favor of the futuristic bounce at the center of the R&B coming out in 1998. Where Whitney had been manufactured for the MTV age, Britney's shimmery dance pop was crafted for the Internet era closing in on us as the millennium approached.

Like Whitney, Britney's beauty had won her adoration (she had modeled in pageants in the South), and her big break came as a young girl. Britney wasn't from a line of talented greats like Whitney. She came from a typical Southern American family where no one had dreams of entertaining but Britney's young ambition and her mother's hubris got her cast on *The Mickey Mouse Club*, which would later prove to be a potent incubator for the young, white talent infiltrating pop music with variations of R&B and dance music at the tail-end years of the nineties. Britney was intensely sexualized, just as Whitney had been, but because Britney debuted in an era when there wasn't much room for subtlety, her emergence as a pop sensation came largely from her positioning as an innocent Lolita. In the music video for ". . . Baby

One More Time," Britney was the doll-faced cheerleader *and* a pigtailed Catholic schoolgirl. There was a perverseness to her image that immediately excited the white-male-dominated music media. *Rolling Stone* put Britney on its cover, laying her atop silk-covered sheets and having her hold a stuffed Teletubby while writing of her "honeyed thigh" when she was all of seventeen. She was a young girl playing dress-up, but so much was projected onto her because she bared her skin and became a teen idol in a country that is incredibly sexist—and incredibly sexually repressed. Britney intrigued America *and* drew the ire of conservatives, who branded the teenager a slut who used sex to mask her limited vocals. Her music was catchy and relatable in the way it explored teenage love and identity, but reporters cared more about asking if she was a virgin and speculating over the authenticity of her breasts. Britney was similar to Madonna in the way she imprinted herself on whatever sounds suited her, making music that spanned dance and electronic and R&B and hip-hop and experimental. But she was much closer to Whitney in the way she was an unknowable enigma. Britney's music was dismissed as sugary sap, but her down-home approachability and beauty made us will her to the top, and then we picked her apart for not being able to handle our punches as we tried to shape her with our expectations. And then we devoured her when the paparazzi and gossip blogs pushed her to the brink. Britney's legacy has gotten washed out in the way she crumbled and the decade-plus conservatorship that has stripped her of any real autonomy over her personal or professional lives, but her arrival in 1999 was essential in marching pop music further into a world of robotic, mechanized creations that started the teen-pop revolution. A crop of young teenage beauty queens inspired by Whitney, like Christina Aguilera, Jessica Simpson, and Mandy Moore, all became superstars. They seemed to come right out of an assembly factory, which in a sense was true given the amount of Svengaliing that went into creating these teen-pop phenoms. Funnily enough, much of this new sound of young America was actually coming right out of Stockholm, where a former heavy metal musician named Max Martin meticulously crafted beats that would move the needle widest for the *TRL* generation. He was smart, the melodies were irresistible, the hooks ubiquitous. Voice didn't matter that much, not when the vocal was going to be digitally manipulated and processed to meld into acrobatic rhythms.

As one Scandinavian shifted the sound of American pop, another was pushing R&B forward. Soulshock, born Carsten Schack, had immigrated to America in 1992 from Denmark to build his career as a DJ. He notched his first production credits making remixes for Queen Latifah, MC Lyte, and Eric B. & Rakim before moving toward R&B. Soulshock linked up with Kenneth Karlin, a keyboardist embedded in Denmark's jazz scene, and they formed a production duo. Soulshock & Karlin combined hip-hop beats and jazzy chords to make a poppier style of R&B that was more delicate than the New Jack Swing dominating the genre during the early nineties. The duo landed their first R&B number one with Monica' s "Before You Walk Out of My Life," a sumptuous ballad built around soft drums, a bit of saxophone, and Monica's rich voice, which was steeped in gospel like Whitney's and earthy like Mary J.'s. Soulshock & Karlin would put their stamp on records from Brandy, Toni Braxton, 2Pac, and eventually Whitney.

Although the second half of her career was a constant play at reinvention, 1998's *My Love Is Your Love* is Whitney's best makeover. This was the album that showed a woman fully embracing her unrefined edges. She had played it too safe on *I'm Your Baby Tonight*, but post–*Waiting to Exhale* Whitney didn't need to work so hard to try to convince us. Post-*Exhale* Whitney had grit and vigor. She leaned away from the regal opulence of ballroom gowns and stepped into chic Dolce & Gabbana couture. Whitney draped herself in furs and showed up in leather minidresses and skinny jeans. She had transformed into a ghetto fabulous diva supreme, and we didn't blink twice since hip-hop made a new Black aesthetic possible when it grew from a niche movement white conservative America reviled into a global superpower that would set the pace for pop music. Hip-hop was a worldview ages before Whitney fully embraced it in her music. She was late to the party, largely at Clive's doing, unlike Prince and Michael and Janet and Madonna. *I'm Your Baby Tonight* was a toe dip, and we all saw right through it. Whitney would have probably arrived there eventually. Two years after *I'm Your Baby Tonight*, Bobby brought her closer to hip-hop's edge when they made "Something in Common" with Teddy Riley, but it's hard to imagine she would have arrived there without *Waiting to Exhale* and without the influence of women in the genre making work that was in direct conversation with hip-hop. In the years before *My Love Is Your Love*, a generation of fierce Black female voices had arrived. We saw the rise of women like Mary J. Blige and TLC and Lauryn Hill and Missy Elliott and Erykah Badu and Jill Scott. These were women offering fierce points of view that countered the violence and misogyny that ran unchecked through much of rap. Nineties R&B was all about looking for a real love and remembering the time and candy rain and just kickin' it and the birth of Neo Soul while too much of the rap at the time was focused on bitches and hoes and pimps. The women emerging in R&B and rap showed visions of Black women that we rarely saw in mainstream spaces. Hip-hop culture normalized the oversexualization and fetishization of women, and those images extended to R&B, most prominently through the rise of R. Kelly. He specialized in sex jams that merged gospel harmonies and buttery-smooth soul with the explicitness of hip-hop, and it made him one of the most successful R&B artists of all time despite an apparent sexual interest in young and underage girls. (The length of time that allegations of R. Kelly's sexual violence went unchecked is possibly our most egregious proof of just how overlooked and ignored the sexualization and abuse of Black women in hip-hop remains.)

Some of the greatest records that came from our sisters with voices throughout the nineties were direct rebuttals to what was being laid down on wax by men. Ladies spun R&B that could be sweet like honey, but they also made acidic, brazen bangers that let them unleash their anger and fury. Gone were the days of women trying to imitate Whitney by packaging themselves as graceful chanteuses and offering delicate pop soul. The rise of hip-hop and the groundbreaking success of *Waiting to Exhale*, and the impact both had on Black commercial pop, made that impossible. As the lines blurred deeply in a new era of R&B and hip-hop, so did its women. There was elegance, but there was also edge, and we got music that laid bare their struggles, their joys, their lust, their passions, and their heartbreaks.

In the summer of 1998, *The Miseducation of Lauryn Hill* dropped, and Lauryn was crowned a modern-day Nina Simone. It was a lot of weight to put on L. Boogie, who, like Whitney, was a Black girl from Newark with boundless magic in her voice. Like Whitney, we were unkind to Lauryn after we lost patience with her creative process and her relationship to her masterwork. That's the burden of a record like *Miseducation*. It had arrived in one of rap's best years and still managed to matter the most. Nineteen ninety-eight, a year so thick with rap greatness: Outkast's *Aquemini*, Jay-Z's *Vol. 2 . . . Hard Knock Life*, and A Tribe Called Quest's *The Love Movement* all dropped on the *same* day. This was the year DMX made his debut and No Limit and Cash Money Records had more than shown us that the South had something to say when it came to this rap shit. But Lauryn scorched the earth when she dropped *Miseducation*. The opening line says all you need to know about what Lauryn had to say: *"It's funny how money change a situation / Miscommunication leads to complication."* This was a record scratch. This was a juggernaut. Lauryn had some *shit* to get off her chest. We gossiped about the shots she fired on the album and the romantic entanglements that inspired it, but we worshipped her, greatly, for baring her soul the way she had. This was an album about joy and pain and motherhood that played like a Terry McMillan novel.

To appreciate the impact of *Miseducation*—and so much of the R&B coming from our queens in 1998—it's vital to remember where we were then. Where hip-hop was. Where Black America was. Bill Clinton had arrived as the Great Black Hope, a youthful conservative Democrat with slick saxophone skills and even slicker charm. Clinton wooed Black America into giving him a lifetime invitation to the cookout. Until an actual Black man made it to the White House, Clinton happily wore the crown of America's first "Black" president even as he passed legislation that would devastate Black households for decades to come. The Clinton age gave us the three-strikes bill and Welfare to Work, federal laws that wreaked tremendous havoc on poor and working-class Black families. Mass incarceration was already putting Black women behind bars at obscene rates compared to white women or left them to carry the weight of a household as their men were locked up—and now there was a draconian crime bill that ensured it would keep going. And then you had Welfare to Work, which ultimately punished Black women for needing government assistance and perpetuated the idea that they were alone in the struggle to raise kids in a single-parent, low-income home. The impact this had on Black men was reflected quite well in hip-hop, but the men only seemed to care about casting women as down-ass bitches who pledged unyielding loyalty to them or as vixens for their pleasures. There wasn't much room for Black women's pain or desire in hip-hop.

Mary J. and TLC and Missy and Lauryn and Badu cut through all the materialism and the archaic sex politics that was rife in male-driven hip-hop and offered blunt answers to all of it. They could be brash and kinky like Lil' Kim or Foxy when they felt like it, but these were women unconcerned with the pressures to be sex warriors or trying to make pussy rap. They made music that interrogated the costs of being Black women at a time when brazen misogynoir and heartless public policy cast them as welfare queens and jezebels and bitches and hoes. When we talk about the costs of all of it—what was happening at home, what was happening on the airwaves and in music videos—it was powerful to witness a Black feminist perspective moving to the center of pop. Yes, TLC gave women the permission to be crazy, sexy, and cool, but they *also* showed them the vulnerability of feeling unpretty. Brandy and Monica and Aaliyah showed little Black girls all over the globe that they could become pop princesses and keep their braids and their tomboy flair and their street but sweet attitude. Badu and Mary J. bared their soul with blues that had punch and heart. *Miseducation* did all that and more, but '98 was a serious year when it came to albums from Black women speaking their piece on the opposite sex with provocative music showing the richness and diversity of the Black female experience. Brandy put out *Never Say Never* after becoming a Black American princess with Whitney as her literal fairy godmother in Disney's 1997 adaptation of Rodgers & Hammerstein's *Cinderella*. Monica had *The Boy Is Mine*. Deborah Cox released *One Wish*. Faith Evans dropped *Keep the Faith*. Tamia and Kelly Price made their debuts, and Beyoncé stated her case as a pop diva to watch with Destiny's Child's first album. Whitney's influence can be easily traced to any of these women, but it would be their work that inspired the transformation that resulted in *My Love Is Your Love*.

Mariah had already closed the gap between pop and soul, and Janet was making some of the lushest R&B of her career post–New Jack. And then there was the juggernaut that was

Miseducation. Whitney really had no choice but to switch it up on us. She was making a comeback in an era that had moved far beyond the tender romanticism of her youth. Whitney's progeny were audacious and brazen and sexual and free and fly. Aaliyah set the mood. TLC and Destiny's Child were the cool big sisters. Badu and Mary J. and Missy were wise and tough as shit. Brandy and Monica carried Whitney's vocal tradition the most, but they also had attitude and verve. Whitney needed to come harder. She needed to bare her blues. All that pretty-girl shit wouldn't cut it as the young women who came after her showed us all the ways Black girls could live in their truths and rule the world (imagine that).

For those of us reared on the soul and gospel of Aretha and the holy spirit of James Brown and Michael Jackson, it was challenging to reconcile the church girl we knew Cissy trained Whitney to be with the creation Clive and Arista peddled to the world. It stings to hear that Clive thought some of her first records were "too Black" and had the music remixed and refined so that she could easily be consumed by the masses—so that white people could rock with her. Whitney had gargantuan hits, but she was still looking for respect from her people, who didn't believe she was living up to the duty bestowed upon Black artists: to live up to and reflect the times. But not everybody wanted to be Nina Simone. Not even Lauryn Hill could live up to the Nina comparisons we lavished on her after *Miseducation,* and we have only now arrived to a place where we are a little more honest about the pressures and burdens placed on Black artists. Whitney sweated and *sang* with the holy spirit of the anointing blessed on her voice. Even when she sang the big pop ballads and took us to the dance floor, she brought the church with her. It was in her voice. It was in her blood. We just wanted an album that plainly made us feel that without pondering.

If *Miseducation* is an album about learning lessons on romance the hard way from the perspective of a young Black woman stepping out in the world, *My Love Is Your Love* is a glimpse of the thornier side of relationships as distilled by a grown woman who had lost her groove and wanted to get it back; a woman who heard all you said about her man *and* had something to say about him too; a woman who had been in Sorrow's kitchen and licked out all the pots; a woman in search of liberation. Post–*Waiting to Exhale* and *The Preacher's Wife*, it had become clear Whitney was struggling. It wasn't *Being Bobby Brown* bad yet, but we knew things were disastrous behind the scenes. And she knew we knew it.

My Love Is Your Love is Whitney's first real reckoning with her public image. Driven by the tabloid drama with Bobby, this was a confrontational album brimming with the level of confession driving the R&B coming out of our women in the last years of the millennium. *My Love Is Your Love* uses the brashness of hip-hop to interrogate the emotional tolls facing modern Black women, and it should be considered Whitney's best work just off the strength of it being the most personal—the most real. So much of our adoration of Whitney, and the marvel of her voice, hinges on "I Will Always Love You" and "The Star-Spangled Banner"—pieces of music that, although timeless, don't offer any insight into what makes her tick. And *My Love Is Your Love* upends all those notions of her white-glove approach to pop music.

She dropped the clichéd stereotypes of love and yearning to make revealing songs that confronted not just the pleasures of sex but the realities of love and marriage strained by the spotlight, our judgment, and old-fashioned domestic drama. We knew Whitney was ticking, and we were waiting for her to implode on record. Whitney needed to exhale and she did, through icy bangers that showed us that Mama had found a brand-new groove. I think a lot about "It's Not Right but It's Okay." It's not her greatest dance record ("I Wanna Dance with Somebody" obviously is), but it is her most sonically interesting. Whitney hooked up with Rodney "Darkchild" Jerkins, a church-raised musician Teddy Riley mentored as a young teenager. Darkchild's music took New Jack Swing and made it sound like it came from another planet by building melodies around stuttering beats that moved in a million different directions (sometimes simultaneously). Darkchild and Brandy had struck gold with *Never Say Never*, a lush album of biting anthems and tender vulnerability crafted over outré beats. The monster duet between Brandy and Monica, "The Boy Is Mine," was on that album, and "It's Not Right but It's Okay" feels like a close cousin with its hypnotic bottom and zigzag vocal performance. Whitney is fiery, and funny, in a way we hadn't heard her on record—made all the more stunning by the glamorous music video where we see her in a buttery leather dress, her hair cut into a razor-sharp bob as she stares down the camera while unleashing a sharp read to her cheating man: *"If six of y'all went out, then four of you were really cheap / 'Cause only two of you had dinner, I found your credit card receipt."*

We hadn't met these sides of Whitney. Hurt. Vengeful. Sexy. Vulnerable. *My Love Is Your Love* showed it all, and she threw a disclaimer on the album as a wink to anybody looking to read too far into the music. "The events & characters depicted in this album are fictitious, & any similarity to actual persons living or dead, or to actual events, is purely coincidental." I like to think of it as yet another reminder of the influence *Waiting to Exhale* had on her. Here was Whitney imagining a world, at least on record, where she could drag her man through the mud and move through various exaggerations of the parts of herself she kept hidden from view. She could take on the chaos of her public persona and the media obsession with her relationship with Bobby (the funky Missy Elliott–produced "In My Business"); she could mourn a lover who's done her wrong ("I Bow Out"); she could make a great sex jam that showed her in command of her pleasures ("Oh Yes"); and she could do the heady dance bangers ("If I Told You That") and creamy ballads ("I Learned from the Best," "You'll Never Stand Alone") that were her signature. This is the Whitney who excited me the most. I loved all the shades Whitney came in, but this was her most vibrant, the one who brought me the most joy to watch. The music was so slick and edgy. It banged the way everything I was listening to at the time did. These were records that felt so perfectly *of* the moment. A moment when two genres I loved had melted together into something so fresh and funky and intoxicating. This was the Whitney I had been waiting for.

Whitney brought gospel ecstasy to the dance floor on *My Love Is Your Love* in a way she hadn't in the past—partially because she was so fierce on this album. Whitney was a powder keg that had exploded. The climax of runs on the bridge of "If I Told You That" alone was a master class in how she could ride a beat. I can't imagine how the record would have sounded as a duet with Michael Jackson, as originally envisioned—he passed on the idea—but her remix with George Michael is just as blistering as the original. It's in the way her voice skitters across the up-tempos that was catnip to a young queer boy who especially loved hearing big-lunged singers spin their voices around unconventional, speaker-rattling beats. As fine as her early music was, Whitney gave us so much here. "Oh Yes" sizzles with an erotic fire her music rarely allowed. Missy is all over the backgrounds, bringing a smolder folks might not have known she had in her from only listening to her debut of avant-garde hip-hop and R&B. But Missy was a church girl, like Whitney, and could write and produce the hell out of a soul melody. She could also craft a freaky beat, which she did on "In My Business," a cheeky clapback acknowledging all the shit talking we did about Whitney, and about Bobby, as Missy hyped her up: *"Too many people say you're fakin' me, they ask what have you done lately? They say we won't last, they're predictin' that it's over."*

By making provocative bangers that made us talk, Whitney at last appeared in control of it all—her image, her sound, our perception of her and her marriage. These were her blues, on record. Finally. That Whitney collaborated extensively on *My Love Is Your Love* speaks to how influenced she was by what was happening in R&B and hip-hop. Of course Babyface and David Foster were going to get the call to go into the studio. But Whitney cast the widest net she'd ever cast for an album. Darkchild took the lead on the up-tempo records, pushing Whitney toward her sharpest sonic direction. Wyclef Jean and Jerry Duplessis delivered the vibrant, gospel and reggae-inspired title track. She called her sisters in voice, Kelly Price and Faith Evans, to make the jazzy breakup anthem "Heartbreak Hotel" with Soulshock & Karlin—TLC actually rejected it first—that would become her last number one R&B hit. The breakout success of *Miseducation* made Lauryn Hill even more of an in-demand savant, and she was called in to produce a stripped-down take of Stevie Wonder's exuberant "I Was Made to Love Her." And Clive made sure the grandiose, gospel-influenced duet Whitney recorded with her perceived pop rival, Mariah Carey, was there for good measure—even releasing it first to ensure the album had a hit *just* in case the public didn't vibe with Whitney's transformation into an icy diva.

My Love Is Your Love didn't break the charts the way Whitney's earlier work did, but the album humanized her and earned her some of the best reviews of her career and has aged better than perhaps anything else she recorded. She had taken risks by drafting young, hip-hop hitmakers and experimental R&B producers to steer her toward her own liberation. This was Whitney letting go of all she needed to be to uphold that image as America's Sweetheart and in turn showing us who she was—a grown-ass woman who was going through some shit.

TELL THE TRUTH
AND SHAME
THE DEVIL

How Trauma, Shame, and Tabloid Culture Broke Whitney

Forty-eight hours before the 2018 release of his third album, *Daytona*, Pusha T got a phone call from his producer—and GOOD Music boss—Kanye West. It was one o'clock in the morning, and Kanye was phoning to tell Pusha he wasn't really feeling the album's cover art. He had a new vision in mind, one that would require spending $85,000 to license an image. Kanye got Pusha on board by assuring his artist that he would foot the bill to secure the rights for the photo. The image is a tawdry yet compelling portrait of drug-induced chaos set against the opulence of wealth: a gilded bathroom littered with the drug paraphernalia of a celebrity addict. The spoon burnt from cooking crack, the cigarette butts, and the empty baggies of cocaine all pointed toward a sad, out-of-control spiral. You've seen the image before, surely. We've all got an appetite for human wreckage and destruction and our hunger for salacious scandal is intensified when those at the center of the drama are rich, beautiful, powerful, or famous. The reason this morbid still life cost $85,000 is because the mess was made by Whitney Houston. That image was splashed on the cover of the *National Enquirer* in 2006 for all to see. That image and all its mess (the pack of Newports, the can of Budweiser, the crack paraphernalia) gave us access to what Whitney's drug use looked like. The *National Enquirer* knew we'd look. Even if they hadn't printed *WORLD EXCLUSIVE! INSIDE WHITNEY'S DRUG DEN!* in bold letters with all the excitement expected of a gossip rag beckoning you at a newsstand or the supermarket checkout aisle, they knew we'd look if we knew what was in its pages. By the early aughts we were all watching, waiting—and some even hoping—for the worst to happen to Whitney.

The worst would come six years after these photos surfaced, when she drowned in the bathtub of her Beverly Hills hotel suite, her use of cocaine and heart disease listed as contributing factors. Yet again a gilded bathroom provided the backdrop of her addiction. And yet again the *National Enquirer* would fawn over the scene. They even got a model and sprawled her out on the bathroom floor. Why? Because they knew we'd look.

And Kanye knew you'd look too. The photo says so much: opulence, fast living, hard partying, despair, abandon, death. The glare in the frame? That's Tina Brown, sister of Bobby, snapping the photo to sell it to the highest bidder. It didn't matter that they were all getting high together off a supply Whitney likely funded—and would continue to after Tina's betrayal, which she now claims Whitney concocted as a cry for help. Whitney *was* the story, and her story was always

worth something to the tabloids—but to further seal the deal,
Tina told the magazine all about doing crack with her superstar sister-in-law. There was always money to be made off
Whitney. We had already stopped regarding her as a radiant,
once-in-a-generation supernova long before her sister-in-law
became the latest in a string of folks to sell her out for a check.
She was an addict, a junkie who squandered her talent and
was perpetually falling further and further into the abyss—her
career defined by her demise. That's how we saw her. Kanye,
better than most, knows our obsession with celebrities in free
fall. The photo only works as a provocative album cover because
most viewers would recognize the tragedy associated with it,
and those who didn't would learn its sordid backstory from the
media attention he knew would come with using it. That photo
is so engrained in the story of Whitney's fall, and its existence
is one of the harshest indictments of our ravenous appetite to
bear witness to the throes of her addiction. *INSIDE WHIT-
NEY'S DRUG DEN!* The excitement of this "world exclusive"
to see one of our heroes in the bleakest light. Whitney was a
cautionary tale, but the price tag on this photographic evidence
of her demons reveals an uglier truth. Whitney's demise—from
her addiction to her tumultuous relationship with Bobby and
her professional missteps—was our entertainment. And we all
took a big bite, at one point or another.

Pusha T's *Daytona* doesn't reckon with any of the harsh
truths of the drug tableau depicted on its cover. It doesn't
reckon with the devastation of Whitney's final years or those
of her daughter, Bobbi Kristina, who passed away under circumstances that were eerily similar to those of her mother's

death after drowning in a bathtub in 2016 with drug intoxication listed as an underlying cause of her death. The realities of slinging crack cocaine have been at the center of Pusha's work with his brother in their duo Clipse and throughout his solo career, but *Daytona* is an album of boastful swaggering—not introspection. *"The only rapper sold more dope than me was Eazy-E,"* he gloats on one of the album's tracks. Kanye has fought hard against the dehumanization of celebrities, particularly Black ones. He'd been in fame's orbit long enough to know its ills. And because he saw how the public tended to consume celebrities, he won our support for the ways in which he pushed back against it. Kanye was a boy from Chicago, so he was ours in the way Whitney was ours and the way Michael was ours. His triumphs were ours, and so we worried about him when he seemed to be on the brink of collapse following the death of his mother and a couple of rough years when the world devoured him after he ruined Taylor Swift's moment in the sun to make a statement about how the art of Black women like Beyoncé are historically overlooked and underappreciated (he was definitely right, but, ya know, there's a time and place); we defended him and his genius furiously. And that's why we have felt so betrayed by him when he did things like disparaging his ex-girlfriend Amber Rose—a Black woman—to make a point about his relationship with Kim Kardashian or when he espoused views on slavery and abortion that were painfully anti-Black and aligned himself with President Trump—smiling for the camera in a MAGA hat as if he wasn't the same man we celebrated for going off-script during a Hurricane Katrina telethon to lambast President Bush's inaction that contributed to so much loss of Black life across the Gulf Coast. But using an image that exploited the shame of a dead Black woman—famous or not—was the gravest of Kanye's trail of egregious offenses. Sure, Kanye didn't take the original photo in Whitney's bathroom. Bobby's sister did. She's the one who trespassed on Whitney's and Bobby's trust and sold out her sister-in-law to the highest bidder, in turn making this scene accessible in perpetuity to anyone who knows how to do a Google search. But it's the why that has stuck with me. Kanye took the ugliest part of Whitney's life—outside of her final moments—and put it on display as an album cover without reason. And for what? Because he knew we'd get the joke. After all, we were all in on it.

Whitney's transformation from America's Sweetheart, the Prom Queen of Soul, into a troubled diva was a slow, sad watch. It took just three words to forever alter the way we looked at Whitney: *Crack is wack*. When Whitney said the words to Diane Sawyer during a 2002 primetime interview special, she made her addiction—an addiction she was still in deep denial of—a punch line. Long before Whitney turned "*Crack is wack*" into the memeable phrase that would define her tragic fall, Keith Haring famously painted the three words on an anti-drug mural out of frustrations with the government.

It was 1986. Reagan's War on Drugs and the crack epidemic were eviscerating low-income communities. Black and brown men and women were being thrown behind bars over the same drug white yuppies were crushing up and snorting through rolled-up $20 bills at higher rates—and for longer sentences—than their white counterparts. Cocaine was perceived as a glamorous party drug that didn't carry the luridness of its cooked-up counterpart, crack. As Whitney told Diane Sawyer in that infamous interview, "Crack is cheap. I make too much money to ever smoke crack." With crack cocaine ravaging urban communities across the country, Keith Haring watched his studio assistant Benny Soto struggle under the weight of addiction. Angry over the bureaucratic red tape that made getting Benny help a challenge as well as the government's inability to respond to the destruction crack was bringing to poor and working-class communities, Haring decided to create a mural as both an act of protest and a warning to New Yorkers about the dangers of the drug. Crack cocaine could put you in a euphoric trance or turn you into an aggressive and irrational version of yourself. It was a powerful drug that hooked you and bled you dry of your spirit and all your riches, and Haring wanted to make a statement that centered the dangers of crack. And so on a hot summer afternoon, he pulled up to the abandoned handball court he often passed on the edge of East Harlem, and with zero legal permission, he painted the mural in a day. Haring eventually got busted for what he did and was looking at jail time and hundreds of dollars in fines, but the quick popularity of the mural's message got him off the hook with only a small fine. And when a vandal defaced the art by turning it into a pro-crack statement, the New York City Department of Parks and Recreation asked Haring to repaint it. The two-sided mural as we know it has monster-like cartoon figures drawn in thick black lines atop a vibrant orange background. The figures are devoid of any discernible age or gender or race, but they are all lost in a zombie-like trance amid a plume of smoke. In the center of the chaos, in bold letters, are three words: *CRACK IS WACK.*

***

John and Cissy Houston were like a lot of hardworking Black parents. Their end goal was getting out of the ghetto, by any means. When they traded Newark for East Orange, they had *moved on up*, but, as Whitney's brother Michael put it, "You can live in a mansion all you want, when you come outside, you gonna be amongst the motherfucking wolves and bears." Those wolves and bears are the temptations that lurk everywhere. It's the drugs and alcohol, the pleasures of the flesh and all the other sinnin' the church preaches against. Whitney's oldest brother, Gary, had already met the wolves and bears that lurked on the streets of Newark. When Gary was ten, he tried heroin for the first time. Gary and his brother, Michael, had seen and done enough and were well aware of what was waiting for their baby sister. "Growing up in Newark . . . you kinda had to grow up fast and furious. We wanted to get the best with the cards we were dealt with," Gary recalled in the 2018 documentary *Whitney*. "I didn't always resort to going to the resources that I had to me to make the best decisions." Gary and Michael got into shit they shouldn't have. Whitney was the baby of the family. Like the youngest tend to do, she followed behind her older brothers. Michael and Nippy were closest in age, and by the time they were old enough to have their learner's permits they were smoking weed—graduating to cocaine shortly after. "If anything was gonna be done, I was gonna be the one to show her," Michael says in the documentary, his voice pierced with regret.

Our desire to know when or where or with whom Whitney got her first high led us to never consider the fact that she was like a lot of people whose recreational drug use spiraled into an addiction. We poked fun at her obvious suffering and looked for someone to blame after it killed her. Maybe having Bobby or Cissy or her brothers or the wolves and bears in her orbit to blame would absolve us from any of the guilt we felt over devouring the smorgasbord of gossip about her addiction, sexuality, family drama, and career failures or laughing at the jokes that cashed in on her spiral. Maybe it would ease the pain over the sadness that settled when we learned the extent of her drug use, that it predated her entry into show business and that all the expectations and pressures—and the criticisms and the ridicule—that came with being Whitney Houston exacerbated her addiction. Whitney's rise as *the voice* offered a potent antidote to the tensions of the late eighties. Crack and AIDS had the nation on edge, and the Reagan administration wasn't making things any better for poor and working-class communities. The collective fawning over a pop virtuoso who felt like a descendant of Aretha, Barbra, and Diana opened new doors for Black women in pop. But look at all it required to make happen. Whitney gave up so much of herself to ensure she could be the *one* to fly above the rest. Where Whitney was headed, there were parts of herself that needed to be shelved. Anything that went against the traditional pop standard needed to be tamed: the full spectrum of her sexuality, her addictions, any overt aspects of Blackness. All that she had minimized to become Whitney, we weaponized against her as she cracked under the pressures to maintain the image. In her 2019 memoir, Robyn Crawford wrote about the first time she and Whitney did cocaine together, days after she got her first hit from one of Gary's friends. Whitney was fourteen when she was introduced to cocaine, she told Robyn. "Where we're going, this can't go," Whitney assured Robyn. But it was too late. The drugs came along for it all. A bandmember even dubbed Whitney's debut world tour in 1986 the Greatest Drug Tour because there was so much weed and cocaine around.

A lot of us get high and drink at our leisure, but we all have had friends or family members or romantic partners who are unable to stop as easily or are unaware that a recreational habit has developed into an addiction. Though it's jarring to hear how young Whitney and her brothers were when they got into drugs, I think of what it must have been like to come of age in the late seventies and eighties, when cocaine and weed were a fabric of life, social lubricants that were freely indulged without much of the shame and stigma that came with the advent of abstinence messaging and aggressive policing. When Whitney and Robyn were teenagers getting high and exploring their sexuality in 1980, they were very much like a lot of teens experimenting with drugs. Though Robyn felt she had a firm grasp on her partying and could stop whenever she wanted, Whitney and her brothers didn't. Robyn attempted to place boundaries around their drug use in order for it to not impact the work and the growing demands coming Whitney's way. *"No getting high when there's work! No getting high after a certain time! No getting high in groups!"* When that didn't work, Robyn went to Cissy, who she knew abhorred her. She confided in Cissy that she and Whitney were doing cocaine on occasion but that Whitney liked it too much and wouldn't stop until everything was gone. "Oh, Mommy, you don't need to worry about any of that," Cissy says her daughter told her when she confronted her about it, brushing off her concerns and telling her that Robyn was simply overreacting.

Our assumption was that Bobby was the one who got her hooked. It was an easy narrative to believe because of the bad-boy image the media cast on him in order to frame his union with Whitney in a particular light and because the Houston camp—and even Bobby, to an extent—was so permissive about it, perhaps out of wanting to protect Whitney from any shame. Bobby was a drinker and he liked to smoke weed, and his introduction to cocaine came from his wife. He'd caught her doing a line on their wedding day, and the next time she offered it to him, he tried it. And then Whitney's brother Michael introduced them to smoking cocaine, which we know as freebasing, as their use heightened. Bobby would have a stroke from his excessive drug use, but it wasn't enough to get him to stop. Nor was the 1993 birth of their daughter, Bobbi Kristina—whom Whitney had the year after suffering a miscarriage while filming *The Bodyguard*—enough to curb their use. One of the sadder revelations in Bobby's 2016 memoir, *Every Little Step*, was detailing how he and Whitney believed they were going out of their way to hide their drug use from Bobbi Kris and his slow realization that that was impossible to do, since they were high all the time, a habit he says intensified for Whitney after being clean during her pregnancy.

We've never been able to be realistic about Whitney's drug use, and that's partially because of our orientation around drug use. Before we moved toward harm reduction, the cultural understanding around drugs that Whitney was exposed to in her formative years went from the glorious, free-spirited hedonism of the seventies to the aggressive policing and shame of Reagan's War on Drugs. But even without the stigma that came with recreational drug use, the line between getting high socially or for fun and full-on dependency isn't easy to pinpoint—especially when it comes to misunderstood and criminalized party drugs. I often wonder what our desire to know the full explicit details of Whitney's drug use is about. Are we wanting to get a better understanding of what she was up against, or is it just too difficult for us to reconcile the fact that Whitney was a brilliant artist who struggled with addiction like many of us? And what does it mean for us that our entire reading of Whitney is complicated by the realization that she had a relationship with drugs before she had a relationship with us?

We don't have the access or data to make the case for when exactly Whitney's drug use crossed the threshold into dependency, but zeroing in on the cocaine overdose from 1995 that was kept out of public view is a critical checkpoint that gives us the clearest picture of when the danger may have begun. After the incident, which happened during the filming of *Waiting to Exhale*, her bodyguard wrote a plea to her camp. In the letter dated May 3, 1995, from David Roberts to Nippy Inc., he outlined concerns over dangers of her dependence after a rough show in Singapore, writing that Whitney "acknowledged to be 'emotionally dependent'" on narcotics and noting his concern that her voice was being damaged from smoking cocaine. A year after that overdose, Whitney was filming *The Preacher's Wife*, and she later told Oprah that she was using daily by then and felt as if she had lost herself. When she pulled out of stops for the film's promotional blitz, it was explained away with careful wording. "Throat issues" were common. We speculated that she was just caving to the pressures of pop stardom and feeling the effects of a strenuous marriage—both were true—but the monster that is addiction was growing more powerful as she fed it. Whitney often said cocaine wouldn't go where she was going, but there was a deep naivete in thinking she could kick the habit after money and fame made indulging easily accessible—that's how addiction works. Whitney shot to stardom at the apex of the crack epidemic, and she was in an industry where hitting the slopes wasn't taboo. Fame can be a drug on its own, and though Whitney was always so clear on her distaste for what came with celebrity, those feelings seemed to only deepen as her troubles developed.

When asked in 1996 how success had changed her, Whitney said it made her "a lot more paranoid." "Success doesn't change you, fame does," she says. "You got to know who you are before you step into this business, because if you're trying to find it, you'll probably wind up being somebody else that you probably don't even like." Whitney was exhausted by the pressures we put on her to uphold the Black Barbie doll image and grew increasingly resentful of the persona expected of her. Becoming Whitney Houston took so much. It was an image that required constant maintenance—even the idea of Whitney chain-smoking or cursing was distasteful. Just imagine if she dared to take the rock star approach and not try to hide her drug use.

As Whitney continued to get lost in her addiction, it put her at odds with Clive. He was frustrated by the lying, the no-shows, her unprofessionalism, and her scandals—behavior that transformed her from a regal pop queen into a petulant diva, at least as far as the public was concerned. Clive wrote in his memoir that he made it a point to not get involved in the personal lives of his artists. "If your help isn't solicited, it's hard to know what you can or should do, so I tried to concentrate on the aspect of our lives that had always gone well: making great music together," he wrote in 2013's *The Soundtrack of My Life*. But he grew tired of Whitney's lack of output, and in August 1997 he wrote her a letter (one of many dispatches to Whitney he published in his book) sharing his concern over her lack of putting out music. "I know that I have absolutely no right to reflect on anything but your professional recording career, so let me address that. You have not done a studio album in seven years," he wrote. "You have been practically missing in action." Clive's letter dances around the obvious. He scolds Whitney for being reckless in her avoidance of her job and tells her that there can no more excuses about her voice or complaints of being tired and needing more time. He had stayed clear of the previous attempts at intervention that had happened behind the scenes, but he expressed his concern over her creative output. There had been the music she did for *Waiting to Exhale* and *The Preacher's Wife*, but it had been years since there was an original Whitney Houston studio album that was unrelated to a film, so Clive did what many record execs would have done by reminding her of that. As if that could be the kick in the pants she needed. Clive believing he had no authority to reflect on her personal life is a cop-out. It lets him off the hook in the chance his artist gets pissed off at the suggestion she needed professional help. Clive ultimately did her a disservice, only adding to the demands that she was, at least partially, soothing with drugs and alcohol. Whitney needed help, not a reminder that she was fucking up the bottom line or her status as the supreme diva. Whitney needed rehab, not the studio. She and Bobby were imploding. Screaming matches and altercations agitated by their substance abuse were now headline news. Robyn's cries went unanswered, and Whitney's father recoiled at the idea of sending his daughter to rehab after she said she didn't feel like going. Whitney needed real support, but the stigma around drug use in America during the eighties and nineties, the complicity of her parents wanting to appease their daughter, the silence of an inner circle trying to protect a brand (and themselves), and the pressures of fame allowed her addiction to metastasize.

Whitney's life was in disarray, but Clive suggested she get back to work anyway, and so she went into the studio, and seven weeks later she wound up with her fiery comeback album *My Love Is Your Love*. But then she'd have to go out on tour, where she and her brothers and Bobby had an excuse for partying and getting high every night. The drugs added to the paranoia and the isolation she felt while holding all the responsibilities that came with being a superstar entertainer. All the people around her, making the Whitney Houston machine churn, depended on her delivering *Whitney Houston* every night. So who would have even told her no when it came to her vices? Her husband or brothers, who were getting high with her? Her mother and father, neither of whom could ever reach her and were tangled in their own denial about how bad things had gotten? Robyn made rules for Whitney when she believed her drug use was out of control, and when that didn't work, she went to Cissy on multiple occasions and dealt with the fallout from Whitney—a cycle that went on for years. When Robyn quit her role as Whitney's creative director in 2000, she did so because she felt there was no other option for her. Robyn didn't actually want to leave, but things weren't changing. She was unyielding in her loyalty to Whitney, but Robyn's distrust of Whitney's father—who worked as his daughter's manager and allegedly stole money from her, according to Kevin Macdonald's 2018 documentary *Whitney*—and the tension between her and Bobby, which Whitney often egged on, had exhausted her. And there was also the constant scorn she got from Cissy and Whitney's brother Gary. Robyn was frustrated. She was fed up with Whitney, who couldn't see the damage she was doing to her career, let alone herself. In January 2000, Whitney and Bobby got busted with half an ounce of marijuana at the airport. We were still in a ridiculous moral panic over weed then, so the story got wall-to-wall coverage as if Whitney and Bobby had cartel weight on them. The Hawaii airport incident then became the backdrop when stories of Whitney's erratic behavior leaked into the press. In March, there was Whitney's no-show at Clive's Rock & Roll Hall of Fame induction and being dumped from an Oscars performance by Burt Bacharach (he was the musical director of the ceremony) because she came to rehearsal high to the point where she was disoriented and couldn't recall the lyrics to "Over the Rainbow." After a botched recording session with George Michael led to Bobby and Whitney lashing out at her, Robyn hit her breaking point. She turned in her resignation and exited the Houston camp—and because we never heard from her until Whitney's death, our speculation allowed us to settle on the narrative that Robyn must have been paid off. But that's our desire to have a culprit to place the blame on. We settled for Bobby because he was the most obvious bad player in Whitney's orbit. And while he certainly exacerbated the worst of her demons, he and Whitney also had the privilege of fame—and fame is a powerful, intoxicating drug. Who was going to tell *them* no? Not anyone on payroll worried that saying no might put their job in jeopardy. Whitney's own bodyguard got canned for writing a letter of concern—the irony of that speaks deafening volumes on its own. Even after Clive lost Janis Joplin in 1970 to heroin when she was just twenty-seven, he was still tiptoeing around the whims of his artist—and to her detriment. But that's fame: People turn their backs and pretend to not see the self-destruction on display.

"She fed everybody," Robyn wrote in her memoir. "Deep down inside that's what made her tired." With the privilege of fame comes a sadder truth: Aside from the riches, there's the spoils of having the world accessible to you. Having her brothers on tour came with the security of family—and the chaos they brought. Gary and Michael had introduced Whitney to drugs, and their appetite carried its own mayhem. When she was younger, they'd get into her stash—looting their baby sister of whatever bit of weed, cocaine, or money she had tucked away for her stolen moments with Robyn. Putting them on payroll, like she did with much of her family, may have come from a place of guilt. Being in a showbiz family and being the *one* who made it the way she had couldn't have been an easy burden. Cissy was proud of her daughter, but there was some resentment from her brother Gary. The eldest of Cissy's three kids had the makings of a star: he was six-five and incredibly handsome, with skin the color of silky dark chocolate and a gorgeous, rich baritone. He was an agile basketball player, but

Gary was certain he'd be the one following his mother's singing path. "I was the one that was supposed to be the singer. My
mother would tell me, 'You're the one to be the performer in
the family.' I loved doing it . . . but basketball took the place," he
told me. Gary made it to the NBA, being drafted by the Denver
Nuggets in 1979. But his shot in the major league was fleeting.
He was dropped after one season when he failed a drug test.
After Whitney took off a few years later, she brought her brother
along to sing background vocals. They had performed with their
mother at club gigs, but this was different. He was navigating
the globe with his sister, who was now singing to thousands
while he stood in the background. It was a perfectly fine (and
frankly steadier) gig, but it was a blow for the "one to be the
performer in the family" to end up in the background. Like his
sister, Gary had his own troubles—and they came along for the
ride. And what a ride it must have been in Whitney's orbit as
she became one of the biggest stars on the planet.

**

Of all the painful truths we've been forced to face about Whitney
in her absence, the most agonizing is that she spent her life carrying the burden of childhood sexual abuse. Her trauma would
have likely remained a buried secret had it not been for 2018's
Whitney, the documentary her estate commissioned to tell her
story. The Oscar-winning filmmaker Kevin Macdonald (*One
Day in September, The Last King of Scotland*) initially passed on
tackling a project on Whitney. Her image had been so prudently
crafted, and her demise had been so well-documented, that there

didn't appear to be anything left to uncover. But after Whitney's death we began having richer conversations around the shame that marked her fame and the parts of herself that she fervently tried to hide. We were interrogating how race and sexuality and addiction and identity and fame impacted Whitney. A firmer understanding of the devil on her back came with the arrival of Nick Broomfield and Rudi Dolezal's 2017 documentary *Whitney: Can I Be Me* and Macdonald's retrospective a year later. Both films sought to shift the narrative around Whitney and restore the reputation of an American icon who had crumbled under scandal and tragedy.

In mapping whatever road Whitney had gone down that led her to self-soothe with alcohol and drugs, the filmmakers behind the documentaries traced the insecurities over her Blackness and sexuality that marred the beginning of her career; the family dysfunction that widened with her fame; her tumultuous relationship with Bobby; and the addiction that crippled her and ultimately stopped her from course correcting for herself or for Bobbi Kristina. *Can I Be Me* showed Whitney amid the height of the *My Love Is Your Love* era. It was a glorious comeback, but she was exhausted from holding her pain and delivering onstage each night. The tension between Bobby and Robyn had reached its peak, and Whitney was struggling to keep it together for herself, and for Krissi, who desperately yearned for her mother's attention without having to share her with the thousands of fans who paid to see her. *Can I Be Me* offered an unvarnished glimpse at the emotional toll fame was having on Whitney as she toured, and her refusal to discuss her substance abuse—which was quite obvious by then—derailed the project until after her death. But it was Macdonald's investigation into Whitney's life and career that painted a clearer portrait of the traumas she had buried deep.

Macdonald suspected Whitney may have experienced childhood sexual abuse after watching interviews she did at the dawn of her meteoric rise in the 1980s. The way she shrank into herself and the discomfort in her physicality reminded him of subjects he'd interviewed in the past who had been sexually abused as children. After working on the documentary for a year and interviewing subjects around Whitney—many of whom were reluctant to be forthcoming despite agreeing to participate in the film—an off-the-record conversation during the last weeks of filming confirmed the director's suspicions. Macdonald reedited the film to build toward the revelation that Whitney and her brother Gary were allegedly abused by their cousin Dee Dee Warwick—an allegation Cissy and Dionne called "unfathomable" in a joint statement that also noted they weren't told about the accusation until two days before the film had its premiere at the Cannes Film Festival.

We struggle with confronting the insidiousness of childhood sexual abuse because it forces us to confront a simple fact that is hardest to reckon with: Statistically speaking, it is family members and those we hold closest in our communities who are typically the ones inflicting harm upon our young and vulnerable. It's our fathers and mothers, sisters and brothers, uncles, aunts, and cousins. Or it's our family friends, teachers, neighborhood elders, or mentors. Regardless of who it may be in our village, we know these crimes largely go unreported and instead become the dark secrets our families carry. Far too many children have suppressed their abuse or had it minimized or questioned out of protection or shame or guilt—and far too often it's the kids doing the protecting because they don't want bad things to happen to the person they love, despite the transgression, so their trauma becomes the burden they keep. We have enough data to know how prevalent this problem is in homes across the globe, and we have enough data to know what can happen to those children when they become adults and the burdens of the secret shame they carry catches up to them. There have been enough studies to draw clear lines between childhood trauma—be it neglect or witnessing domestic violence or the loss of a parent or emotional, physical, or sexual violence—and addiction. About two-thirds of adults battling addiction have experienced some type of physical or sexual trauma during childhood, according to the National Institute on Drug Abuse. And a study from the National Survey of Adolescents found that teens who have experienced physical or sexual abuse or assault were three times more likely to report past or current substance abuse than those without a history of trauma.

There's an old interview of Whitney that Macdonald inserted into his film that is the most overt clue to the trauma she held deep inside. She's asked what makes her angry, and an unmistakable rage takes hold: "Child abuse makes me angry . . . 'Cause I hate to see kids . . . It bothers me that children who are helpless, who depend on adults, for their security and for their caring, and for their love . . . It just . . . It bothers me. It makes me angry." Whitney was haunted by her childhood. There was speculation that the friction between her parents and their split wounded her, and while that is certainly true, there always appeared to be something else beneath the surface—which is maybe why we were questioning her authenticity.

Gary unburdened himself in his interview for the film, connecting his drug addiction to the trauma of his childhood. He disclosed that he was between seven and nine when the molestation began. We don't know what age Whitney may have been. Gary, Michael, and Whitney spent periods of their childhood floating between relatives and the homes of family friends as their parents worked. Cissy was often on the road touring; John had a handful of gigs and sometimes traveled with his wife. These were parents working to get their kids out of the ghetto, away from the wolves and bears that lurked outside.

***

Like her big sister Dionne, their auntie Cissy, and most of her kinfolk, Dee Dee Warwick had a voice that was blessed by the glory of God's touch. Dee Dee struck out on her own shortly after her sister did, cutting records with Jerry Leiber and Mike Stoller before signing with Mercury Records. In 1966, Dee Dee reached her apex when "I Want to Be with You" hit number nine on the R&B charts (just missing the Top 40 by one spot), but she's mostly known for her stunning rendition of "I'm Gonna Make You Love Me." Dee Dee didn't go as far as her sister. Dionne went the pop route. She smoothed the grit she got from singing in the church and allowed her voice to sweetly glide into an ethereal crescendo. But Dee Dee held on to her grit and her fire and sang with the full power that she learned in church. Her voice didn't float like her sister's, it commanded. Like a lot of soul singers of her generation, Dee Dee spent her career bouncing around labels and recording with nominal success. She struggled with an addiction to narcotics for a period of her life and was in failing health when she passed away in a nursing home in Essex County, New Jersey, in 2008 at the age of sixty-six. The year prior to her death, Dee Dee and the Warwick and Houston women—Dionne, Cissy, Whitney, and Bobbi Kristina—recorded "Family First" for the soundtrack to the Tyler Perry drama *Daddy's Little Girls*. It's the only time we've ever heard the entire clan on a record together.

The disclosure of the alleged abuse from Dee Dee comes from one of Whitney's last trusted confidants, her assistant Mary Jones. "We was talking one day, 'cause she knows my sister, and my sister was molested at an early age. And she looked up at me, and she says, 'Mary, I was too.' . . . And she had tears in her eyes," Jones told Macdonald in *Whitney*. "She says, 'Mommy don't know the things we went through.'" The allegations were vehemently dismissed by Dionne, Cissy, and Robyn, who wrote in her book that Whitney worshipped Dee Dee and would have confided in her if anything like that had ever happened. Neither Whitney nor Dee Dee are here to speak for themselves, but we have learned enough about intrafamily child sexual abuse to understand that Gary and Whitney could have experienced this violence and never disclosed the trauma until adulthood—and even then, they were likely selective about who they disclosed to. Jones believed Whitney was deeply ashamed of what had happened, and that it played a role in the ways in which she struggled with her own sexuality. That Gary got into drugs when he was so young falls right in line with what studies have revealed to us about how the trauma of sexual abuse can impact children as they mature. Cissy taught her boys to be protectors, but what do you do when you're a child and the person you need protection from is your own blood? That's a profound burden to carry. "My mother would hurt somebody if I told her who it was," Whitney confided as tears streamed down her cheeks, according to Jones. Jones said she advised Whitney to free herself of her secret, if only to release herself from the suffering of carrying her dark truth. "One day, when you get the nerve, you need to tell your mother," she told her. "It will lift the burden off you."

The burden of the secrets we carry can be enough to kill us if we let them. Some of us are able to tuck our trauma away and place it on the highest shelf in the library of our minds—out of reach and completely inaccessible to our current self, never to be opened. Others have melted the memory away from their brain in an act of self-preservation, only to find it slowly re-form like a hazy fever dream. The weight of the burden can collapse your spirit, driving you to depression or self-destruction or igniting a righteous fury underneath you. Some of us piece ourselves back together through therapy and meditation and self-love and faith and worship. And some of us go to the brink and never return. How we shoulder the burdens of our trauma varies. For Whitney, it may have been following her older brothers and dabbling in drugs when she was young, getting hooked, and then self-soothing when the pressures of fame and the bitter criticisms that came with it reactivated the part of herself she believed she had tucked away on the top shelf of her mind. It's a profound burden to carry, the memory of innocence lost at the hands of someone you loved and worshipped.

Whitney kept her secrets buried, and she paid the price for it. A heavy one. The toll of the burdens she carried is a sad throughline of *Can I Be Me*. Cameras were rolling in the quiet moments when she was so depleted from being *Whitney Houston* that she had to search for herself in her own reflection in a mirror backstage. *Can I Be Me* is the most extensive sight we got into her relationship with Robyn. The two had settled into a friendship punctuated by love and understanding of what they meant to each other, but it's hard not to clock the way in which their bodies respond to each other when they are alone and imagine the history these women once shared before Nippy became a superstar and Robyn was no longer able to protect her. When cameras rolled on Whitney and Bobby for *Being Bobby Brown*, the public didn't care as much about the Whitney who exhilarated us with spine-tingling ballads and euphoric dance anthems. The Whitney who conquered the world time and time again had descended into a cautionary tale that captivated us as much as any of her music had. Before the *National Enquirer* put photos of Whitney's bathroom counter trashed with empty beer cans and spoons burnt from cooking crack on the front page, the world was already enthralled by her downfall. The sensational headlines when she and Bobby got caught with weed at an airport, the rampant speculation when Burt Bacharach fired her from the 2000 Academy Awards after she showed up to rehearsal out of it and forgot her cues, the rumors of her demise after emerging onstage at Michael Jackson's anniversary celebration alarmingly thin, and that infamous *Crack is wack* interview. Eventually her denials felt ridiculous. She worsened the ridicule and speculation when she sat across from Diane

Sawyer and demanded Diane "show [her] the receipts" as it pertained to the hundreds of thousands of dollars she was rumored to have spent on cocaine. Her defensiveness is understandable, but the public was growing tired of watching her pretend—and watching everyone around appear complicit. Her film agent, Robyn, CeCe Winans, and Cissy once staged an intervention, but Whitney talked her mother out of it, instead begging her to move in with her to help her kick her habits. Who was going to push her after she said no? Whitney had her faith and it was all she needed. God would get her through.

In her 2017 memoir, *The Mother of Black Hollywood*, Jenifer Lewis recalled a moment she had with Whitney as they filmed *The Preacher's Wife*. The legendary actress played the sharp-tongued mother to Whitney's character. Lewis picked up on a vibe from Whitney, that she was perhaps unwell. Whitney was using daily at this point, as she admitted to Oprah in 2009, a reality that was surely impossible to hide on set given how much she loathed the early-morning call times required of film shoots. Between the scenes, Lewis pulled Whitney aside. She gave her some motherly advice by suggesting she consider therapy to help her cope with whatever might be troubling her. "Before I could say another word she whipped her head around and said, 'Oh no Mama! My Lord and Savior Jesus Christ will take care of me,'" Lewis wrote. Whitney was a woman of ardent faith, but she was mistaken to believe she could simply pray it all away. But that's how faith works, right? Whitney believed she could heal herself with her prayer. Through prayer, she could overcome this—especially with her mother at her side. And Cissy, unwavering in her faith, obliged. But Whitney immediately went back to her ways, locking herself in her room as addiction closed in before Cissy freed herself of her denial and pushed for Whitney to get treatment for drugs.

***

We have to be honest about how ravenous our appetite is for watching stars shoot into orbit and come crashing back down to earth. Whitney had the great misfortune of being the product of a time when our relationship with celebrity changed under the rise of MTV and of tabloid culture, *and* the advent of gossip blogs and social media. Our appetite for celebrity destruction flourished under the rise of tabloid talk shows and the dawn of reality television. It should come as no surprise that MTV—which was still very much the quintessential hub for youth counterculture—was pivotal in the birth of the latter when it launched *The Real World* in 1992. "This is the true story of seven strangers picked to live in a house, work together, and have their lives taped—to find out what happens when people stop being polite and start getting real" was the tagline. It was simple yet revolutionary. We hadn't seen people live their lives in front of the camera in this way. *The Real World* was ground zero for a genre of television that fed on our desire to see how other people, regular or famous, lived—for better or worst (and of course the worse usually made for better viewing). The growing popularity of reality and talk show hosts that specialized in controversy like Jerry Springer, Maury Povich, Jenny Jones, and Ricki Lake created a market for humiliation that allowed tabloids to thrive. And the feeding frenzy was magnified with the Internet shifting celebrity news into a 24/7 churn. Celebrity access was no longer finely controlled by print and television empires as the Internet gave anyone with a connection the power to gawk and feed off the drama, and paparazzi went through exhaustive lengths to feed the beast. They violated starlets by snapping portraits of their crotches. They dived in trash bins to rifle through their waste. And they invaded their morning hikes, Starbucks runs, and lunch dates to get the perfect shot of them doing mundane things. *Stars—They're Just Like Us!*

Gossip rags allowed us to see celebrities without the sheen we were used to, but celebrity tabloid culture became more voracious in the early 2000s as our access to tragedy and scandal widened. We went from having a few trashy gossip rags at the supermarket to thousands of blogs online that promoted the self-destruction of celebrities. That it was TMZ and not CNN that told us Michael Jackson was dead of a cardiac arrest felt like a pendulum swing. We had already consumed him and all his eccentricities and scandals to the point that his death felt like the overdue conclusion to a film we had fallen asleep watching. Tracking the downfall of our heroes was now a sport as the lines between mainstream media and celebrity blogs blurred. Before Amy Winehouse succumbed to alcohol addiction, her slow spiral was documented on a near-daily basis—paparazzi hounding her at every stumble. Amy's story is as classically tragic an industry tale as they come. Her talent was profound, but the British press pounced on the vulnerability that was the bedrock of her music. Her alcohol and drug dependency overshadowed her sheer brilliance. We were in awe when she cleaned herself up and gave a spectacular performance via satellite for the 2008 Grammys after achieving international crossover success. But we watched in horror as her addiction sent her careening on the streets of London or onstage and as her toxic relationship with husband Blake Fielder-Civil unraveled her further. The relationship had inspired her magnificent breakthrough album *Back to Black,* a perfect mishmash of Motown-era soul, sixties girl groups, and contemporary R&B. Amy was a beautifully emotive singer, with a voice that could absolutely devastate you, but her spats with the press and her addictions became the focus. Amy blew up right as celebrity tabloid culture was experiencing its digital boom. There was Perez Hilton and Dlisted and Oh No They Didn't and Just Jared and endless blind items and pages and pages and pages and pages of blogs and forums discussing and picking apart the intimate lives of anyone with a taste of fame. The Internet intensifying our appetite meant artists who took their time to create ran the risk of falling into oblivion, unless of course we were feeding on their scandals. The constant churn from blogs devoured every blunder and low point of Amy's short orbit. There was even a dedicated website that polled visitors on when she would perish—with a free iPod for the winner.

Whitney wasn't a stranger to the darker side of fame. Some of the secrets she tried to keep out of public view had made it into a few sordid tell-all exposés released in the early nineties, when she was reaching the apex of her fame. Books with juicy titles like *Good Girl, Bad Girl* and *Diva* arrived amid Whitney's nineties peak and were deep dives into the gossip in her personal life and her career—and were written with all the breathless tawdriness one might expect. It all fed into the narrative that Whitney was a diva in peril and our thesis that the problem was Bobby and the drugs and her ego. And now the talk of her drug use was supplemented with paparazzi snaps of her looking haggard and unwell, confirming our belief. We gleefully consumed her humiliation. But even if we turned and looked the other way, there would always be an audience watching and waiting for the next stumble, for the next headline to devour. Whitney would tell Diane Sawyer about her penchant for partying and would tell us that she smoked weed and drank and used cocaine. But that's not what stuck with us. It's when she uttered those three words—*Crack is wack*—and solidified our view on her. Those three words went instantly viral, burying her in infamy. She had told *some* of her truth and shamed the biggest devil that lived inside her, but we were too busy feeding on her humiliation to actually notice.

THE UNDOING OF WHITNEY HOUSTON

Virtue, Vice, and a Requiem for Redemption

Whitney had a recurring dream in which she was standing atop a bridge that swayed back and forth from the weight of stormy weather. She was trying to flee a giant that was chasing after her. *That's nothing but the devil; he's just trying to get you,* Cissy told her. The words rang true to Whitney. She was constantly fleeing in her dreams, always getting away from the monster and waking up exhausted from all that running. The Diane Sawyer interview hardened our view of Whitney. As it related to her issues with drugs we saw an addict in denial. Her rebuttals were sharp and defensive, and she didn't hide her irritation at the questions being asked. Diane wanted to know about the drinking, the weed, the pills, the cocaine, the weight loss, and Bobby. She wanted to know it all because she knew the world wanted to know. In retrospect, agreeing to the interview was not the sharpest move. Whitney and Bobby were sweaty and shifty, which made most of her refutations sound ludicrous. "We're rock 'n' rollers, man," Whitney says, with Bobby quickly chiming in: "That's the life we live here, you know?" They weren't wrong. That they did drugs wasn't that remarkable. A lot of people do drugs. But what Whitney and Bobby always failed to realize was the behavior that was generally permissible to the music industry didn't extend to either of them. Her letting us know that she made too much money to ever smoke crack was her separating herself from our association of crack with the poor Black and brown folks strung out in the streets. Whitney and Bobby were rock stars, but they were still a Black man and woman on national TV talking about getting high. And one thing the War on Drugs taught us was that it's impermissible for Black people to be high in this country without consequence. It's in this talk about Whitney's drug use where the most revelatory moment of the interview comes. Diane asks Whitney to name the biggest among her devils. "That would be me," she replies soberly. "Nobody makes me do anything I don't want to do. It's my decision. So the biggest devil is me. I'm either my best friend or my worst enemy. And that's how I have to deal with it." Whitney was always running from that devil on her back. It had stripped her of so much. It had stolen her dignity and robbed her of much of the beautiful instrument we all hoped would return to its former glory. We wanted to blame the man sitting next to her on the couch during that trainwreck of an interview, or the parents who might not have always had their daughter's best interest at heart, or the brothers who used her—we didn't want to blame Whitney. She had given us too much. Even as we derided her, we pointed our fingers at Bobby and at Cissy but never at Whitney—and never at ourselves. Whitney wasn't ready to let the world in on the extent of her troubles, but she shamed the devil, even if it was herself.

**

What Whitney needed was a hit. After her glorious comeback with *My Love Is Your Love*, Whitney became a heartbreaking reminder of what once was. She had slowly extinguished the fire required to deliver the signature records that put her in the upper echelon of pop. Her vices and the burdens she soothed with weed, cocaine, and alcohol had taken a toll on her voice. It was harder for her to sing the way we expected—pristine and otherworldly, like she sounded when the record-breaking string of hits at the beginning of her career cemented her as *the voice*. But she was bound to her early successes, a prisoner of her own achievements. No one wanted to see Whitney without hearing a signature, defining record like "I Will Always Love You," even if her lungs could no longer sustain the rigor of floating sky-high into the rafters. In performances far after her peak, you can see Whitney trying to push through the notes, struggling to muster the strength to deliver the crescendo runs from the top of her head voice. Those were the money notes she knew everyone was holding their breath to hear. Footage from a 1999 show in Frankfurt that made it into *Can I Be Me* shows Whitney working her way through "I Will Always Love You." You can feel her exhaustion through the screen. Her eyes are sunken; she's damp with perspiration and appears disconnected from the moment. She was in the final stretch of the *My Love Is Your Love* World Tour—a run that was ultimately her last victory on the road—and she was drained. Whitney braces for the moment she knows everyone is waiting on. That great big boom *"and Iiiiii"* that launches out her throat, like a volcanic blast, powered by damn near every muscle in her five-foot-eight frame. It's where she works the hardest on the original recording and is, perhaps, the most famous vocal run in pop music. But onstage in Frankfurt, Whitney doesn't deliver with the assured grace of an Olympic athlete somersaulting effortlessly through the air, the way we were used to. She lets out a sigh, catches her breath, and wipes her face as her eyes dart around in search of something only she knows. She's paused long enough that folks in the audience wouldn't have been mistaken in wondering if the big climax would go unmet. But she motions for the band to fire up the *boom* that signifies the assault of runs so many of us have attempted to do in our cars and in our bedrooms and in the shower while listening to the *Bodyguard* soundtrack. The notes are labored, but there's still so much splendor and elegance that the performance is magical simply because she wills it to be so.

But Whitney's magic was fading. We watched it slip further away from her grasp after she had reclaimed much of her glory with *My Love Is Your Love*, a biting album that pushed her deeper into the contemporary R&B that critics and Black music purists felt her work was devoid of. The album subverted her pop-queen image into something closer to who she was at the moment—a woman fed up with the man she loved and fed up with the world's opinions of her. It made for records that were fierce and sexy and vulnerable and brimming with rage and pain; deeply lush and soulful records that saw her exploring reggae and hip hop soul sounds that allowed her voice to flourish and set moods and not always have to climax toward the earth-shattering heights that were now laborious to replicate. Whitney had been waiting to exhale and she finally did, over hot tracks from Wyclef and Missy and Darkchild and Babyface and Soulshock & Karlin and Lauryn Hill. It was the best music she ever made, but that doesn't stop the devil from running after you.

What makes *Can I Be Me* so devastating is watching the tour footage with all that we know now. It guts you to see Bobbi Kristina just wanting a little more time with her mommy and the guilt from Whitney knowing she doesn't have more to give; to see Robyn gritting her teeth and trying her damnedest to hold it together as Whitney and Bobby descended further into addictions that were painfully evident to everyone *except* them; to feel the distance between Cissy and her daughter and imagine the strain brought on by the burdens they both carried. What's hardest to watch, though, are the performances. The joy Whitney was having leaning into the drama of the icy bangers that reinvigorated her countered by the sheer will she had to find to deliver those big, showy ballads that at this point imprisoned her by revealing the limitations of a voice damaged by years of drug use.

My Love Is Your Love was the beginning of a career stretch constantly defined by comeback attempts. In 2000, Clive and Whitney revisited the idea of assembling her classic records for a greatest hits collection. Guilting her into returning to the studio had resulted in enough material for a new album, and the retrospective set took a back seat to promoting *My Love Is Your Love*. Pairing her timeless hits with a handful of new records was the victory lap Whitney needed amid the flurry of negative press she was constantly bombarded with. But Clive was soon on his way out of Arista, and his protégé would be left to figure out her next move without her guiding light.

Arista reinvested in Whitney handsomely with a lavish $100 million multi-album deal, a mind-blowing sum unseen by a female singer at the time that was their way of showing their commitment to Whitney after her longtime mentor departed. The pressure was on the moment the contract was announced. She needed to show the world that she could score big without Clive, that she could do it despite the talk swallowing her career. That silly weed scandal in Hawaii, her frail appearance at Michael Jackson's comeback concert, skipping Clive's induction into the Rock & Roll Hall of Fame, getting fired from the Oscars—these all fed into the bigger story of a slow decline that was getting more attention than her music. But nothing makes bad press evaporate quicker than a hit. And so Whitney needed another smash. Another comeback. Building on the groove-heavy hip-hop soul that made her sound perkier and exciting again on *My Love Is Your Love*, Whitney got in the studio to record her fifth album, *Just Whitney*, with Missy Elliott, Kevin "She'kspere" Briggs, Kandi Burruss, and Charlene "Tweet" Keys—a crop of young songwriters and producers who were integral in steering the fusion of R&B and hip-hop into the twenty-first century—and with Rob Fusari, who crafted funky records for Destiny's Child before going on to shape Lady Gaga's seminal debut. Whitney also worked with trusted longtime collaborators like Babyface and Ricky Minor. The theme of the music, as Whitney told the press, was about survival and being a multifaceted woman. It was an approachable thesis that, like her last album, showed a woman in search of presenting herself as someone a little more real than her earlier music had. Whitney had abandoned the prissy pop-princess façade—in part out of necessity, but largely because she just stopped bothering to hide the rougher edges that came out when she drank or got high. Whitney eased into an elder stateswoman role. She doesn't get enough credit for the comradery she carried with her throughout her career, but she was a woman who lifted as she climbed, as Black creatives often tend to do. Sisterhood was everything to Whitney. It was in the way she lifted up Brandy and Monica in her name and called on Faith Evans and Kelly Price to sing with her and forged bonds with Natalie Cole and CeCe Winans and Mariah Carey—putting to bed years of being pit against each other by the media with a blockbuster duet and a lasting friendship (and let us not forget that *epic* dress moment at the 1998 MTV Video Music Awards).

Next to the blatant homophobia, the most offensive thing about the way in which people spoke of Robyn was the dismissal of her presence and influence in Whitney's life. The media framed Robyn as someone who wasn't as integral to Whitney's success as Clive or Cissy. She was seen as someone whose sole purpose was linked to whatever may or may not have happened romantically between them when, in fact, Robyn and Whitney built the Nippy Inc. brand together and Robyn was a driving force in Whitney's creative direction—the two even managed a short-lived girl group named Sunday under their banner.

But like Clive, Robyn was no longer around to offer creative guidance—or career support. She had grown tired of Whitney's self-destruction, and she was tired of fighting with Bobby and the Houstons, so she walked away from the job in 2000. For the first time in her career, Whitney was without the two people who had the most influence in it.

Just Whitney is quite an innocuous listen, all things considered. The grittier edges she embraced on *My Love Is Your Love* were polished to move Whitney back to her adult contemporary core by focusing on R&B ballads, smooth pop-soul grooves, and dance records. Babyface and legendary singer-songwriter Carole Bayer Sager crafted the album's centerpiece ballad, "Try It on My Own," an empowering record very thinly based on the personal struggles in Whitney's own life that were playing out publicly. Even if she wasn't ready to fully admit the truth, she was incapable of hiding the drama with Bobby and the denials and spin from her camp about her erratic behavior was antithetical to what we read in the news. What made her interview with Diane Sawyer so infamous, aside from the sharp-tongued one-liners, was seeing Whitney literally perspiring as she's being grilled. That interview didn't humanize Whitney, as her obliviousness to how her defensiveness would be received—and scrutinized—was embarrassing to witness. And the Diane Sawyer interview directly impacted the way *Just Whitney* was received. We saw a woman in trouble, and we looked to the music for answers or insight into how she was doing. "Try It on My Own" sounded like the words she needed to sing to confront where she was at the time, or at least that's what the writers were aiming for. *"I'm wiser now, I'm not the foolish girl you used to know so long ago /*

I'm stronger now, I've learned from my mistakes which way to go," Whitney sings in the first verse. There's an even raspier tone to her voice, from both natural aging and the effects of substances, and it's that grit that makes a record like "Try It on My Own" feel more emotive now that you can actually hear her pushing through the lyrics. A savvier move would have been to release that as the album's first single and not "Whatchulookinat," the missive she co-wrote as a response to the media coverage over the rumors surrounding her. *"Same spotlight that once gave me fame, trying to dirty up Whitney's name,"* Whitney sings with a voice that's borderline sneering.

It was gutsy and full of venom, but a grossly miscalculated move. Making a record essentially blaming the negative press on lies opened her up to further criticism considering all that had been in public view—beyond the Bobby drama and the Oscars mishap and escaping arrest in Hawaii, she showed up hours late to photoshoots, struggled to keep her eyes open during interviews, and exhibited erratic behavior. It all made the news because she was Whitney Houston and a chaotic record like "Whatchulookinat" sounded like the half-baked, paranoid manifesto from someone who didn't realize *why* we were giving them the side-eye. It's the biggest miss of the album, next to her sappy, overwrought take on "You Light Up My Life," the inclusion of which feels entirely based on it being the sole powerhouse ballad from Whitney, who otherwise spends much of the album belting in the lower registers that were now more comfortable for her to rest in. She'kspere took the melody from the Isley Brothers' smoldering classic "Between the Sheets" and mixed it with honey until he got the groovy "One of Those Days," a breezy R&B jam that allowed Whitney to float gracefully without having to strain her vocals. There were grown and sexy and *real* records like the downbeat "Things You Say" and the rock-leaning "Tell Me No," and there was the frothy dance pop of "Love That Man," which felt like a tribute to the euphoric bangers of her early years, and the resilient anthem "Unashamed." Recording no longer came as easy as it once had. Whitney would lock herself in the hotel room for days or weeks at a time. She wasn't ready. People around Whitney knew she wasn't ready. But Arista spent millions on travel and studio time for Whitney. Aside from the drug use, she wasn't always disciplined about caring for her instrument. She wasn't really ready for any of this, but Whitney had something to prove—to herself, and to us.

Just Whitney was a moderate hit, which is to say it was a flop by Whitney Houston standards. Fingers pointed at the lack of Clive by her side and the lack of focus on her part, but there aren't enough bangers in the world that could have distracted us from the trainwreck of the Diane Sawyer interview, which aired just days before the album was released. We all wanted to know what was going on with her, and with Bobby, and the drugs, and the fallout with her father when the president of his company sued Whitney for the entire $100 million of her renegotiated deal in a breach-of-contract claim (the suit was tossed out shortly after John died in 2003). We all watched and saw her in denial of so many truths, the depths of which couldn't have been more obvious to anyone watching at home. "Crack is wack" and "Show me the receipts" have logged permanence in our minds, but it's painful to consider all she was running from—betrayal from her dying father, her and Bobby's drama, the departure of Robyn, the devil on her back waiting to catch her in a moment of weakness. Between *Just Whitney* and *One Wish*—the holiday album she released the following year—it felt as if this was a performer reaching the end of her career.

Just Whitney was the beginning of Whitney's unending cycle of comeback attempts. Every release was now seen as her trying to prove to herself, and to us, that she still had *it*. That she could still move through the lavish gospel-rooted belting that made her the Queen of Pop. But neither *Just Whitney* nor *One Wish* did much to move her any further from the perception that the fire was slowly but surely burning out. She was living in Atlanta after seeking counsel from her sisterfriend Perri Reid, who had left music behind to become a minister. "She took me under her wing," Whitney recalled to *Essence* in 2003. "I stayed in one room, and she took me through a transition of deliverance and prayer. You need somebody to give you tough love, people to remind you that you are a child of God and you don't belong to the devil." Being in the South, away from her connections to the industry on the East Coast, allowed Whitney to be out of the spotlight for the first real time in her life. But it also allowed her to descend further into darkness, spending her days with Bobby smoking joints laced with cocaine as time slipped away from them.

Whitney, Bobby, and Bobbi Kristina settled in Alpharetta, a suburb outside of Atlanta. Although *Being Bobby Brown* would be an embarrassment to Whitney, it did show us how much she enjoyed life out of the spotlight. But the cameras weren't rolling for the stretches of time when she was closing the world out with drug binges. The wear and tear of her addiction was clear when she confronted Wendy Williams live on-air in January 2003. Before Wendy had her catchphrases and doled out celebrity news for the daytime TV crowd, she was an OG radio jock who spilled the tea with reckless abandon. Wendy told her audiences what she heard in the streets or through the grapevine of the industry or from old-fashioned reporting. Her enemy list was long and mighty, and for years Wendy talked about all the speculation around Whitney and Robyn, and she talked about her marriage with Bobby and all the gossip that was on the front page of the tabloids. Wendy rarely spoke in innuendos, and she gave it to the audience straight. And Whitney called her up—which speaks to the era we were in—and got in her ass about all of it, cursing Wendy out for asking about the drug use and how much money she was giving her family, as there were rumors that her drug habits had put her in dire financial straits. Whitney calling into Wendy Williams's radio show was like her Diane Sawyer interview in the sense that both moments showed us the overt cracking of a façade that could no longer be performed.

There were several interventions to get Whitney help. Clive wrote in his memoir that he intervened after she was fired from the Oscars and skipped his induction at the Rock & Roll Hall of Fame in 2000 and urged her to go to rehab, but she told him her personal matters were under control, and even though he saw the denial on her face, Clive was resigned that there wasn't much for him to do if she didn't want the help. He reached out again after seeing her at Michael Jackson's celebration concert the following year. Clive penned Whitney an impassioned letter asking her to stop living in denial about her struggle. "I know somewhere down deep there is the real you that knows that you are being confronted this time by everyone who loves you, who cares for you and who wants you well," his letter read. "You are now being begged by these same people who know that this problem is bigger than you can deal with alone." Clive was certain Whitney received the letter and read the letter, but a response never came. Whitney always believed she could get through with prayer. She went to rehab for the first time in 2004. And then she relapsed. Cissy intervened again in 2005, showing up to Whitney's home with deputies and a court order granting her the power to have her daughter involuntarily committed to a treatment facility. In Cissy's memoir, she detailed the state of Whitney and Bobby's home as being in shambles: "Somebody had spray-painted the walls and door with big glaring eyes and strange faces. Evil eyes, staring out like a threat . . . In another room, there was a big framed photo of [Whitney]—but someone had cut [her] head out. It was beyond disturbing, seeing my daughter's face cut out like that," Cissy wrote. When Bobby's sister Tina sold the details of the drug binges she went on with Whitney to the *National Enquirer* in 2006, she spoke of the paranoia Whitney's drug use activated. How she saw demons when she was high. How she believed someone was after Bobby and that they were under surveillance. Tina told it all for a pretty coin while Whitney was trying to get clean—even if it was forced on her. Whitney needed support and empathy, but she got our shame and judgment. Her fall from grace had become such a scintillating drama, and Tina knew there was an audience waiting to devour every detail. A few months after the *Enquirer* splashed

Whitney's "drug den" all over its front page, she separated from Bobby and was working on her sobriety with a drug counselor. She filed for divorce a month later and was awarded full custody of Bobbi Kristina. At last, it appeared Whitney had freed herself from *all* the drugs that imprisoned her. Or so we hoped.

***

There's a reluctance to paint Whitney as a hero. One of the costs of addiction is we tend to place asterisks next to our titans who don't die dignified deaths or have the tragic luxury of becoming a martyr. Her final chapter didn't end with either, so we've filed Whitney under Pop Music Cautionary Tales, along with Michael Jackson and Amy Winehouse and the rock gods and goddesses of the 27 Club. It doesn't help that much of her music told us nothing of who she was or the pain she was carrying. Whitney was our great entertainer. Her music didn't have the radical power that made us worship Prince and Michael. Nor did it have the intimacy that came with a Mariah-penned record or offer any revelatory perspectives on feminism in the way Madonna and Janet constantly did with their provocative, ambitious work. Whitney's gift was her voice, and the way she interpreted lyrics. The choices she makes with her voice—that was her magic. We can agree that there was a lack of singularity in her records, but we can't forget that Whitney was a girl from the church and to her this was about reaching and touching people with the majesty of her voice, making us *feel* even if the words weren't her own. The brilliance of a voice that forever changed the way we heard "The Star-Spangled Banner" and reworked an Annie Lennox B-side into a spiritual disco and turned a Dolly Parton tune into perhaps the greatest pop ballad of all time. This was a voice that could exhilarate in one moment and bring you to your knees the next. And we spent so much time telling her that it wasn't enough. That she wasn't good enough. Interesting enough. Artistic enough. *Black* enough. Straight enough. Years of goading from the press and her toxic love with Bobby gave us *My Love Is Your Love*, but much of the world was already waiting for the next stumble. The next bit of hot tea to sip on. The next scandal that reminded us how far she had fallen from those glory days when she was flying so close to the sun. *Being Bobby Brown* and those last tumultuous years of her marriage had brought her even more public shame and ridicule. Whitney was already a punch line, but we made her a laughingstock and it continued as her output failed to hit like her old shit. But that's the pitfall of flying as high as Whitney had. The fact that she's the *only* artist to have seven consecutive number-one singles speaks to not only how high she had soared but how difficult a feat it is to duplicate.

Whitney achieved so much. No one can sustain that kind of success. When we praise Whitney and the glory of her voice and all she did, the conversation is almost intrinsically connected to her performance of "The Star-Spangled Banner" or "I Will Always Love You" or the record-breaking stretch of hits she earned in the late eighties that made her the gold standard—a standard that still very much applies today. Just look at how many people show up to *American Idol* or *The Voice* or whatever variation of singing show trying to sound like Whitney. And because she couldn't ever replicate her original successes, we saw her as broken. We saw her as a failure who was unable to score another big hit. We expect our greats to never miss, even when time and shifting tastes and a new generation of innovative talent make it harder to take a shot and win. Whitney was a woman in the pop industry pushing forty—and a Black one at that. Her records were being judged against Destiny's Child and Brandy and TLC and the litany of younger acts that now got most of MTV's and BET's attention. And then there was Clive's first post-Arista success, Alicia Keys, a classically trained pianist who poured her heart and soul into records that fused together R&B, jazz, hip-hop, blues, classical, and gospel. Keys was the hot new sensation to emerge during the height of the Neo Soul era, and she was the anti-diva: she wore her hair in cornrows, she didn't hide any of the hardness she got while growing up in Hell's Kitchen, and her swag was East Coast tomboy. Keys wrote and produced her music—a rare occurrence in contemporary R&B—and her 2001 debut, *Songs in A Minor*, was a critical and commercial smash that would yield her five Grammys. Clive had done it again; his ear had led him to another Black girl with magic in her throat (and in the case of Keys, also in her fingertips). The way we all saw it, if Whitney was to ever find magic again, she needed Clive.

Recapturing that glory was at the core of Whitney's second big comeback attempt after Clive came back into the fold in 2004 when he accepted an offer from BMG to head the entire RCA Music Group, which included Arista. That same year he

was being honored at the World Music Awards for his contributions to the industry, and he wanted Whitney to perform.
Though she had been touring overseas with Dionne and Natalie
Cole, this would be the first time she was on national television
in two years. Clive kept the plans secret until he had a chance
to lay eyes on her and confirm for himself that she appeared
healthier and more sober than she had while promoting *Just
Whitney*. She delivered an incandescent performance of "I
Believe in You and Me" and "I Will Always Love You" that ended
with a two-minute standing ovation from the crowd. They
announced their plans to reunite, but Whitney went back to
living her life and the old habits that tempted her. Their reunion
would have to wait until Whitney cleaned herself up enough
to try again. In 2007, Clive called her up. "Okay, are you ready
now?" he asked over the phone. Whitney hadn't released any
music since putting out a holiday collection after *Just Whitney*
fizzled. She was off and on with her sobriety, but Clive wanted
his girl back. He needed *the voice* back. We all did, even if we
didn't think she had it in her. She was afraid, but she told Clive
she knew it was time to go back to work. Because Clive tended
to shy away from pushing about her personal life, they didn't
discuss where she currently was with her sobriety, but he did
lecture her about cigarettes.

As much as we ridiculed and criticized Whitney, we all love
a comeback story. Redemption stories are the heartbeat of the
entertainment industrial complex. We root for the hero as they
get placed on a pedestal, gasp at their fall, and feel inspired when
they rise again. That's the cycle. Time and time again. Actors,

athletes, politicians, singers, or whoever we launch into fame's orbit. Clive wanted the world to see the hero triumph again. Whether she was ready was another thing.

In those last years, Whitney was always *one* hit away, and so Clive got to work doing what Clive does best—assembling hitmakers. Grammy-, Emmy-, and Golden Globe–winning songwriter Diane Warren imagined the depths of Whitney's struggles and channeled that into a powerful ballad about rebirth and resilience that David Foster produced and Whitney sang better than anything she'd sung in years. R. Kelly—still in demand despite a miles-long trail of sexual abuse allegations—contributed a set of records, and Whitney worked with some of the leading hitmakers in R&B at the time, including Harvey Mason Jr., Danja, Norwegian production team Stargate, Johntá Austin, Akon, Tricky Stewart, Eric Hudson, Claude Kelly, Swizz Beatz, and Alicia Keys. It was a ferocious set of hired guns, but the magic was always Whitney and *that* voice. The impact of her vices had reduced her instrument to a hoarse rasp. But between stretches of sobriety and working with a vocal coach, Whitney was able to regain a great deal of strength in her voice. "People have standards that they expect you to live up to," she confided to her vocal coach Gary Catona during a session. "I have a problem with that, myself, trying to live up to what I once was."

Though Whitney's full range wasn't there, there was still wonder in her voice, and she used all of it to make *I Look to You*, a joyful collection of gospel-drenched ballads and slick contemporary R&B that perfectly merged the approachable side that became the center of her persona post–*The Body-guard* with the regal pop queen of her youth. The lower, raspier register that had become her safety net makes the old-school vibes and deep disco grooves on the up-tempo records feel more vibrant than anything she'd done since *My Love Is Your Love*. But the bread and butter of Whitney Houston are the big powerhouse ballads and hearing her tackle those swooping, masterful belts. *I Look to You*, like *Just Whitney*, is light on ballads. The R. Kelly–penned title track, which Clive picked as the first single, and the Warren and Foster collaboration "I Didn't Know My Own Strength," became the centerpieces of the album, as they both vaguely dance around the tumultuous decade that set the stage for this latest comeback. "I Didn't Know My Own Strength" was particularly potent with its message of willpower and redemption.

Released in August 2009 to a flurry of Clive-orchestrated hype, *I Look to You* started as the triumphant return we hoped for Whitney. The record debuted at number one, the first time she'd done it since *The Bodyguard*. This was the victory she needed to restore herself from the years of ignominy that had tarnished her image. We had lost Michael Jackson two months earlier, dead of cardiac arrest brought on by the Propofol his doctor pumped into him so that he would sleep. It was an awful conclusion to a life and career defined by so much genius, chaos, and tragedy. Michael was dead before he could perform any of the shows booked as part of the splashy comeback that was to double as his final curtain call. The warning of Michael's tragic demise hung in the air as Whitney hit the promotional trail for *I Look to You*. They were cut from a similar cloth in terms of their fame—both had reached zeniths in the eighties as once-in-a-generation talents; both carried the weight and the wounds of having to break down so many barriers as Black artists; and both had their brilliance overshadowed by scandals and an inability to recapture their former glories as they aged in an industry that favored youth above all. They carried much of the same pain. There's a powerful moment in *Whitney* where Debra Martin Chase, Whitney's longtime film collaborator, shares how Michael would occasionally call and she would go visit him at his hotel. Whitney and Michael would just sit together, in complete silence. "They were . . . two of the few people in the world who could understand what their circumstances were," Chase explained. It's a devastating image. Two of the biggest superstars in the world finding companionship in the silent understanding of their shared isolation. Both had been through the wringer. At a point they were the easiest, most dependable punch lines in entertainment—bizarre eccentrics who had squandered their talent and riches to drugs and their own whims and couldn't make a hit anymore. We lived in the nostalgia of who they *once* were and didn't appreciate the flashes of brilliance they showed on late-career albums like Whitney's 2002 comeback attempt, *Just Whitney*, or Michael's 2001 album *Invincible*, his first record in six years and ultimately his last project. They both had made it so easy to stop rooting for them—Whitney with her resentment toward the press and self-destructive behavior, Michael with his mania and allegations that he was sexually abusing the young boys he befriended and paraded in front of the world. But they were still our heroes, and we want to see our heroes rise again. So we propped Michael back up to king status after he died. We drove up his streams and bought copies of the old shit we loved so much and the newer shit we ignored, and we came out in droves to see the film that stitched together the rehearsals for the concerts that never happened. And we showered Whitney with our love when she came back to us with *I Look to You.*

***

The sight of Whitney making her big comeback knocked me into a daze. She was wrapped in the most elegant white chiffon that draped from her shoulders down to the floor, vanishing under a plume of stage fog. It reminded me of the first time I had fallen in love with her, watching her run through heaven like an angel in *The Bodyguard.* There she was, statuesque and graceful. My eyes bounced around the monitors displaying Whitney's angelic silhouette and then her voice came in: *"Lost touch with my soul, I had nowhere to turn, I had nowhere to go / Lost sight of my dream, thought it would be the end of me."* I relished in the moment. After a lifetime of experiencing Whitney by proxy of her recordings, TV performances, and films, I was witnessing her brilliance in real life—albeit from the posh backstage lounge where the journalists covering the 2009 American Music Awards worked. I was a cub reporter at the *Los Angeles Times* and had gotten the assignment mostly because no one else cared much about the AMAs. It didn't have the prestige of the Grammys or the fun irreverence of the Video Music Awards, but I was a kid from the hood who grew up desperately hoping to one day get a chance to cover all the award shows I'd spent years watching in my bedroom. And now I was here. And so was Janet. And Mary J. Blige. And Jay-Z. And Whitney. Heroes who had defined my childhood and were part of what drove me toward pursuing music journalism. The grief over Michael was still fresh, and there was Whitney, showing that she had the strength to survive it all. There she was, singing the hell out of "I Didn't Know My Own Strength" and proving that she could still send you into orbit with the sheer beauty in her voice. I stood in awe, taking in the myriad of angles being beamed onto a half-dozen screens, each of which were larger and sharper than the set that rested on the floor of my first L.A. apartment. The sight of Whitney standing in triumph, after all she had been through—and all she had put herself through—made my eyes flood with tears that I didn't care to hide. I wasn't alone. All around me were journalists, publicists, handlers, and production crew members weeping at the performance happening in the next room over. Whitney had dazzled once again, ending the performance with a graceful bow as the building shook from the standing ovation she received. The hero had risen again, and I saw it with my own eyes.

The initial success of *I Look to You* restored some of what Whitney had lost, but the feat was short-lived. She wasn't 100 percent ready to be back in the spotlight. Beyond her voice, which strained now more often onstage, Whitney wasn't entirely sober. The devil was chasing her again. But instead of getting clean, she went on the road again. She hadn't toured since *My Love Is Your Love*, and she didn't really want to. But the pressure of a comeback means there's too much on the line. Clive didn't think she should go on the road, but she needed the money.

In 2010, the *Nothing but Love* World Tour kicked off in Moscow before hitting Asia, Australia, and Europe. Reviews were brutal, and much of the footage living on YouTube shows why. The tour wasn't the hero's victory lap it was supposed to be. The shows were hard on her—she struggled to keep up with the choreography that punctuated her breezy up-tempos, and she often strained to hit notes in the top range of her voice, taking breaks to catch her breath or let a fit of coughs escape. Though she was far removed from the vocal perfection of her youth, she had never before appeared in this rough of shape onstage. We all assumed she was in the midst of a relapse, given her history. Her performances, once so full of poise, were now being mocked for the notes she failed to land and the steps she couldn't hit. Fans walked out, demanding their money be returned. In the past, an off night onstage got you a bad review and a few folks talking shit about you in the streets. But this was the age of YouTube and Twitter and Facebook. An off night now went viral for the world to see—shared with just a few clicks. Less than a year after the tour, Whitney returned to rehab for a third time.

***

I Look to You gave us a glimmer of hope—but addiction doesn't care about hope. In May 2011, Whitney voluntarily checked into an outpatient treatment for drugs and alcohol. She wanted to get clean not just for herself and for Bobbi Kris, but because she wanted to work. Whitney and Debra Martin Chase had finally gotten their remake of *Sparkle* off the ground, a passion project of Whitney's that was halted after the death of its original lead, the stunning, shape-shifting R&B powerhouse Aaliyah. When the original film came out in 1976, a teenage Whitney spent months going to the theater to watch it every weekend. In the new version, *American Idol*'s Jordin Sparks assumed the titular role, with Carmen Ejogo and Tika Sumpter playing her sisters and Whitney easing into the role of their mother, a failed singer who hit rock bottom and turned to the church. There was anticipation over Whitney's first film role in fifteen years, which would again see her contribute new material to a soundtrack. That anticipation came with questions, though. Was she ready for any of it? Could she get it together? Clive had already communicated to the world that there would not be another album until *the voice* returned by going on the record with a radio host and saying just as much during a 2011 interview. But Whitney wanted the world to see her win. She also knew that as much as people loved a comeback story, there were only so many chances she was going to get.

Whitney was all in. She did the routine drug screenings required of her during the film's production. She had fully cleaned herself up and became *Whitney Houston* again, but it would be short-lived. "On the last day [of filming *Sparkle*], she said: 'I got an idea for our next movie,'" Chase recalled in *Whitney*. "I just don't think she wanted to leave. Because she had purpose and people who loved her. And I can just see her going back to Alpharetta and waking up in the morning—or more likely, in the afternoon—with no reason to get out of bed and nothing on the horizon."

In early February 2012, Whitney checked into the Beverly Hilton using her grandmother's name for the anonymity required of a superstar (and tabloid magnet). "Elizabeth Collins" was given a presidential junior suite on the fourth floor.

Whitney had just landed in Los Angeles, a small entourage in tow. It was the eve of Grammy week, and those electric days ahead of music's biggest night were abuzz with schmoozing and bottle popping and party hopping. Whitney's presence at Clive's annual gala was expected. She dazzled there, the year prior, with one of those triumphant performances of hers that offered the briefest reminder of the brilliance we all had desperately hoped would stick around. It was always a night where she could be our pop queen, she could be Whitney Houston, and not have to worry about the judgment of the public—because there's no one who wants to see the hero rise more than a roomful of artists and producers who have all weathered their share of success and failures while trying not to drown in the finicky waters of the music industry. At Clive's gala, Whitney was always the belle of the ball. She was in L.A. to cut her vocal on the duet she was doing with Sparks for the *Sparkle* soundtrack. Recording in town gave her the chance to play the music for Clive, and she was eager to get his read on the retro soul number she'd recorded with Harvey Mason Jr. He loved the upbeat record, but he also loved Whitney enough to lecture her about the smoking habit she still hadn't managed to kick and have an honest conversation about her taking better care of herself. Whitney saw *Sparkle* as the beginning of her return. And as much as Clive wanted his girl to make a comeback, she couldn't return like she had last time. She had to be ready this time—really ready—and she'd have to prove it.

Two days before the gala, I arrived to the ballroom of the Beverly Hilton to interview Clive, Brandy, and Monica. The R&B divas had reunited to record a follow-up duet to their 1998 smash "The Boy Is Mine" and were going to perform at Clive's gala as a way to tease a reunion that would bury the hatchet from a nineties beef born simply out of the media's intense comparisons of them. They were two young Black girls, deeply inspired by Whitney and the church, who paved exciting lanes for themselves as R&B prodigies at a time when the genre was meshing with hip-hop. Their music defined an era, and after being savvy enough to team up and create a smoking-hot duet where they vocally sparred over a ladies' man, the media and their fanbases wanted a cat fight in real life as the record became a megasmash. Brandy and Monica worshipped the gospel of Whitney, and I worshipped the gospel of Brandy and Monica, so I basically levitated into the ballroom off the fumes of my own excitement as the band set up for rehearsal. Their teenage peaks were in the past, and I was one of the few reporters in the room who truly cared about the women onstage nervously running through "The Boy Is Mine." The room was thick with national and international press, most of whom were there to talk to the man with the platinum ears about his legendary party. I was given the last slot of the day because I had requested (well, begged) for maximum time with Brandy and Monica. I balanced my notebook with a Flip cam to capture the first full run-through the ladies did with the entire band. As they sang, there was a chorus of gasps from the back of the room. From the corner of my eye I caught the figure of a woman shuffling toward the front of the stage. It was Whitney. She was not the Whitney who first mesmerized me in her music videos or the Whitney who captivated me in *The Bodyguard* and *Waiting to Exhale* and *The Preacher's Wife* or the Whitney I had seen bow to thunderous applause just two years prior. The woman before me was unfamiliar. She was visibly intoxicated, her clothes disheveled, and her hair soaking wet from the pool. But her face was plastered with that wide, familiar smile of hers. So radiant and warm. It's the smile I'd seen a million times by then. The discomfort growing in my stomach as chatter took over the ballroom was reassured by that smile. I was arm's length from these women who had meant so much to me and my love of R&B and pop music, but before me was a woman who appeared so lost in her addiction that she didn't even have the frame of mind to reconsider showing up to a room crowded with news crews or the ability to see how she was being received by a room of people. Whitney had presented herself on a silver platter at a time when social media had become our primary source of consuming celebrity news, and it felt like a Tweet was about to go live at any moment. No one in the room bothered to mask their whispers as Whitney flailed her arms frenetically while speaking to Monica or shuffling across the stage to talk to Brandy and hug Ricky Minor (he'd been her musical director for ages) as they attempted to run through their performance.

When Whitney returned to the ballroom roughly an hour later, people were sharing their bewilderment at seeing her outside doing handstands by the pool. She looked stoned, but aside from being deeply embarrassed over her appearance, no one would have thought they were witnessing someone in the last forty-eight hours of her life. Bobbi Kristina trailed behind her mother this time. She was now a gorgeous teenager who had weathered the weight of fame's orbit *and* all the tabloid drama that came with having superstar parents who struggled with addiction and a toxic codependence. I took mental note that Whitney only greeted the group of Black reporters I stood with in this room full of mostly white journalists. Even though her relationship with the press, especially the Black press, could be tenuous, Whitney very well knew the difficulties Black press had when it came to representation in spaces like that. I was still learning the depths of privilege I had as a reporter for the *Los Angeles Times* as it related to celebrity access, but I think more than anything Whitney was genuinely enthused to see a group of young Black journalists standing together who were excited to see her and had zero judgment on display. She felt safe enough with us that she instructed Bobbi Kristina to hang tight near us as she went into a side room where Brandy, Monica, and Clive were receiving reporters. When I look back on that afternoon, I often think about a pair of white reporters I saw discreetly filming Whitney on their cell phones, laughing to themselves over her appearance. It's a surreal sight to feel a room swell with embarrassment because one of the biggest pop stars on the planet showed up high and disheveled. I didn't like the snickers or the whispers, but I couldn't pretend to not see the obvious. Watching those two reporters slyly pointing their phones toward Whitney, knowing full well they were probably going to post their video or embed the footage in their story, filled me with shame and sadness for Whitney. She was always the story, even when she wasn't the story. I believed the most righteous thing was to write nothing of the bad stuff. Yes, my motivation was fueled by a desire to protect Whitney, but I also felt it unfair. I was there to write about Brandy and Monica's reunion and not the strange disruption at rehearsal. I asked my editor how to best cast her appearance in the most respectful way that got at the newsworthiness of Whitney's unexpected presence without sounding salacious. We settled on "loose and lively." Though I believe Whitney greeted us simply because we were young and Black and happy to see her, I also think she felt protected by us. We were not only her people; we were the only ones not gawking or giggling at her. Everyone could hear Whitney in the other room, hamming it up for the cameras, and a publicist for the Grammys very politely suggested to Bobbi Kris that she go in and grab her mother and take her away. And she did just that. Whitney and Bobbi Kris came bouncing out of the room, smiles splashed across their faces as they skipped away toward the exit. It felt messy to ask Clive or Brandy and Monica about the afternoon's surprise visitor, but it would have been just as strange to pretend the day hadn't been colored by Whitney's disruption. Everyone offered gracious sound bites into my tape recorder, and Clive indulged me by allowing me to take his place in between Brandy and Monica while he got back to prepping for the gala. A half hour later I was in the hotel lobby when I felt a tap on my shoulder. It was Whitney. "Are they still inside?" she asked. Her voice was but a gentle rasp. I nodded and told her how much I loved her, the influence she had on me and my love of music. That her existence was largely one of the reasons I ever wanted to write about pop stars. There was a sadness in her eyes that forever imprinted itself on my memory when I got the call that she was dead. Though her eyes were sad, there was that smile, so radiant and warm. Whitney gently pressed her hand into mine. "Thank you, baby.

God bless you." And then she was gone just as quickly as she had popped up.

That night, like every night of the week leading up to the Grammys, I hopped from party to party with the close circle of friends I'd made in the industry. We were still buzzed from Mary J.'s set at a party where Belvedere flowed endlessly (they were a sponsor) when we stumbled to Tru nightclub. Kelly Price was hosting an event celebrating R&B, a genre the Grammys historically overlooked on its live broadcast, relegating it instead to the non-televised preshow that happens across the street from the big ceremony. R&B hadn't yet entered its next wave of mainstream resurgence, so the night at Tru was largely about solidarity for a community that had seen its influence continually diminished despite its prevalence across all facets of pop music. There was a commotion when we arrived. The club had hit capacity, and the bouncer was arguing with someone in Price's camp. Word spilled outside that Whitney had shown up, but we gave up on trying to get in and opted to load our bellies with pancakes. Another night of revelry awaited. By morning, the blogs were lit up with headlines from the party at Tru. Whitney had unleashed a drunken tirade on former *X Factor* contestant Stacy Francis over Ray J and was photographed with blood dripping down her leg after falling inside. And there was a brief, impromptu performance of "Jesus Loves Me" with her friend Price that, yet again, showed how much of her voice had been lost. Deciphering what was going on between her and Ray J had replaced her Bobby drama in terms of enticing the press. There was the seventeen-year age difference and his sex tape with Kim Kardashian and Whitney's role in his big sister Brandy's life.

Neither of them ever divulged the nature of their friendship and yet we made assumptions anyway. It was never interesting, or even groundbreaking, that a divorcée found someone to spend time with, but we judged her like we always did.

***

Whitney's assistant Mary Jones laid out the gown Whitney was to wear to Clive's gala. She had spent much of her time in L.A. partying and finding herself on the blogs. But tonight, she would be the belle of the ball. This was the one room waiting to receive her with unyielding love and appreciation for all that she was—even if that meant turning a blind eye to all that she had become. That's not a judgment, but let's not pretend as if part of what keeps the entertainment industrial complex churning isn't complicity. Everyone wanted Whitney to win again. Her presence at the gala was always a moment of triumph. Clive's golden girl had inspired so many of the young acts who grace that stage each year. Brandy and Monica were direct descendants. Without her shattering barriers, they wouldn't have been able to become teenage dreams who ruled pop and R&B. A label wouldn't have taken a chance on church-singer-turned-background-vocalist Kelly Price had Whitney not opened the door for Mariah, who then opened the door for Price. It's nearly impossible not to trace any facet of contemporary pop or R&B back to Whitney. At Clive's gala he would remind her—and the entire room—of just that. At the gala, all that she had accomplished would be celebrated. She would be exalted, not reminded of what she could no longer do—or what she no longer achieved—but of who she inspired and the lives she changed with her music. And so Mary laid out the gown Whitney would wear and left to run errands. When she returned, the room was dark. Water slowly seeped from the bathroom. Inside, Whitney was floating facedown in the tub. It was too late. She had gone to the same party she went to so many times before, but this time she didn't make it out. There would be no celebratory rise. The hero had fallen, just before she was supposed to be received by an adoring audience waiting to be awed by her splendor.

I felt the air escape my lungs when I got the call from my editor. A colleague was at the Staples Center watching Rihanna rehearse when a producer was informed. Word was making its way across town the old-fashioned way as her team went into action to do the one thing they couldn't for so long—control the story. Confirmation came by way of my phone vibrating from the reporter trusted to break the news and stave off TMZ.

Whitney was dead. It felt unfathomable yet inevitable. Her story had become too familiar, a cycle of tragedy in an industry that seemed unconcerned with breaking it. I have still never reconciled the thought of her body resting in her room—the gown she would never wear off in the distance—as Clive's party continued. "Simply put, Whitney would have wanted the music to go on," Clive told the audience. It was a cruel, Shakespearian ending. One of the greatest performers the world had seen was dead before her mentor's annual gala, and the party goes on anyway as her body lies in her room upstairs. Clive was brokenhearted, certainly, but the decision to continue the party and not send everyone home is such a grotesque reminder of the old showbiz adage: *The show must go on.* And so the show went on as a coroner waited to remove her body from the hotel. Onstage, Clive did what he does best—he reminded the room of all that Whitney had accomplished and all she had inspired with *that voice*. That magical, transcendent voice that sent her flying into orbit and took us along for the ride. Whitney never got her big comeback, but she was still our hero, and so we did what we always did after we lost one of our heroes. We placed her back on her pedestal.

WON'T THEY ALWAYS LOVE YOU?

Reflections on Meaning and Legacy

Nearly a century ago, Langston Hughes wrote "The Negro Artist and the Racial Mountain." The essay is essentially his philosophy for Black creatives navigating a world that constantly places expectations on their art because of their race. He starts with an anecdote about a promising young poet who confided to him that he just wanted to be considered a poet. Not a Negro poet. "And I was sorry the young man said that, for no great poet has ever been afraid of being himself," Hughes wrote. "This is the mountain standing in the way of any true negro art in America—this urge within the race toward whiteness, the desire to pour racial individuality into the mold of American standardization, and to be as little negro and as much American as possible." *To be as little negro and as much American as possible.* Those words have punctured my thoughts the most while reconsidering the ways in which Whitney was perceived the first time around.

The way we read her, and judged her, and criticized her music. The mountain that stood in her way wasn't just her shit, but the shit we put on her. *To be as little negro and as much American as possible.* It's a heavy burden, and we placed it upon Whitney the moment we found out who her mama was and who her cousins were. She was a young Black girl stepping into an industry where there weren't girls who looked like her at the top, and it took the tragedy of her demise for us to ever consider the price she paid to get up there. To be the one to break the ceiling.

Whitney Houston represented the common American dream, but there has always been a divergent experience when it comes to Black and white people realizing that dream. The way Whitney's family tracks mainstream Blackness—from her grandfather leaving the South during the Great Migration and her mother's contributions to the emergence of Black gospel and the ground Dionne broke in pop music—is a brilliant coincidence that paved the way for her. It made *us* root for her. This was her birthright. Her family had endured the way so many of our families had endured while trying to get a piece of the American dream. Because Whitney was from Newark we were able to see her as one of us. It mattered that she was from a city where our people endured so much, the same way it mattered to us to see the Jacksons come out of Gary, Indiana, and change the world or watch Prince put Minneapolis on the map. It matters because so much of the American songbook was built off the backs of Black folks pouring the sorrows of a country that has never loved them into song. The blues and jazz and gospel of the Deep South. The Motown sound Berry Gordy and Holland-Dozier-Holland innovated in Detroit. The Philly soul sound Gamble and Huff established. The house music that came out of Chicago. The go-go music from Washington, D.C. The funk that poured out of Dayton, Ohio. And the birth of hip-hop in the Bronx. All genres of music intrinsically linked to the Black experience that has influenced pop music and white cultural tastes for over a century. Whitney was envisioned as a voice for the post–civil rights era, a position she solidified when she took all the complicated, racist history of the national anthem and transformed it into a moment so full of beauty and grace and power that she moved the world. Whitney was *ours*, but all that she represented to us—and all that we put on her—became a mountain that grew as we projected our expectations for how we wanted her to show up. In the end she didn't make it over the mountain, but she got so damn close.

***

"Was my life not a cautionary tale for you," Whitney says while channeling her fiercest church elder sass in a scene from *Sparkle*. She was playing the role of Emma Anderson, a failed singer who had hit rock bottom and turned her life over to the Lord. Emma didn't want her three girls making the same mistakes she did, so she forbade them from pursuing music altogether. Sister Emma didn't want her daughters anywhere near the business as her life was proof of the dangers of chasing fame. It was easy for Whitney to fall into this role. Much of her life had already been a cautionary tale before she got clean and shot *Sparkle* in Detroit toward the end of 2011, and the film would be made all the more tragic when she died three months after working on it—her addiction ultimately getting the best of her on the eve of her mentor's big gala, where her presence was sure to dazzle a room of people she had once inspired.

Sparkle arrived in theaters in August 2012. It had been six months since her passing. Whitney was no longer here to relish in the hype surrounding her big comeback—though much of that hype morphed into a chance to celebrate what once was. The idea of listening to her music still felt too painful, but I slipped into an early screening of *Sparkle* because I wanted to mourn. I *needed* to mourn. An affliction had developed in the depths of my spirit once the dust settled on writing about the days and weeks following her death. There was a heaviness of being in her presence in her final days, of sharing space, and having a moment of human connection with this woman I had spent so long loving and worrying about *and* judging. It had consumed me. Documenting her in death after loving her for so long cut me deeper than it hit after Michael or Amy or Prince. I had seen her. Touched her. Connected with her. Felt her smile wash over me. I met my hero, and she died some forty-eight hours later. Watching her have one last victory was how I felt I should grieve. Her performance of "His Eye Is on the Sparrow" in the film would be her final curtain call, and I needed to bear witness to it.

The performance begins with just a whisper of piano and organ. So much had been said about the condition of Whitney's voice in her last years, but it's actually the rasp in her voice that makes her rendering of "His Eye Is on the Sparrow" so moving. Whitney desperately wanted another comeback, which is part of what drove her to get herself together for the movie. She wanted redemption and she wanted to inspire Bobbi Kristina, who was soothing the wounds of all she had endured as a child of superstar parents who were also addicts by turning to the same drugs that undid her parents. Whitney wanted the world to see her as a hero again. And we did too. So we propped her right back up to queen status after her death. We streamed her music and bought copies of all the old stuff we loved so much, the newer stuff like *Just Whitney* and *I Look to You*, and the compilations Clive and her estate have issued in her absence. We came out in droves to see her final curtain call in *Sparkle*, and we've been showering her with all our love—and our empathy—ever since.

In death we think of Whitney so much differently. We tend to do that with our fallen heroes, when time and unlocked secrets and critical reevaluation and public discourse lead us to different understandings and opinions than we had before. There was a period when even the kindest of us may have gawked and laughed or wondered what the hell was going on with her or with Bobby. Whitney was one of our greatest voices. A Black church girl from Newark became one of the greatest—a culture-shifting talent. But the stumbles, all of them, reduced her into a punch line. The cracked-out diva who had squandered her money and talent and become a disgrace. That's how we talked about her for so long. It took losing her for us to finally take the time to calculate the cost of what it took to become *Whitney Houston* and break down the door for legions of Black girls from the ghetto with Afro curls and gospel in their blood. It took losing Whitney for us to reconsider her and *finally* see her for who she was and not who we believed she should or could have been. Learning the full scope of her secret agony helped us understand the burdens she carried as she made pop history. Her death gutted us, our grief worsened by watching Bobbi Kristina quickly spin out. The night before

Whitney died, she found her daughter passed out in the tub of her room at the Beverly Hilton. We don't know if she was drunk or high or both, but everything about Whitney's last days points to a woman on a freight train of her addiction, and although her instincts as a mother kicked in and she pulled Bobbi Kris out of the water before the situation could turn dire, Whitney was still too high to do anything to stop the train she was on from going off the rails, and the next day she'd be the one dead. Krissi should have had the space to heal, but she never got that. Instead, she got cameras in her face as her grief was documented for a Lifetime docuseries the Houston family announced three months to the day after Whitney's death.

It was unfathomable that the Houstons would invite us into their grief in this way. Whitney had given so much of herself to us, and her family had too. They had done all the interviews and shared their pain and their regrets and the lessons they learned from Whitney's tragic fall. We didn't need any more. Though the series was largely centered around Pat Houston, Whitney's manager, sister-in-law, and closest confidante as she worked to strengthen the estate, Krissi was the reason anyone would be enticed to tune in. Everyone wanted to know how Whitney's daughter was managing. She had been a mainstay on the blogs, and it was painfully apparent she was running from something, just like her mother and father had. It was apparent from how often the cameras captured a clearly intoxicated Bobbi Kris in the presence of her entire family that she was incredibly unwell and needed help—real help. Her chaotic relationship with Nick Gordon, a close friend of the family whom Whitney had taken in as her own, had drawn eerie parallels to her parents, and putting the cameras in front of her as she was trying to find her way felt like it placed yet another cruel burden on a young woman who, in retrospect, never really had a chance.

When it debuted in October 2012, *The Houstons: On Our Own* showed us family history repeating itself. Krissi was signaling for help. She was nineteen and in a haze of grief that allowed her growing dependency on alcohol and drugs to thrive, and that vulnerability set the stage for this codependency with Nick—who she previously referred to as her big brother—to morph into an engagement. The Houstons cast him as a leech who planned to dig his claws into the estate Whitney left for Krissi by marrying her. Nick became another Bobby to them—someone else to point the finger of blame toward as they avoided the reality that Krissi was on a path that had only one outcome. I often think about the last time I saw her, skipping with her mother arm-in-arm out of the ballroom of the Beverly Hilton. They were both trying to find their way, even then, but it's sad to think of all that Bobbi Kristina gave up. All she couldn't be because of who her parents were and what they had exposed her to. Her entire life had played out on the world's stage as Whitney and Bobby's baby. It was a heavy burden, made insufferable by losing her best friend. We will never know what happened to Krissi before she was found floating facedown in her tub at home in 2015, just a few weeks ahead of the three-year anniversary of her mom's death. Nick and a friend they often partied with were the ones to find her, and the similarities between Whitney's passing and how Krissi was found reignited the conspiracy theories that something more sinister was at play. Our suspicions of the circumstances and the rumors of physical abuse from Nick told us he was responsible in some way for what happened to Krissi, who had morphine, cocaine, alcohol, and prescription drugs in her system when she was pulled out of the tub. We held vigil for months, hoping a miracle would bring her back from the induced coma she was placed under while a media circus enveloped the Brown and Houston families, who were—yet again—pointing the fingers at one another. But Bobbi Kristina never awoke from her coma. She died on July 26, 2015, at the age of twenty-two. The cause of death was lobar pneumonia, and though the medical examiner was unable to determine if her death was due to intentional or accidental causes, the cloud of suspicion over Nick grew as he became more unhinged under the scrutiny. Bobbi Kristina's estate went after Nick, and while he was never charged with any crimes related to her death, in 2016 a judge did order him to pay the estate $36 million in a wrongful death lawsuit. We likely won't ever know if Nick actually played a role in Krissi's death, because he's gone now, having died of a heroin overdose at the age of thirty on January 1, 2020.

***

Wondering where Whitney would have gone had she outrun her demons and made it to the other side of that mountain standing in her way haunts me more than witnessing the tragic haze of her last days. I think about who Whitney would have become had she lived long enough to see the world shift to where it is today, culturally speaking. What it may have been like if she was around to experience the immense shift the Black Lives Matter and #MeToo movements have brought to our society and all the ways in which we have reframed our relationship with celebrities—particularly women. It's laughable now to think of all the ink that was spilled over Whitney's same-sex relationship or about her music not adhering squarely to the soul and gospel expected from her Black voice or getting caught with the same amount of weed that you can now get delivered anytime via app or pick up at a boutique dispensary. When we look at the tick-tock of her downfall, it's all rooted in shame—the shame of her relationship with Robyn and with drugs and with the way she was seen, and not seen, by her own people. If all that was off the table, what would have been different? Would there have been a great third act that saw her rise back to prominence? Would she have retired and lived a quiet life, stepping out every few years to rake in millions on the Vegas strip or for the occasional film project? Would she have focused her energy on shaping Bobbi Kristina, who wanted to break into music like her parents had, and helped her move out of their shadow? I wonder if she would have done a big interview and unburdened herself about her secret teenage years with Robyn. And I wonder if she would have disclosed what happened to her as a child under Dee Dee's care. Whitney had a favorite saying: *Can I be me?* She said it so much that one of her band members recorded her saying it and turned it into an audio sample that they would play at rehearsals. Of all the things I think about in regards to who Whitney could have become, I most often find myself wondering who she would have been if we just let her *be* from the beginning. If Clive and Cissy hadn't done any grooming. If we hadn't spent so much time telling her she wasn't good enough or interesting enough or sexy enough or artistic enough or Black enough or straight enough for us. If we hadn't shamed her so much, who would Whitney have become?

***

A life-size digital likeness of Whitney glowed in front of me. She wore a gorgeous white gown and her hair was up in a bun, with two tufts framing the sides of her soft face, similar to how she was styled during the *Bodyguard* era. Whitney had been dead for five years at this point, but here she was with the push of a button, singing "I Have Nothing" as majestically as she had when I fell madly in love with her as a child seeing her in *The Bodyguard* for the first time. I got up from my seat and moved closer to inspect Whitney—and better understand whatever witchcraft made her likeness appear like an actual ghost gliding across the stage. I was profiling Alki David, an eccentric Greek billionaire who had sunk millions of dollars into a technology that allowed him to stage "hologram concerts." David was thrilled to show me the pièce de résistance in his multimillion-dollar portfolio of hyper-realistic avatars, most of whom had been dead longer than either of us had been alive. Though the woman before me sounded just like Whitney, courtesy of an old recording, upon closer inspection the digital avatar was more in the spirit of Whitney than a passable likeness. But that wasn't the point of David's master plan. It was all about the *feeling* that these shows evoked, and for an artist like Whitney, who didn't have the gargantuan creative output of someone like Prince that can be endlessly repackaged and reintroduced to the public, it offered her estate an innovative chance to exploit her catalog. David had been working with Pat

Houston on a concept that would revive the singer for a world tour fashioned after the intimate show Whitney had been dreaming of giving her fans. Plans fell apart, and the estate went with Base Hologram to get *An Evening with Whitney* off the ground. The digital spirit of Whitney kicked off its world tour in February 2020 and played a handful of dates in Europe before the coronavirus shut the production down. It's a ghoulish idea for some to watch a show with a digital likeness of a dead performer projected onto a real stage for their entertainment. I had been in the audience at Coachella a few months after Whitney died and watched a very real-looking 2Pac pop up and rip the stage as if he'd been cryogenically frozen since his 1996 murder. And now I was watching Whitney, or at least a rough sketch for what the finished product would be—a product David hoped people would spend big bucks to see for themselves. The word "product" made me shudder every time he said it. David could have been successful in selling me on the vision had the avatar at least bore any semblance to Whitney from her time on earth. She looked like an actress in costume, and that was *after* digital tweaking. But what did it matter? People paid to see Whitney's resurrection even if the finished version still looked nothing like her (aside from nailing her hair and her costumes). My curiosity got the best of me, and I scoured YouTube for footage of the shows. The final version looked much closer to the real Whitney. And of course the digital Whitney sounded incredible, as the shows lean on performances from her peak and are supplemented with a live band. Replicating Whitney in perfect form for our consumption feels strangely poetic. She couldn't duplicate her early brilliance in life, but in death an audience can be teleported to the apex of her fame—before she spiraled too far out of reach—courtesy of twenty-first-century technological advancements. With just the touch of a button Whitney could be triumphant night after night for as long as people wanted to see her. And someone will *always* want to see Whitney.

A Whitney hologram says a lot about where we are today and speaks to the lengths her estate is willing to go to move us back toward regarding her as *the voice* without the operatic tragedy that silenced it. But sending a digital likeness around the globe is only a reminder of what we lost—and how we lost her. We're in a place where we're ready to do the work and look at who we are now compared to who we were in our past. There have been great cultural reappraisals of our most controversial figures courtesy of sympathetic docuseries, big-budget biopics, and extensive scholarship. It would be deeply ironic that the same ecosystem that once destroyed women like Whitney and Amy and Mariah and Janet and Britney is now responsible for uplifting them if it weren't for the fact that it taps into our pattern of rooting for a hero, watching them fall, and cheering for their comeback. The collective outrage that now resides over the way we read these women vis-à-vis the gossip coverage that never treated them like humans doesn't change the fact that we consumed their falls for our enjoyment. Shifting cultural attitudes have helped us see just how ridiculous it was that we were so deeply unkind to famous women while looking the other way when it came to Michael and R. Kelly and Russell Simmons and Bill Cosby and every other powerful man who used their position and influence to abuse. The double standard has always been clear. Men are celebrated for what they accomplish, regardless of how perverse their transgressions are, while women are roundly punished for theirs, and unfortunately, we lost Whitney before we learned to be better.

I've thought long and hard about my position in an industry that has prospered greatly from the marginalization of those who look like me. A big part of why I left the *Los Angeles Times* after a decade of covering pop music was knowing I would always be limited in what I could do and who I could be. This book wasn't just born out of my frustration over the way Whitney was seen, but also the way in which the genres of music she contributed so much to continue to see so little scholarship around its Black visionaries. There was a fullness I wanted to give to Whitney and the pop and R&B she transformed, and I couldn't do that from the seat I sat in, regardless of the access it gave me. And in leaving to write this book and rediscover my love of Whitney's voice, I found my own.

This book is really a debate between who we used to be and who we are now. Our treatment of Whitney would be unacceptable and abhorrent if she were alive today. The pain of losing so many of our great talents has pushed us to raise a mirror to see ourselves and our culpability in contributing to their demise and, thankfully, we have chosen a way forward that has led us toward accountability. If Whitney were alive today, she would be more protected. We have learned enough to be sensitive of a celebrity's right to heal, and although TMZ and gossip blogs still thrive, their frothy coverage is often rejected and detested by us. But we cannot let ourselves off the hook if we are going to create a different environment—not just for our celebrities, but for ourselves. The rich and famous rarely see the shitty things we say about them on Twitter and Instagram, but your friend who's afraid to live in their truth or struggling to find their identity or dealing with addiction or the trauma of sexual abuse does. Will we ever create a better world for them? Will we continue to repeat our history?

***

Technically, "I Will Always Love You" is a farewell song between creative partners and not an aching parting between lovers. That was Dolly Parton's inspiration when she wrote it—a sweet goodbye to her partner Porter Wagoner, whose show she was leaving to pursue her own solo career. Whitney had other plans. She took those lyrics and let them spill out with such tender longing. But the money is in that moment. You know the one. That BOOM *"and Iiiii"* climax that stretches into the heavens, her voice exploding into a series of sweeping runs. None of it was supposed to work. Not the languid intro. Definitely not the shmaltzy dramatics or the sax solo that sounded like elevator music. But it worked. Whitney's range, bountiful and pristine, made it work. She had spun gold the way she did at the Super Bowl and during those glorious years when she was flying so high in the sky. Whitney's voice was such a dominant force in pop music before her troubles—and our disappointment—undid her. She could make records feel holy and sacred, or she could sing us into a euphoric high. That's the glory of a once-in-a-lifetime talent like hers.

In 2020, the power of Whitney's voice had once again placed her in the history books. She became the first Black recording art-ist to land three Diamond-certified albums after her sophomore record, 1987's *Whitney*, crossed the 10× platinum threshold. The achievement came right around the time Whitney was inducted into the Rock & Roll Hall of Fame, a massive validation of her artistry that had evaded her for so long—even after her death—that will likely open the door for other women like Whitney, great vocalists who shaped music with the instrument in their throats, to be included among the rock gods and goddesses and the rappers they have started making room for long after the genre's influence became a worldview of its own. The scholarship and discourse around Whitney's life and career after *Can I Be Me?* and *Whitney* gave us a better, clearer view of all we didn't see the first time around. There was something profound about Whitney getting her flowers in a time when there was so much chaos, loss, and transformative change happening to us between the end of the darkness that was the Trump administration, a devastating global pandemic, and social unrest giving way to America's latest reckoning with its racism. Much of this was written in the thick of it as Whitney's voice poured into my earbuds. Twenty-twenty was a year suspended in isolation as the coronavirus raged destruction unseen in these modern times of ours. We lost more than 2.8 million people across the globe during the first year of the pandemic, a number that may very well have doubled by the time we've made it to the other side of it. Our emotional and financial livelihoods hung in the balance for much of the year as we also watched the nation grapple with a chaotic election and a wave of racial reckoning. There were enough new images of Black death at the hands of police officers or white strangers to send hundreds of thousands of us into the streets to make noise and get in some good trouble. Necessary trouble, as John Lewis would say. The summer of 2020 looked like 1967 Newark and 1992 Los Angeles and 2014 Ferguson, and writing this as Whitney's voice—and all the sisters with voices she inspired—blasted directly into my eardrums was the self-care that got me through it all. It was her voice—sweet, euphoric, full of gospel ecstasy and beauty and *power*—that got me through a year of such unrelenting bleakness. But a burst of light came on a Saturday night in November when Kamala Harris became the first woman elected as vice president of the United States. Harris was breaking so many barriers. She was a Black woman who was also of South Asian descent who had just become the highest-ranking woman in America's 244-year existence. It was a remarkable, once-in-a-lifetime moment many of us thought was impossible. As Vice President–elect Harris and President-elect Joe Biden stood on a stage with their families, amid a flurry of fireworks and glowing drone lights—a socially distanced audience cheering their victory from atop their cars—it was Whitney's voice that was chosen as part of the chorus of Black women who soundtracked the coronation of a sister making history. The year prior, Norwegian DJ and producer Kygo breathed new life into Whitney's 1990 cover of Steve Winwood's late-eighties hit "Higher Love." She had recorded a whimsical take with longtime trusted collaborator Narada Michael Walden for *I'm Your Baby Tonight*, but the track landed only on the Japanese version of the album. Pat Houston says she was compelled to commission a remix of the rarity because the times called for something uplifting and inspiring. Trump was ramping up his reelection efforts, and we were buckling up for the nasty rhetoric and venom he was about to spew to whip his cultish base into a fury. Pat's instinct to reintroduce Whitney's voice via a fresh remix was right. Kygo took her old vocals and built a blissful tropical house record around them. It shouldn't have really worked at all—but of course it did, because Whitney's voice worked on damn near anything. Since there isn't a vault of unreleased material to work with, the "Higher Love" remix is one of the few posthumous releases Whitney's estate has been able to pull off since her death. It was the rare opportunity to reintroduce that voice to a younger generation of listeners, and the record shot to number one on the dance charts. Whitney was right back to where we hoped she'd be: on top. As bursts of light danced against the darkness of the night's sky, her voice roared against the grand display of patriotism, like it had on that winter night in Tampa that changed everything back in 1991. It was a year of chaos and destruction, and there was Whitney's voice, spilling from the heavens and lifting us higher, as it had so many times before.

ACKNOWLEDGMENTS

Thank you to my agent, William LoTurco, for your unwavering commitment. To my brilliant editor, Samantha Weiner, you were such a gift to this book—thank you for your patience as I found my way. I am deeply grateful to the extraordinary minds that helped keep me focused and became the brain trust I needed: Elizabeth Broussard, Whitney Coble, Dr. Yaba Blay, Maori Karmael Holmes, Josh Begley, Eddie Hemphill, dream hampton, Brianne Pins, Chad Miller, Jessica Herndon, Kevin Nelson, and Yvonne Villarreal. Thank you to Tarana Burke for always nurturing me and lifting my spirit to the heavens and to Dr. Chanté D. DeLoach for steering me toward healing. To my family and friends, I am grateful for your support.

To Brandy, I have spent a lifetime loving you. Having you be a part of this book surpasses even my wildest dreams. Thank you for your trust and for opening your heart so wide.

To Merv, *you are the greatest love of all.*

And finally to Nippy, thank you for inspiring us all and changing the world with your gift. I hope you finally feel seen.

NOTES

Under His Eye, Blessed Be the Sound

Cissy Houston with Jonathan Singer, *How Sweet the Sound: My Life with God and Gospel* (Doubleday, 1998).

Steve Hochman, "Mom Can Carry a Pretty Mean Tune," *Los Angeles Times*, February 28, 1995.

Whitney Houston (foreword), in *How Sweet the Sound*.

Home

Archived Whitney Houston interview, in *Whitney*, directed by Kevin Macdonald (Lionsgate, 2018).

Frances Grill interview, in *Whitney: Can I Be Me*, directed by Nick Broomfield and Rudi Dolezal (Dogwoof, 2017).

The Merv Griffin Show, directed by Dick Clarkson, aired June 23, 1983.

Stuff That You Want, Thing That You Need

Clive Davis interview, *Weekend Edition Saturday*, NPR, aired February 23, 2013.

Michael Cavacini, "A Conversation with Dionne Warwick," August 13, 2014.

Kenneth Reynolds interview, in *Whitney: Can I Be Me*.

Mark Anthony Neal, *What the Music Said: Black Popular Music and Black Popular Culture* (Routledge, 1998).

David Foster with Pablo F. Fenjves, *Hitman: Forty Years Making Music, Topping the Charts, and Winning Grammys* (Gallery, 2008).

My Lonely Heart Calls

Archived Whitney Houston interview, in *Whitney*, directed by Kevin Macdonald (Lionsgate, 2018).

Robyn Crawford, *A Song for You: My Life with Whitney Houston* (Dutton, 2020).

Richard Corliss, "The Prom Queen of Soul," *Time*, July 13, 1987.

"Interview with Whitney Houston," *Dateline NBC*, aired December 10, 1996.

Pat Houston, interviewed by the author, June 20, 2018.

Anthony DeCurtis, "Whitney Houston Gets Nasty," *Rolling Stone*, June 10, 1993.

Gary Houston, interviewed by the author, June 20, 2018.

Miss America, the Beautiful

Touré, *I Would Die 4 U: Why Prince Became an Icon* (Atria, 2013).

Whitney Houston interview, in *Whitney: The Greatest Hits* (DVD, Sony Legacy, 2000).

Lynn Norment, "Whitney Houston Talks About the Men in Her Life—and the Rumors, Lies and Insults That Are the High Price of Fame," *Ebony*, May 1991.

"Interview with Whitney Houston," *Dateline NBC*, aired December 10, 1996.

W. E. B. Du Bois, *W. E. B. Du Bois: Writings: The Suppression of the African-Slave-Trade / The Souls of Black Folk / Dusk of Dawn / Essays and Articles* (Library of America, 1987).

Trey Ellis, "The New Black Aesthetic," *Callaloo*, 1989.

Ta-Nehisi Coates, "I'm Not Black, I'm Kanye," *Atlantic*, May 7, 2018.

Bolder, Blacker, Badder

Chris Willman, "How Whitney Houston Got Hooked on Singing," *Entertainment Weekly*, November 24, 1995.

Jamie Foster Brown, "Whitney's Love," *Redbook*, March 1996.

Mark Seal, "The Devils in the Diva," *Vanity Fair*, May 8, 2012.

Tell the Truth and Shame the Devil

Michael Houston interview, in *Whitney*, directed by Kevin Macdonald (Lionsgate, 2018).

Gary Houston interview, in *Whitney*.

Robyn Crawford, *A Song for You: My Life with Whitney Houston* (Dutton, 2020).

Cissy Houston with Lisa Dickey, *Remembering Whitney: My Story of Love, Loss, and the Night the Music Stopped* (Harper, 2013).

"Interview with Whitney Houston," *Dateline NBC*, aired December 10, 1996.

Clive Davis with Anthony DeCurtis, *The Soundtrack of My Life* (Simon & Schuster, 2013).

Gary Houston, interviewed by the author, June 20, 2018.

Kevin Macdonald, interviewed by the author, June 28, 2018.

National Institute on Drug Abuse, "Exploring the Role of Child Abuse in Later Drug Abuse," July 1, 1998.

Dean G. Kilpatrick and Benjamin E. Saunders, *Prevalence and Consequences of Child Victimization: Results from the National Survey of Adolescents, Final Report*, U.S. Department of Justice, National Institute of Justice, 1997.

Mary Jones interview, in *Whitney*.

Jenifer Lewis, *The Mother of Black Hollywood* (HarperCollins, 2017).

The Undoing of Whitney Houston

Primetime Special Edition: Whitney Houston, directed by Paul George, aired December 4, 2002.

Isabel Wilkerson, "God Is Still Working on Me," *Essence*, July 2003.

Clive Davis with Anthony DeCurtis, *The Soundtrack of My Life* (Simon & Schuster, 2013).

Cissy Houston with Lisa Dickey, *Remembering Whitney: My Story of Love, Loss, and the Night the Music Stopped* (Harper, 2013).

Harriette Cole, "Whitney Houston: A Star Is Reborn," *Ebony*, October 2009.

Chris Connelly, Glenn Ruppel, and Alice Gomstyn, "Whitney Houston Insider Reveals Singer's Anguished Fight to Win Back Her Voice," ABC News, February 17, 2012.

Debra Martin Chase interview, in *Whitney,* directed by Kevin Macdonald (Lionsgate, 2018).

Won't They Always Love You?

Langston Hughes, "The Negro Artist and the Racial Mountain," *Nation,* June 23, 1926.

Gerrick Kennedy, "Meet the Man Determined to Make Celebrity Holograms a Major Hollywood Draw," *Los Angeles Times,* October 9, 2017.

INDEX